DATE DUE

MR 19 '93			
MR 0 '94			
DE 23 '94			
AP 17 '95			
FE 23 '99			
FE 9 '06			
NO 7 '07			

DEMCO 38-296

NUCLEAR
PROLIFERATION

OPPOSING VIEWPOINTS®

Other Books of Related Interest in the Opposing Viewpoints Series:

NUCLEAR
PROLIFERATION
OPPOSING VIEWPOINTS®

David L. Bender & Bruno Leone, *Series Editors*

Charles P. Cozic, *Book Editor*
Karin L. Swisher, *Assistant Editor*

OPPOSING VIEWPOINTS SERIES ®

Greenhaven Press, Inc.   PO Box 289009   San Diego, CA 92198-9009

Library of Congress Cataloging-in-Publication Data

Nuclear proliferation : opposing viewpoints / Charles P. Cozic, book editor; Karin L. Swisher, assistant editor.
    p.   cm. — (Opposing viewpoints series)
  Includes bibliographical references and index.
  Summary: Presents differing opinions on the threat of nuclear proliferation, the need for arms control, the role of NATO, the elimination of nuclear weapons, and other related topics.
  ISBN 1-56510-005-0 (lib. : acid-free paper) — ISBN 1-56510-004-2 (pbk. : acid-free paper)
  1. Nuclear nonproliferation—Juvenile literature. [1. Nuclear nonproliferation. 2. Disarmament.] I. Cozic, Charles P., 1957-   . II. Swisher, Karin, 1966-   . III. Series: Opposing viewpoints series (Unnumbered)
JX1974.73.N83 1992
327.1'74—dc20   92-23065
                                                            CIP
                                                             AC

Copyright © 1992 by Greenhaven Press, Inc.

"Congress shall make no law . . . abridging the freedom of speech, or of the press."

First Amendment to the U.S. Constitution

The basic foundation of our democracy is the first amendment guarantee of freedom of expression. The Opposing Viewpoints Series is dedicated to the concept of this basic freedom and the idea that it is more important to practice it than to enshrine it.

Contents

Why Consider Opposing Viewpoints?

"It is better to debate a question without settling it than to settle a question without debating it."

Joseph Joubert (1754-1824)

The Importance of Examining Opposing Viewpoints

The purpose of the Opposing Viewpoints Series, and this book in particular, is to present balanced, and often difficult to find, opposing points of view on complex and sensitive issues.

Probably the best way to become informed is to analyze the positions of those who are regarded as experts and well studied on issues. It is important to consider every variety of opinion in an attempt to determine the truth. Opinions from the mainstream of society should be examined. But also important are opinions that are considered radical, reactionary, or minority as well as those stigmatized by some other uncomplimentary label. An important lesson of history is the eventual acceptance of many unpopular and even despised opinions. The ideas of Socrates, Jesus, and Galileo are good examples of this.

Readers will approach this book with their own opinions on the issues debated within it. However, to have a good grasp of one's own viewpoint, it is necessary to understand the arguments of those with whom one disagrees. It can be said that those who do not completely understand their adversary's point of view do not fully understand their own.

A persuasive case for considering opposing viewpoints has been presented by John Stuart Mill in his work *On Liberty*. When examining controversial issues it may be helpful to reflect on this suggestion:

9

The only way in which a human being can make some approach to knowing the whole of a subject, is by hearing what can be said about it by persons of every variety of opinion, and studying all modes in which it can be looked at by every character of mind. No wise man ever acquired his wisdom in any mode but this.

Analyzing Sources of Information

The Opposing Viewpoints Series includes diverse materials taken from magazines, journals, books, and newspapers, as well as statements and position papers from a wide range of individuals, organizations, and governments. This broad spectrum of sources helps to develop patterns of thinking which are open to the consideration of a variety of opinions.

Pitfalls to Avoid

A pitfall to avoid in considering opposing points of view is that of regarding one's own opinion as being common sense and the most rational stance, and the point of view of others as being only opinion and naturally wrong. It may be that another's opinion is correct and one's own is in error.

Another pitfall to avoid is that of closing one's mind to the opinions of those with whom one disagrees. The best way to approach a dialogue is to make one's primary purpose that of understanding the mind and arguments of the other person and not that of enlightening him or her with one's own solutions. More can be learned by listening than speaking.

It is my hope that after reading this book the reader will have a deeper understanding of the issues debated and will appreciate the complexity of even seemingly simple issues on which good and honest people disagree. This awareness is particularly important in a democratic society such as ours where people enter into public debate to determine the common good. Those with whom one disagrees should not necessarily be regarded as enemies, but perhaps simply as people who suggest different paths to a common goal.

Developing Basic Reading and Thinking Skills

In this book, carefully edited opposing viewpoints are purposely placed back to back to create a running debate; each viewpoint is preceded by a short quotation that best expresses the author's main argument. This format instantly plunges the reader into the midst of a controversial issue and greatly aids that reader in mastering the basic skill of recognizing an author's point of view.

A number of basic skills for critical thinking are practiced in the activities that appear throughout the books in the series. Some of the skills are:

Evaluating Sources of Information. The ability to choose from among alternative sources the most reliable and accurate source in relation to a given subject.

Separating Fact from Opinion. The ability to make the basic distinction between factual statements (those that can be demonstrated or verified empirically) and statements of opinion (those that are beliefs or attitudes that cannot be proved).

Identifying Stereotypes. The ability to identify oversimplified, exaggerated descriptions (favorable or unfavorable) about people and insulting statements about racial, religious, or national groups, based upon misinformation or lack of information.

Recognizing Ethnocentrism. The ability to recognize attitudes or opinions that express the view that one's own race, culture, or group is inherently superior, or those attitudes that judge another culture or group in terms of one's own.

It is important to consider opposing viewpoints and equally important to be able to critically analyze those viewpoints. The activities in this book are designed to help the reader master these thinking skills. Statements are taken from the book's viewpoints and the reader is asked to analyze them. This technique aids the reader in developing skills that not only can be applied to the viewpoints in this book, but also to situations where opinionated spokespersons comment on controversial issues. Although the activities are helpful to the solitary reader, they are most useful when the reader can benefit from the interaction of group discussion.

Using this book and others in the series should help readers develop basic reading and thinking skills. These skills should improve the reader's ability to understand what is read. Readers should be better able to separate fact from opinion, substance from rhetoric, and become better consumers of information in our media-centered culture.

This volume of the Opposing Viewpoints Series does not advocate a particular point of view. Quite the contrary! The very nature of the book leaves it to the reader to formulate the opinions he or she finds most suitable. My purpose as publisher is to see that this is made possible by offering a wide range of viewpoints that are fairly presented.

David L. Bender
Publisher

Introduction

*"It is essential . . . to prevent nuclear prolifera-
tion, which poses one of the greatest risks to the
survival of mankind. "*

President George Bush, March 1990.

*"We should be like the Chinese—poor and riding
donkeys, but respected and possessing an atom
bomb. "*

Libyan president Mu'ammar Qaddafi, 1987.

On November 21, 1991, Secretary of Defense Dick Cheney announced, "We are convinced that North Korea is developing the
capability to build a nuclear weapon." Cheney and leaders from
around the world feared the worst: the possibility that the
Communist dictatorship could build and one day launch a nuclear weapon. But North Korea is not alone. A growing number
of primarily Third World nations are suspected of seeking nuclear weapons. Nearly all Western nations agree that if Third
World nations obtain these weapons, they could use them to
threaten global security.

Concern about the spread of such weapons dates back to
World War II. After the detonation of two U.S. atomic bombs
over Japan in August 1945, the United States understood how
massively destructive these weapons could be. The United
States also realized the powerful security value of nuclear
weapons. Through the threat of nuclear retaliation, the United
States could deter almost any nation from attacking it or its allies.

These security benefits were not ignored by other nations. In
1949, the Soviet Union, head of the Warsaw Pact alliance in
Eastern Europe, became the second nation to develop and test a
nuclear weapon. Thus began the nuclear arms race. In the ensu-
ing years, the two superpower foes built the largest nuclear arsenals in the world. But they managed to refrain from using
them, a restraint that was tested most severely during the 1962
Cuban missile crisis that brought the United States and the

Soviet Union to the brink of war. Ironically, many experts believe that nuclear weapons helped prevent such an outcome: neither side dared risk initiating hostilities that could lead to a devastating nuclear strike.

Today, with the demise of communism in the Soviet Union and the end of the Cold War, concern over the threat of a nuclear confrontation has shifted to other nations, primarily those of the Third World. In 1974, India became the sixth nation to test a nuclear device. And in 1979, U.S. satellite photos revealed that Israel, in collaboration with South Africa, also may have tested a nuclear device. Both Israel and India, located in volatile regions with long histories of war and aggression, apparently sought nuclear weapons for many of the same reasons as the United States and the Soviet Union, to increase their security and protect their borders.

In the Middle East, the tiny nation of Israel has long been embroiled in conflict with its surrounding Arab neighbors. Terrorism and uprisings stemming from Arab-Jewish differences mark the region as one of the most unstable in the world. Since 1948, Israel has been directly involved in six wars or invasions with neighboring enemies. In southern Asia, India, too, is flanked by traditional enemies—Pakistan and China. Here, regional disputes frequently erupted over the possession of Kashmir, a territory north of India now divided and occupied by all three nations.

The potential nuclear capability of Israel and India has prompted some of their adversaries to conclude that they, too, cannot afford to be without nuclear arms. Following the Persian Gulf War in 1991, inspections in Iraq confirmed that Saddam Hussein, who had once threatened Israel with chemical weapons, had nearly been successful in completing a nuclear device. Western nations suspect that other Islamic states, specifically, Iran, Syria, Libya, and Algeria, are now following in Iraq's footsteps. And in Asia, after years of having been suspected of possessing nuclear weaponry, Pakistan finally admitted to it in 1992.

The idea of these volatile nations possessing nuclear weapons has prompted much concern among the United States and other Western nations. They fear that a nuclear device in the hands of an irrational, militaristic dictator in Syria, Pakistan, or other Third World state could be used to threaten neighboring enemies, the United States, or one of its allies. They are concerned, too, with the possibility of a crude nuclear device falling into the hands of terrorists, who could then detonate it or use it as a form of blackmail. Western nations are convinced that if these regional enemies obtain such destructive weapons, they will inevitably use them. If this were to occur, many analysts believe it

13

would lay the groundwork for the next world war, most likely between Arab nations and the West.

But many Third World nations suspected of developing nuclear weapons assert that they should be allowed to obtain them for the same reason the United States and Russia have them: to defend their territories as best they can. As Iran's vice president, Sayed Ataollah Mohajerani, stated in 1991, "Since Israel continues to possess nuclear weapons, we, the Muslims, must cooperate to produce an atomic bomb, regardless of UN attempts to prevent proliferation." Leaders such as Mohajerani contend that nonproliferation efforts by primarily Western nations amount to hypocritical discrimination against the Third World and the Arab world in particular. Arab leaders argue that their nations are victims of a double standard: the West condones the ownership of nuclear weapons technology and materials by the United States, Russia, and others but denies it to Arab states. Arab states assert that they, too, would never use the weapons, but would merely have them to deter their enemies.

Whether Third World nations obtain these deadly weapons and use them in peace or in war is a vital issue. The contributors to *Nuclear Proliferation: Opposing Viewpoints* address this and other questions surrounding the spread of nuclear weapons in the following chapters: How Serious a Problem Is Nuclear Proliferation? Are International Measures Effective Against Proliferation? Which Nations Contribute to Nuclear Proliferation? How Can Nuclear Proliferation Be Prevented? As the reader examines the viewpoints in this book, one issue becomes clear: the management of nuclear weapons must ensure that they are never used again.

How Serious a Problem Is Nuclear Proliferation?

Chapter Preface

In 1991, a United Nations investigative team began uncovering the extent of Iraq's success at building a nuclear bomb. Their discoveries refocused world attention on the problem of Third World nuclear proliferation. Accounts such as this one have led many to believe nuclear proliferation is a serious problem.

Those who consider nuclear proliferation a serious threat to international peace point to the number of countries that have attempted to and, in some cases, succeeded in constructing nuclear weapons. Israel, Pakistan, India, and South Africa are all widely believed to possess at least one functioning nuclear weapon. In addition, Brazil, Argentina, North and South Korea, and, of course, Iraq have all made progress toward attaining nuclear weapons. If any of these countries, critics maintain, exploded a nuclear bomb in their enemy's territory, a full-scale nuclear war could result.

Others, however, maintain that this threat is more appropriate to fiction. These critics point to the success of international proliferation prevention efforts. They argue that only five nations legally possess nuclear weapons, and the number has not increased in more than twenty years. They also maintain that, of those states that attempted to attain nuclear weapons illegally, many are now giving up their weapons programs and are willing to abide by international nonproliferation rules. They also suggest that international pressure would be sufficient to prevent even the most desperate terrorist nation from using a nuclear bomb. The viewpoints in the following chapter debate the seriousness of nuclear proliferation.

"A new and much more dangerous era of nuclear proliferation has begun. "

The Threat of Nuclear Proliferation Is a Serious Problem

Stephen Budiansky

In the following viewpoint, Stephen Budiansky maintains that the threat of nuclear proliferation is growing. According to Budiansky, repressive nations such as North Korea and Iraq have been working secretly to develop nuclear bombs. By developing atomic bombs, renegade nations threaten the entire world. Budiansky is a senior writer for *U.S. News & World Report*, a weekly newsmagazine.

As you read, consider the following questions:

1. According to the author, how have nations such as Iraq and North Korea developed nuclear weapons?
2. How should the United States respond to the increasing threat of nuclear proliferation, according to Budiansky?
3. How have control measures designed to prevent nuclear proliferation failed, according to the author?

Don't blame it on penurious Russian physicists selling their souls for 5,000 rubles and a Big Mac, or on accommodating German trading companies that are only too happy to ship sensitive electronic triggers under the label "automobile parts."

The North Koreans, who CIA Director Robert Gates warned may be only a few months away from building an atomic bomb, did it all by themselves. Saddam Hussein's Iraq got much closer to the bomb than anyone realized. And if the North Koreans and the Iraqis can do it, anyone can do it. "Things that were very difficult for the smartest people in 1943 are easy for ordinary people now," says Richard Garwin, a physicist at IBM's Thomas J. Watson Research Center and a former nuclear-weapons designer.

The Collapse of the Soviet Union

At the same time, the collapse of the Russian economy is unleashing a flood of uranium ore and other nuclear materials onto world markets; it may be only a matter of time before more dangerous products, including tons of plutonium from spent Soviet reactor fuel and perhaps even uranium-processing technology from the Central Asian republics, reach the black market. The West's attempt to prevent the spread of nuclear weapons, based on the premise that a combination of secrecy, export controls and inspections of civilian nuclear reactors could thwart the world's nuclear wannabes, has failed, and a new and much more dangerous era of nuclear proliferation has begun.

U.S. officials privately concede that the system has failed—and that America blew an important opportunity to strengthen it after the gulf war. "We should have pointed to Iraq as proof positive that the system doesn't work and that something much more aggressive must be put in place—an assertive nonproliferation policy instead of the passive one we have now," admits a senior U.S. official.

Now America and its allies may be facing a painful choice: Either use military force to prevent North Korea and others from going nuclear, or learn to live in a world in which nearly every nation that wants nuclear weapons has them. U.S. officials fear that a North Korean bomb could destabilize all of Northeast Asia, triggering a nuclear arms race that could bring South Korea, Japan and Taiwan into the nuclear club as well. A white paper issued by the South Korean Defense Ministry ominously warned that North Korea's bomb program "must be stopped at any cost."

But it would be much harder to muster allies for an attack on North Korea than it was to round up support for driving Saddam Hussein out of Kuwait. A commando raid, a cruise missile attack or a Stealth bomber raid on the North's nuclear installations could trigger another Korean war. In addition to its million-man Army, North Korea has thousands of artillery pieces and hundreds of Scud missile launchers lined up just across the demilitarized zone—well within range of Seoul, just 35 miles away. Japan would be likely to oppose the use of bases on its soil for such a mission; using them anyway could jeopardize the U.S.-Japan Security Treaty and magnify the growing tensions between Washington and Tokyo. "We'd like to see a political solution to this," says U.S. Under Secretary of Defense Paul Wolfowitz. "It's not the time to start discussing military options. But we haven't ruled anything out."

The Wrong Door

North Korea's approach to building the bomb is a case study of how a determined country can evade international controls—and without much outside help, either. The primary aim of the nuclear safeguards regime, first developed in the 1950s, was to let developing countries have commercial nuclear-power plants without allowing their byproducts to be funneled into bombs.

As a result, almost all of the International Atomic Energy Agency's inspection and monitoring efforts are devoted to keeping tabs on the uranium fuel that's fed into nuclear-power plants and on the plutonium-containing waste that comes out of them. Inspectors attach seals to the reactor vessel of a power plant after fuel is loaded or install cameras to monitor the cooling pools where spent fuel rods are kept after being removed from a reactor. The safeguards regime did not anticipate that instead of trying to divert nuclear raw materials from power plants bought from abroad, even technologically primitive countries such as North Korea might simply build their own, complete nuclear infrastructures—in effect, reproducing the Manhattan Project.

In fact, every country that has built a bomb or even come close has done it the same way—not by hijacking the operations of a civilian reactor but by building a dedicated bomb-making complex. That means the IAEA safeguards are largely focused in the wrong direction.

The hardest part of building a bomb is obtaining plutonium or highly enriched uranium to fuel the explosive chain reaction. Neither substance exists in nature. Plutonium is formed when uranium fuel is bombarded by neutrons inside a nuclear reactor; it must be extracted from the spent fuel, a step called reprocessing. Highly enriched uranium is made in an industrial process that selectively concentrates the isotope uranium-235 from 1 percent or less—its abundance in natural uranium ore—to the 20 percent, or ideally 90 percent, that is required for a nuclear explosive.

North Korea picked the plutonium route, which meant it needed a nuclear reactor. IAEA rules control the sale of reactors, as well as the hard-to-come-by materials needed to fuel and operate most power-producing reactors: low-enriched uranium fuel, which is needed for the water-cooled reactors typical in the United States and Europe, and heavy water (a combination of deuterium—a heavy isotope of hydrogen—and oxygen), which is needed for reactors fueled by more easily obtainable natural, unenriched uranium.

...AND NOW FOR THE REAL TRICK!

Paul Conrad, © 1992, Los Angeles Times. Reprinted with permission.

The North Koreans sidestepped these obstacles entirely. The design they chose went back to the dawn of the nuclear age. It uses natural uranium fuel and, in place of heavy water, graphite—which North Korea has in abundance. "The first reactor, which we built at the University of Chicago football field, was a graphite reactor," notes Michael Golay, a professor of nuclear engineering at MIT [Massachusetts Institute of Technology]. "It was built by stacking blocks [of graphite]" on a wooden scaffold. North Korea, like just about every country in the world, also has its own source of uranium ore.

The North Korean reactor, completed in 1987, is tiny by commercial standards, with a power output of 30 megawatts compared with 1,000 megawatts for a typical electric power plant. Yet it can produce at least 20 pounds of plutonium a year—more than enough to build one nuclear weapon.

"If you're in a weapons program, you don't want to tie in to your electric power system; you want a reactor that's especially for that purpose," says A. David Rossin, a nuclear engineer and a former U.S. assistant secretary of energy. Trying to divert plutonium from a power reactor presents a host of technical hurdles. Fuel in a power reactor is left in the core for a long time to maximize energy production; that makes it highly radioactive and hard to handle. Then it has to be reprocessed by remote control behind heavy shielding.

Undesirable Reactions

Moreover, long irradiation leads to undesirable nuclear reactions that complicate the bomb maker's task. When the neutrons produced in a nuclear reactor strike uranium-238—the abundant and otherwise uninteresting isotope of natural uranium—it is converted to plutonium-239, the stuff that bombs are made of. But in subsequent reactions the Pu-239 can in turn capture more neutrons itself, forming Pu-240 and -241. These isotopes not only are highly radioactive, but because they tend to undergo nuclear fission spontaneously, they can cause the nuclear chain reaction of a bomb to begin a fraction of a second too soon—making a whimper instead of a bang. To overcome this problem, a bomb has to be designed so the conventional explosives that squeeze the plutonium together to create a critical mass do their job much more quickly, an extremely difficult technical challenge. "But if your whole thing is oriented to production of the bomb, you avoid some of the headaches," says Leonard Spector, an expert on nuclear proliferation at the Carnegie Endowment for International Peace.

The obstacles that secrecy and technical backwardness once presented to the world's would-be bomb makers have largely vanished, too. Perfectly legal assistance has provided countries such as North Korea with a cadre of skilled technicians. Technicians from the former Soviet Union are working in Libya and Algeria. North Korea even received technical aid from the IAEA in uranium mining and assaying, and had reactor operators trained by the Soviet Union as part of an IAEA-sanctioned deal during the 1960s in which the Soviets provided a small, safeguarded research reactor at Yongbyon, the site of North Korea's burgeoning nuclear complex.

Uncontrolled Proliferation

Whatever happens to the nuclear weapons in the disintegrating Soviet Union, the old nightmare of uncontrolled atomic proliferation is moving measurably closer to reality—and it would not be dispelled even by an arrangement to destroy many of the Soviet nukes and keep the rest under responsible control. The Bomb may soon be brandished by a whole new class of countries—Third World regimes far more radical and unpredictable than any of the eight present members of the nuclear club.

George J. Church, *Time*, December 16, 1991.

Even designing a nuclear weapon, once the most closely guarded of secrets, is now not a terribly difficult task for a physicist anywhere. "What's classified today is how to build a *good* weapon," says Golay, "not how to build a weapon." Mathematical problems that challenged some of the best minds in the world during the Manhattan Project can now be solved on a personal computer. What's more, not all the best minds in the world are in the West anymore. Citizens of Taiwan, South Korea and India, for example, account for more than 2,600 of the science and engineering Ph.D.'s awarded annually by American universities.

The United States has been pressing its allies and the IAEA to tighten up export controls and inspection procedures to eliminate the kind of loopholes that North Korea exploited. All the major nuclear nations—with the notable exception of China—have now agreed that they will not sell *any* nuclear technology to a nation that refuses to open all its facilities to IAEA inspection—so-called full-scope safeguards. Under the nonproliferation treaty, the only obligation of a supplier nation is that the particular plant or material it sells be placed under safeguards. That loophole allowed Pakistan, India, Algeria and Israel, none of which have signed the treaty, to receive nuclear help from abroad while pursuing nuclear-weapons programs at uninspected sites.

Germany, embarrassed by the prominent role played by German companies in the legal, quasi-legal and blatantly illegal sales of nuclear technology to Pakistan, Iraq and other proliferators, has tightened its export controls. And a new IAEA policy has affirmed the agency's right to conduct inspections at undeclared facilities in countries that have signed the treaty or otherwise accepted full safeguards. Such inspections might have detected Iraq's clandestine nuclear program, for example, and may be invoked soon in an IAEA demand to see North Korea's undeclared production reactor and reprocessing plant.

But with the equivalent of only 40 full-time inspectors to cover close to 1,000 *declared* nuclear installations, the IAEA has its hands full already. And what especially concerns many nuclear experts is the increasing ease with which a determined nation can gain direct access to the critical technologies needed to enrich uranium or reprocess plutonium, as well as to weapons-grade materials themselves. Once a nation has the ability to manufacture its own highly enriched uranium or plutonium, no inspection regime is worth very much. It takes only a few weeks to make plutonium from a sealed and monitored storage depot into a nuclear bomb. Argentina, Brazil, Pakistan, India, Israel and South Africa all have declared or undeclared reprocessing or enrichment plants in operation. "Good intentions in peaceful times last for years; plutonium lasts forever once it's separated into weapons-usable form," says Paul Leventhal of the private Nuclear Control Institute. . . .

In the case of North Korea, U.S. officials are especially worried that Pyongyang may continue its foot dragging on allowing IAEA inspections just long enough to reprocess a couple of bombs' worth of plutonium, which it could then hide—or sell to the highest bidder.

But if the North Koreans try to peddle plutonium, they could face stiff competition. Russia has recovered at least 20 tons of plutonium from power reactors, in addition to military stockpiles of 115 tons of plutonium and 500 tons of highly enriched uranium, all of which the government is eager to sell as reactor fuel.

Peaceful Uses

"It could conceivably be sold to companies and consumers, as can any other valuable commodity. Hopefully it will be used in a beneficial method," says Boris Nikipelov, first deputy minister of Russia's Ministry of Atomic Power and Industry. "We see no technical or political restrictions against utilizing the materials." The fact that they have a market value of close to $1 billion is no doubt a factor, too. The Soviet Union sold 12 million pounds of uranium in the United States in 1991, worth $110 million, nearly 30 percent of the entire U.S. consumption; Russian shipments reached as much as 5 million pounds in the first month of 1992 alone. American uranium producers have filed an antidumping suit against the Russian sales.

The plutonium trade, meanwhile, is getting a boost from Japan, which is reprocessing reactor fuel in France and Britain, and plans to ship a *ton* of plutonium aboard a freighter escorted by a single Japanese patrol boat armed with a light cannon and machine guns. Japan plans to reprocess a total of 100 tons of plutonium over the next 20 years.

"You have an impossible task of accounting for it all," says Leventhal, "and ensuring that the 15 pounds you need to blow up a city doesn't fall into the wrong hands" through theft, terrorism, or black-market sales.

Leventhal argues that a global ban on the production of weapons-grade material would shut this door. "We haven't produced any plutonium for two or three years because our production reactors are all unsafe or broken," adds physicist Richard Garwin, "and we haven't produced any highly enriched uranium since 1964." The only remaining use the United States has for HEU is as fuel for reactors in ships and submarines, a demand Garwin says could easily be met from the U.S. stockpile of 500 tons. Russia says it no longer makes HEU and will stop plutonium production by 2000.

But it is unclear whether France and Britain, eyeing lucrative Japanese reprocessing contracts, would go along. And even some U.S. officials, while acknowledging that the nation no longer needs to produce weapons-grade material, are apathetic about a ban on the production of weapons-grade nuclear fuel. "I don't believe that I see any downside to it," says Everet Beckner, an official at the U.S. Department of Energy who works on defense programs, "but there are more important problems to consider."

In any event, nuclear experts are virtually unanimous in believing that no "technical fix" alone can do the job. "It's effectively impossible to keep the lid on," says MIT's Golay. "The only way you're going to control these things is to make them uninteresting." Unfortunately, some of the most unsavory regimes in the world are just now discovering that their motives and their opportunities for going nuclear are converging.

"The actual scope of the current proliferation threat is smaller *than is generally perceived."*

The Problem of Nuclear Proliferation Is Exaggerated

Thomas W. Graham

Thomas W. Graham is policy research coordinator at the University of California's Institute on Global Conflict and Cooperation in San Diego. In the following viewpoint, Graham argues that global nonproliferation efforts—from export controls to enforcing the Nuclear Nonproliferation Treaty (NPT)—have been successful. He maintains that these controls will continue to be successful and will continue to eliminate the threat of nuclear proliferation.

As you read, consider the following questions:

1. Why does Graham speculate that "winning" the nuclear nonproliferation battle is possible?
2. What evidence does Graham give to show that nonproliferation efforts have been successful?
3. Why does the author conclude that the threat of nuclear proliferation has been exaggerated?

As the Cold War dissipates, the spread of nuclear weapons has risen to the top of the international security agenda. After the *laissez-faire* nonproliferation policy of the Reagan era, the Bush team—initially reluctant to embrace a strong nonproliferation policy because of a mistaken perception that little could be done—has substantially upgraded its nonproliferation effort.

Nonproliferation Victories

Since then, six substantial nonproliferation victories have been won. France has announced its intention to sign the Nonproliferation Treaty (NPT), thereby codifying its transformation into a supporter of nonproliferation, which began in the mid-1970s. China, the last declared nuclear-weapon state hold-out and once one of the harshest critics of the NPT as a conspiracy against the developing world, has announced its willingness to sign. South Africa has actually signed the NPT, a step which could result in the first case of genuine nuclear disarmament—a state with a nuclear weapon capability dismantling that potential—and help assure that the African continent remains free of nuclear weapons. Argentina and Brazil have agreed to establish a mutual system of comprehensive safeguards and to take steps to implement the Treaty of Tlatelolco, Latin America's nuclear-weapon-free zone agreement. The International Atomic Energy Agency (IAEA) has successfully conducted several challenge inspections against a hostile country (Iraq), demonstrating that international safeguards can be extremely effective if backed by strong political support and intelligence information from the major powers. Finally, in the course of the gulf confrontation, the United Nations has established many potentially important precedents which could help reverse proliferation in other volatile regions of the world. If the North Korean nuclear program can be brought under control by a U.S.-led international coalition, the Bush administration will be able to lay claim to the most effective nonproliferation policy in U.S. history.

In the midst of these successes, there has been a growing debate over the future of U.S. nonproliferation policy. Some, including this author, believe that many current trends, especially the increasing delegitimization of nuclear weapons for all forms of extended deterrence, provide an opportunity to think about "winning" the nonproliferation battle—freezing or reversing the nuclear programs of the four current *de facto* nuclear-weapon states (India, Israel, Pakistan, and South Africa), and ensuring that no additional states are added to this list for at least the next 20 years. . . .

Fundamental to the winning strategy is the belief that many current conventional wisdoms about nuclear proliferation are wrong. The primary reason for this is that many discussions of proliferation take place on a very abstract level, focusing on the nuclear fuel cycle or the NPT regime. Most of the actual business of nuclear proliferation, however, relates to the often highly classified specifics associated with the "sensitive" nuclear programs of a handful of "problem" countries. Accurately assessing the options for an effective U.S. nonproliferation strategy for the 21st century requires a detailed knowledge of the successes and failures of these countries' nuclear programs over the last 30 years. Unfortunately, few individuals have had the historical perspective, breadth of detailed knowledge, or time to reflect on the key lessons learned over these three decades of international nonproliferation efforts.

The primary lesson—considered radical by some—is that getting the bomb is much *harder* than most strategists believe, and that international nonproliferation efforts have been extremely successful, especially given the meager resources that have been devoted to the task. As a result, today U.S. policymakers can and should realistically think in terms of "winning the battle." The intellectual logic that supports a winning approach is set out in a series of propositions.

A Finite Problem

The first and most important proposition is that the proliferation problem is finite, involving only a comparatively small number of serious problem countries, and that number is unlikely to grow in the foreseeable future. The fatalistic assumption that proliferation will continue indefinitely to all regions of the world, and that 20 or more countries will get the bomb, is not supported by either historical evidence or detailed analysis. The rate at which nations have become nuclear-weapon states or even *de facto* nuclear-weapon states has been slower than predicted by most of the Kennedy administration advisers in the early 1960s or the energy crisis analysts in the mid-1970s.

More importantly, for the last 10 years the proliferation problem has been limited to approximately a dozen nations. Despite wars, revolutions, conventional arms races, and the increasing spread of nuclear and high-tech military technology, these problem states have *not* increased appreciably in number. While 40 to 45 countries are sometimes cited as having the technical capability to begin a nuclear weapon program, most countries have clearly and deliberately "opted out" of the nuclear proliferation game. Virtually all of the nations of the world have calculated that acquisition of nuclear weapons would not strengthen their national security. Not only are more than 140 countries parties to the NPT, but all but a few of those countries (i.e., Iran, Iraq, Libya, and North Korea) are genuine parties to the treaty and represent no nuclear proliferation problem. Many nations that were considered potential problem countries 15 to 30 years ago are no longer of proliferation concern, a testament in part to the success of the international nonproliferation regime. Today, it is remarkable to remember that Egypt, Germany, Indonesia, Japan, Saudi Arabia, Spain, Sweden, Switzerland, Turkey, and Yugoslavia, were all once considered potential problem countries.

"We got a good deal on the warhead, but unfortunately there wasn't enough left over for a state-of-the-art delivery system."

In addition, since many countries also have opted out of nuclear energy research and production, any decision by most states to produce nuclear weapons would now face extremely long lead times and an international export control environment that makes procurement of complete sensitive nuclear facilities extremely difficult. . . .

The second major proposition supporting a winning nonproliferation strategy is that the actual scope of the current proliferation threat is *smaller* than is generally perceived. In addition, the capabilities of the dozen or so problem countries fall into distinct categories, and this has important implications for policy.

As mentioned earlier, despite the formal denials of several governments, four nations' nuclear weapon programs have progressed to the point that they must be considered *de facto* nuclear-weapon states—India, Israel, Pakistan, and South Africa. These countries either have nuclear weapons or could build them in days or weeks. Behind this group are four "advanced threshold countries"—Argentina, Brazil, South Korea, and Taiwan which have the technical capability to become *de facto* nuclear-weapon states in only a few years; because of international nonproliferation efforts, however, it appears that none of them is now likely to do so. Five "potential threshold states"— Algeria, Iran, post-war Iraq, Libya, and North Korea—are further away from having the technical capability to build a nuclear arsenal, but appear to have an interest in pursuing the nuclear weapon option. Only the four *de facto* nuclear-weapon states have produced nuclear weapons or could move quickly to do so. All other problem states will have to take clear and often difficult steps to become *de facto* nuclear-weapon states. And again, there is no evidence that this list of problem countries is lengthening; in fact, new opportunities are opening to shrink it.

Proliferation Can Be Rolled Back

A third proposition is that nuclear proliferation is not a one-way street. Reversing the tide is possible. Indeed, U.S. policy interventions both in the mid-1970s and recently have already succeeded in shortening the list of active problem states from approximately a dozen to about seven.

In the 1970s, the United States forced South Korea and Taiwan to take steps which reversed their nascent nuclear weapon programs. In the early 1980s, the United States took steps that have had the effect of significantly reducing Libya's nuclear proliferation potential. With the substantial recent progress made in diffusing the nuclear competition between Argentina and Brazil, these two long-time problem states have moved into the category of probable success stories. The complete implementation of U.N. Security Council Resolution 687, if achieved, could force Iraq into remission for a substantial period. With international attention focused on Iraq, rebuilding a covert nuclear weapon program there will be far more difficult than it was in the past.

South Africa's signing of the NPT could set an even more remarkable precedent. If South Africa ratifies the NPT, presents a credible accounting of its stockpile of highly enriched uranium to the IAEA, and places its entire stockpile under safeguards, it would become the first case of real nuclear disarmament in history—the first former *de facto* nuclear-weapon state. . . .

In short, active policy initiatives taken by the United States, by other nonproliferation leaders, and by domestic political leaders opposed to nuclear weapon development within various problem countries have created a new category of states that are "in remission." This list of successes is impressive: Argentina, Brazil, Libya, South Africa, South Korea, Taiwan, and potentially Iraq. It attests to the fact that winning the nonproliferation battle is possible, even in difficult cases. While constant attention will have to be paid to ensure that these countries stay in remission, one should not be surprised to find all of them free of nuclear weapons 20 years from now.

A fourth thesis challenges the conventional wisdom that the diffusion of technology makes it relatively easy to produce a nuclear weapon capability. A corollary is the belief that the continued spread of technology makes it much easier to produce nuclear weapons today than it was several decades ago, and that eventually it will become impossible to control sensitive nuclear technology. These impressions, common though they may be, are largely false—and they tilt the policy debate in a dangerously fatalistic direction.

A review of problem countries' efforts to build nuclear weapons reveals that lead times between a decision to build a nuclear device and the actual acquisition of a nuclear weapon capability remain quite long for virtually all Third World states of proliferation concern. The fact is that it remains extremely difficult to build a bomb. It requires a wide array of advanced technology, and a huge and expensive industrial infrastructure. . . .

This means that the international community continues to have "timely warning" in which to take action to stop a potential proliferator. In the process of building a nuclear weapon capability, proliferating states are highly vulnerable to cut-offs of technology and equipment, diplomatic pressure, and covert action.

In sum, the imperfect success of nonproliferation efforts to date has been due not to the inherent difficulty of controlling nuclear technology and equipment, but to the extremely limited diplomatic, intelligence, and military resources that have been devoted to the problem.

Export Controls Work

The fifth pillar of the winning strategy is the conclusion that nuclear export controls have substantial utility even against states with advanced industrial capabilities.

At a minimum, export controls ensure that a nuclear weapon program will be correctly identified as such early on. In every known case, export controls have forced proliferating countries to take steps in acquiring equipment and materials that clearly label their effort as being directed toward a military program. There is no need to set up a covert purchasing system or to acquire various specialized equipment if one wants only a peaceful nuclear power program. While proliferating states may hide behind the peaceful atomic rhetoric popular in the Atoms for Peace era, informed government officials in dozens of countries now have sufficient intelligence and analytical capability to differentiate between peaceful and military activities. . . .

Nonproliferation Success

Despite dire predictions in past years that 20 or 30 countries would have nuclear weapons by the 1990s, only one additional nation, India, is known to have detonated a nuclear device since the NPT came into effect. The two nuclear-weapons states that did not originally adhere to the treaty, France and China, have now decided to join as we work toward the indefinite extension of the pact when it is reviewed again in 1995.

Ronald Lehman, *The Washington Times*, February 2, 1992.

The sixth thesis is that from the point of view of potential proliferators, nuclear weapons are not cheaper than conventional weapons, as was once argued to be the case in the United States. A complete economic analysis shows that production of nuclear weapons for most potential proliferators is expensive.

As mentioned above, proliferators have generally been forced to spend billions of dollars to build a serious nuclear weapon program. Moreover, since nuclear weapons have not replaced conventional weapons for any state that has them, expenditures on nuclear weapons must be added to expenditures for modern conventional forces. As a result, while the phrase "more bang for the buck" did justify nuclear reliance in the specific context of the United States in the 1950s, the historical record of the nuclear age shows that most states correctly do not see nuclear weapons as a cost-effective way to deal with the security threats they face. Thus, economics provide a limited disincentive for developing nuclear weapons. . . .

Seventh, proponents of a winning strategy challenge the idea that the United States has to be "realistic" about its nonproliferation goals and has to acknowledge that stemming proliferation is only one aspect of foreign policy.

The historical record shows just the opposite: highly idealistic nonproliferation initiatives have always challenged the conventional *realpolitik* view of the day, and in essentially every case have been more effective and less costly—in both diplomatic and economic capital—than even their advocates predicted. . . .

The final tenet of the winning strategy is simply that we are now faced with several golden opportunities that may never come again. First, the United States has an unprecedented opportunity to show the world through its own actions that nuclear weapons are only useful for deterring the use of nuclear weapons, not for extended deterrence. With the collapse of the Warsaw Pact, the United States no longer requires extended deterrence to protect its vital interests in Western Europe. The current conventional balance on the Korean peninsula is sufficiently stable (from the West's point of view), that the United States could consider quietly removing U.S. nuclear weapons from South Korea. Similarly, some retired naval officers have concluded that the fighting efficiency of the fleet could be improved if tactical nuclear weapons were removed from our surface ships. . . .

Effects of Political Change

The unprecedented combination of political change and new technologies that can improve transparency has produced new possibilities for confidence-building measures in several regions around the world. These potentially could be applied as a first step toward reducing nuclear tensions in areas ranging from the Koreas to South Asia. . . .

As a result of all of these factors, it is now time to think "big" concerning a multilateral initiative to "solve" the proliferation problem in these key states. One first step would be to put together an international coalition and a package of incentives to convince these states to "STOP"—simultaneously terminate operation and production—at all their nuclear facilities that produce unsafeguarded weapons-grade material. A STOP initiative would be an excellent multilateral confidence-building measure. The fundamental value of a STOP approach is that it would serve as a first step to bring countries that have already proliferated and are unwilling to immediately roll back their nuclear programs into the arms control arena, capping their nuclear weapon potential. A STOP initiative would be easier to verify than a nuclear-weapon-free zone proposal because a state would only have to show that a specific facility was no longer operating. This could be done in a variety of ways, including the use of the national technical means of third parties, without initially going through the politically difficult step of applying full-scope IAEA safeguards. A STOP agreement could be made for a limited time period and continued if other states in the region took parallel steps which the initiating state believed would be needed before the initiative were made permanent.

> *"With the advent of [a] burgeoning free trade in technical ideas and the people who think about them, we have entered a new era in the history of proliferation."*

Nuclear Proliferation Is Inevitable

Tom Clancy and Russell Seitz

Tom Clancy is the author of the best-selling novels *Patriot Games*, *The Hunt for Red October*, and most recently, *The Sum of All Fears*. Russell Seitz is an associate of Harvard University's John M. Olin Institute for Strategic Studies in Cambridge, Massachusetts. In the following viewpoint, the authors argue that technological progress in computer science and physics has given most of the world the knowledge needed to make nuclear weapons. Because of the spread of information and the availability of technology, the proliferation of nuclear weapons will continue, the authors conclude.

As you read, consider the following questions:

1. The authors believe that an increasing number of people in less developed nations obtaining degrees in the sciences will in turn increase nuclear proliferation. Why?
2. Why are existing attempts to control nuclear proliferation a failure, according to the authors?
3. According to Clancy and Seitz, how have increases in the sale of advanced technologies contributed to nuclear proliferation?

From Tom Clancy and Russell Seitz, "Five Minutes Past Midnight—and Welcome to the Age of Proliferation," *The National Interest*, Winter 1991/1992. Copyright Tom Clancy, 1991. Reprinted with permission of *The National Interest*, Washington, D.C.

An H-bomb in Iraq? Chinese uranium enrichment hardware in Iran? It's just not the same world as that in which the study of disarmament and proliferation began. Generations have passed since the completion of the Manhattan Project—generations not just of people but technologies. Progress, a concept that generally resolves us to endure the terrors that the future holds, is upon us, and with its arrival we find ourselves confronted with that most ancient and malevolent curse: "May you live in interesting times.". . .

A generation later still, much that is unspeakably classified in the context of weapons design and fabrication is merely the common knowledge of other disciplines that have undergone a separate evolution in the unclassified world of international scientific endeavor. And circulating today within the scientific community is a wealth of expertise that dwarfs the amount of intellectual currency that existed in the 1940s and 1950s. The number of newly minted Ph.Ds and Sc.Ds entering the marketplace each year is transforming the global R&D scene in ways difficult to comprehend and impossible to reverse.

In the two generations that have grown to adulthood since World War II, the sociology of science and technology has been transformed. A once Eurocentric enterprise has become a global one. In 1939, German was the *lingua franca* of science—of physics in particular. Scientists were far fewer than today. Apart from America, Europe, Japan, and the USSR, few nations could boast of dozens, let alone hundreds, of Ph.Ds in the pure or applied sciences. Whenever individuals of scientific promise arose in the British or French colonies, they tended to be educated at those empires' hearts, there to spend their careers rather than return to the impoverished or nonexistent technical cultures of their homelands.

The Transformation of the World of Technology

The intervening years have witnessed a transformation of the world of technology. What was extremely demanding then—building a few bombs stretched the "high technology" of World War II to its limits, and beyond—has ceased to be state-of-the-art or even demanding. In the 1940s, the Third Reich's atomic weapons program barely got off the drawing board. Its experimental program ended before a chain reaction was achieved. Yet today, little of the equipment, instruments, and materials (fissionables and explosives excepted) needed to develop the first generation of atomic weapons is alien to the research establishments of a large university or a Fortune 500 company. High technology has become a global enterprise and the scientific database that underlies it has become almost universally accessible.

With the advent of this burgeoning free trade in technical ideas and the people who think about them, we have entered a new era in the history of proliferation. It is cautionary to note that what the Germans could and did accomplish at the limits of their wartime high-technology binge—the V-2 rocket—has been successfully emulated by Iraq and North Korea. Perhaps the most fitting adjective to apply to the scientific and technical resources of most nations, with or without nuclear ambitions today, is "overqualified.". . .

Warm, Wet, and Gray

For four decades, the United States and Europe have been engaged in exporting to the developing nations the most sensitive of nuclear materials. This uncontrolled trade has grown exponentially, increasing ninefold in the last thirty years and doubling in the last decade. The matter in question is warm, wet, and gray—a small tonnage of human brains freshly armed with doctorates in nuclear physics and all its related disciplines. Most of them go home.

A high-tech cadre of thousands has returned to the Third World with First World advanced degrees. For example, both India and Taiwan now have more than 2,500 American-educated Ph.Ds. Even more remarkable, South Korea is now acquiring more than 1,000 American doctorates *annually*. Similar numbers have stayed behind in the West to participate in state-of-the-art research in disciplines as varied as plasma physics, materials science, chemical engineering, and computer science. The percentage of the world's scientists and engineers resident in developing countries rose from 7.6 percent to 10.2 percent between 1970 and 1980 and today exceeds 13 percent.

More than mere numbers is at issue. The strength of science has grown to a point where a comparative handful of scientists and engineers can successfully pursue tasks that once required the concerted effort of hordes of the best and brightest. Interdisciplinary areas of research are fertile ground for the rediscovery in the open literature of the technical factors that were originally cultivated in secret and kept thereafter in the well-guarded vaults of the superpowers' weapons establishments. Many, perhaps most, of the concepts, techniques, materials, and machines originally developed to enable the production of the first generation of thermonuclear devices have been reinvented, rediscovered, or spontaneously spun off into the world of civilian R&D and purely scientific endeavor. . . .

In the aftermath of the information explosion, the component technologies of nuclear proliferation are no longer identifiably labeled as such. What is evolving spans the spectrum of scientific work—but with the advent of computerized databases a macroscope for visualizing such a 360 percent field of view is becoming available on line.

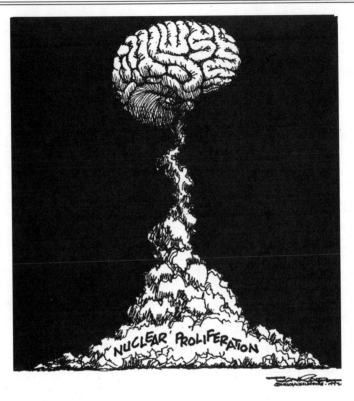

Paul Conrad, ©1992 Los Angeles Times. Reprinted with permission.

As high-technology ramifies, appropriate technologies multiply: the most engaging illusion of proliferation control arises from the temptation to believe that its central goal is to prevent the duplication of *existing* technology. Before the first prototype of a weapons system comes into existence at the level of conceptual design—before its component technologies have been fabricated—one cannot determine which alternate concept for each component will prevail in the long term. . . .

A current example involves the calutron, a bastardized descendant of a Depression-era atom smasher (the original Berkeley cyclotron). Relative inefficiency doomed the early calutrons, and the strength of existing materials limited gas centrifuges in the 1940s. But the Atomic Energy Commission and its successors blithely created a new discipline, materials science, and massively funded it for another half-century. The result: the materials science community naively solved those problems associated with the gas centrifuge and irremediably changed the context of separation technology. This is significant, because such initially dismissed branches of technology as the calutron can take root and flourish in the shadow of their "mature" competitors. Thus the western scientific community was taken by surprise when the calutron, a woefully inefficient device for electromagnetic uranium isotope separation, was reborn in Iraq. This second life testifies to the difference between the undoable and the merely obsolete. At ground zero it matters not if an H-bomb has fallen from a B-2 or a Zeppelin.

Welcome to the Future

In the near future it will be possible to duplicate almost all past technology in all but the most forlorn of Third World backwaters, and much of the present state-of-the-art will be both intellectually and practically accessible. It is no longer safe to assume that looking for the paper trail of a nation attempting to emulate the work of the Manhattan Project will lead us to the laboratories of those with nuclear ambitions. The scope of technical enterprise in today's world prevents a rigid definition of what to look for. The motto of today's ambitious bomb-smiths might be, "These are our weapons technologies—if you don't like them, we have others." Teach a man to make microwave ovens and you've opened the door to radar and calutrons alike. CO-COM (the Coordinating Committee on Exports Control) can list and monitor trade in "critical" components; but available tools and materials, and the ubiquity of iron, copper, sand, and vacuum, doom the exercise to futility in the not-very-long run. . . .

The Russian Yard Sale

We are partly to blame: consider the proliferation risks inherent in our emphasis on classifying data rather than protecting technology from exposure. It is edifying to attend the manufacturers' displays that accompany many large technical meetings sponsored by engineering associations or the Department of Defense. There, proudly displayed, are the first fruit of Pentagon R&D—components whose exotic materials and advanced electronic, thermal, and optical performance seem unparalleled in the civilian sector, and which are very often offered before their end-use systems (the B-2 and SDI, for instance) have even been tested or publicly displayed. Silicon carbide laser mirrors or stealth carbon foam, it's all on offer in the West—albeit without reference to what it has been developed for. And now in the East, even more is on sale.

The Iron Curtain did more than isolate the citizens of the Warsaw Pact nations from the Free World. It also functioned as an impermeable barrier, a containment that kept in a mass of militarily important high technology often rivaling the best in the West. Now that containment has been breached, and the most secretive of military powers is spilling its technology into a new and multipolar world where nuclear ambitions have multiplied. Throughout the former Warsaw Pact, we are witnessing the Yard Sale at the End of History. The Soviet Union is selling jewels more precious than the Fabergé eggs of the Romanovs—at distress-sale prices. . . .

Proliferation Will Continue

The shocking experience with Iraq's nuclear program has brought two clear conclusions. The first is that knowledge of how to construct nuclear weapons is now so extensive that the spread of nuclear weapons cannot be stopped by controlling information on the subject. UN inspections have revealed that Iraq acquired its nuclear expertise through educating its own citizens in physics and engineering programs in foreign universities and through published literature.

Second, current multilateral controls on nuclear materials and components, as well as national intelligence means for monitoring the nuclear programs of other states, are wholly inadequate to stop countries from acquiring nuclear weapons capability.

Union of Concerned Scientists, *A Program for World Nuclear Security*, February 1992.

The response of Soviet laboratories to the outbreak of peace has been even more disturbing. Invoking glasnost and perestroika, they are ready and willing to sell off the fruits of decades of innovation and development for hard currency abroad, rather than seeking means of converting it to civilian use in a land where the ruble is despised. Despite the supposedly continuing vigilance of both the KGB and the military, a virtual sampler of military technology—some of it arising from nuclear weapons research—has been put on the table for Western entrepreneurs and Third World shoppers. . . .

As glasnost mutates into an unbridled high-tech sell-off, we must revise our perception of how the technologies of mass destruction may soon spread across the globe. For what is on sale is not Manhattan Project surplus, but systems explicitly made for fighting the World War III that never was.

Some of the architects of the present regime of proliferation controls will protest that such speculations are moot. They will argue that, given iron-clad sanctions against trade in ^{235}uranium and ^{239}plutonium and vigilant monitoring of the technological basis for their enrichment and separation, traffic in weapons-building expertise is unlikely to result in anything being built, because of the sheer lack of the critical materials of construction. But such complacency is foolish.

The common wisdom is that, having been stripped of its uranium and plutonium, waste from spent nuclear reactor fuel assemblies poses only the problem of finding a safe means of long-term storage. However, the waste is still pregnant with elements like neptunium which, despite their never having been used in deployed American nuclear weapons, are every bit as fissionable as the better-known trans-uranic elements. . . .

Nuclear Ambition

Very often we forget how the imperatives of nuclear ambition can warp normative perceptions of safety and cost-effectiveness beyond recognition. Many a terrorist has made his own nitroglycerine. Some of the spent fuel residue is already four decades old and has decayed to a point where its once ferocious radioactivity has fallen nearly a thousandfold. Today, using technologies as diverse as robotics and zeolite ion exchange separation, a group bent on quarrying rad-waste for weapons—a patently suicidal notion three decades ago—might live to tell the tale.

More ominous still is the risk of the qualitative escalation of proliferation, of nations following Iraq's example in proceeding directly to the H-bomb. The assumption that "strategic" yield devices are vastly more demanding technically has been undermined by two factors: first, numerically controlled machine tools of optical levels of precision and almost unlimited versatility; second, the availability of computers and attendant software that bridge the gap between the level of sheer genius needed to innovate thermonuclear devices and the less demanding task of getting them built once their operation is understood from its first principles. This hypothesis has been chillingly corroborated by the UN's recent discovery of Iraq's possession of precision machine tools as well as isotopically purified ^{6}lithium, with evident intent to develop a hydrogen bomb.

When the Einstein-Szilard letter brought the possibility of the atomic bomb to President Franklin Roosevelt's attention, the American Physical Society had just 4000 members. About half of this cadre of (mostly) Ph.Ds joined the Manhattan Project, which at its height employed roughly 10,000 scientists with advanced degrees, principally in chemistry and chemical engineering. Some of its veterans have reflected on the acceleration of their research efforts relative to the pace of their pre-war endeavors. They all concur that the program's relatively unlimited budget contributed mightily to its rapid progress. It took a great deal of money, some $2 billion in an era when the largest of industrial research establishments—General Electric or Du Pont, for example—had annual budgets on the order of $10 million. That acceleration has more modern examples, such as the Apollo program in the 1960s and the Iraqi nuclear program of the 1980s. It is a tacit principle of research management that money buys time, and having spent a billion dollars a year for a decade, Iraq's progress should surprise no one. . . .

Death of the Illusion

The hermetic secrecy of the Manhattan Project gave way in the 1950s to the public emergence of nuclear science and information technology. Half a century later, there are more secrets than ever inside the weapons laboratories, but few that remain novel to the unclassified realm of science and technology that has been burgeoning uncontrollably on the outside. The continuing inflation of an already sprawling high-technology sector that spans the globe is leading us into a future that may be beyond economic repair. It is one in which the growing similarity of civilian and military technologies may lead to the extinction of their meaningful difference.

Information is the universal solvent of secrecy. And secrecy is not to be regarded as a permanent thing. The more that is known, the less remains that can be kept unknown. With the exponential growth of the technologies of information, the pressure of the known can exceed the strength of a secret technology's containment, and secrets can implode into irrelevance. Two thousand years before Columbus, Heraclitus gave us fair warning: *He who does not expect the unexpected cannot detect it.* Contemplating the realm of science and technology today, and considering the prospect of what intelligence, human and artificial, can accomplish in the century to come, we arrive at the depressing conclusion that the present regime of proliferation control may be among that rare set of entities—a fit object for catastrophe theory.

"The continued spread of nuclear weapons to additional countries is not inevitable."

Nuclear Proliferation Is Not Inevitable

Center for Defense Information

The Center for Defense Information in Washington, D.C., works to reduce the military's influence on U.S. domestic and foreign policy and to prevent nuclear war. In the following viewpoint, the author argues that controls on the spread of nuclear proliferation have been successful. New proliferation problems such as those in the Third World can be prevented by strengthening existing proliferation controls like the Nonproliferation Treaty, the author maintains. The author concludes that if these measures are enforced, the spread of nuclear weapons will not be inevitable.

As you read, consider the following questions:

1. Why have existing nonproliferation controls been effective, according to the author?
2. According to the author, how has the threat of nuclear proliferation been exaggerated?
3. How can the Nonproliferation Treaty and the International Atomic Energy Agency prevent nuclear proliferation, in the author's opinion?

From the Center for Defense Information, "Stopping the Spread of Nuclear Weapons: Still Time to Act," *The Defense Monitor*, vol. 21, no. 3, 1992. Reprinted with permission.

Since the beginning of the nuclear era there has been apprehension about the possible spread, or "proliferation," of nuclear weapons. In 1962 President John F. Kennedy warned that "fifteen or twenty or twenty-five nations may have these weapons" by the middle of the 1970s. But thanks largely to a complex assortment of national and international institutions, policies, and agreements established to counter nuclear weapons proliferation, this has not yet happened.

Iraq's Secret Program

However, disclosures about Iraq's secret nuclear weapons program have revived concerns that the "nuclear club" is expanding and damaged confidence in traditional nonproliferation measures. In 1991 Defense Secretary Dick Cheney reported to Congress that eight Third World countries "either have or may be near to acquiring nuclear weapons." In his 1992 State of the Union address, President Bush said of the multibillion-dollar Star Wars missile defense plan, "We must have this protection because too many people in too many countries have access to nuclear arms."

But to what extent is this most recent proliferation scare warranted? Is it mere coincidence that the sudden high-level attention being given to this issue coincides with a post-Cold War scramble by the Pentagon and the CIA to identify new threats? And if their security interests are threatened, what should be the reaction of the United States and other concerned countries?

The U.S. responded to proliferation concerns about Iraq by bombing suspected nuclear weapons facilities. Substituting military force for a nonproliferation policy, however, will not prevent nuclear weapons from spreading. Nor will it help to retreat behind unproven Star Wars technologies.

A far more effective response would be to strengthen peaceful nonproliferation mechanisms, in particular the systematic inspection procedures, or "safeguards," of the International Atomic Energy Agency (IAEA). In addition, if those countries that already possess nuclear weapons are serious about preventing further proliferation, they must dramatically reduce their reliance on such weapons. As long as they continue to assign importance to nuclear weapons, it should come as no surprise that other countries may also want them.

Going Nuclear

The know-how required to design a simple atomic bomb is now widely disseminated. Many of the technologies needed to develop a bomb, according to CIA Director Robert Gates, "are simply more available and more easily absorbed by Third World countries than ever before." Because some technologies are "dual-use," having both military and civilian applications, it is difficult to restrict trade in them without hampering the ability of developing countries to modernize.

One might expect countries that lack sophisticated industrial bases to be highly vulnerable to export controls and sanctions. However, several such countries have demonstrated that through a variety of means, including front companies, false documentation, and third-country transshipments, external constraints can be overcome. A black market in nuclear equipment and materials waits to serve would-be possessors of nuclear weapons.

Nonproliferation Programs Deserve Attention

The spread of the bomb is not inevitable. Preventing proliferation is an achievable goal in many cases and, given the stakes involved, deserves to be pursued vigorously.

Leonard S. Spector, *The National Interest*, Spring 1992.

The primary technical obstacle to making a nuclear weapon is acquiring the fissile material needed to fuel the chain reaction in a nuclear explosion. About 25 kilograms of highly enriched uranium or 8 kilograms of plutonium are generally regarded as the necessary minimum, although more sophisticated designs may enable a bomb to be built with less material. Weapons-grade uranium is produced by enriching the concentration of U-235 in natural uranium to 90 percent or better. Plutonium is obtained by chemically separating (reprocessing) spent (irradiated) reactor fuel.

Of course, it is one thing to have a nuclear weapon, but it is another matter entirely to have nuclear weapons plus missiles capable of delivering them to targets thousands of miles away. In this regard the U.S. remains fortunate. In January 1992 Gates told Congress that "only China and the successors of the former Soviet Union now have the physical capability to strike the United States directly with weapons of mass destruction. We do not expect direct threats to the U.S. to arise within the next decade.". . .

The Nuclear Club

The most tangible demonstration of a nuclear weapons capability is a nuclear explosion. It is something only six countries are known to have accomplished: the U.S. (960 explosions since 1945), the former Soviet Union (715 since 1949), the U.K. (44 since 1952), France (192 since 1960), China (36 since 1964), and

India (1 in 1974).

The first five—collectively known as the "nuclear club"—were until 1991 the only countries with "declared," or acknowledged, nuclear arsenals. Now Soviet nuclear weapons are spread among the new nations of Russia, Ukraine, Kazakhstan, and Belarus.

Meanwhile, India, Israel, Pakistan, and South Africa are widely believed either to have some undeclared nuclear weapons or to be able to produce a limited number of them within weeks or months of a decision to do so. Several additional countries—Algeria, Iran, Iraq, Libya, and North Korea—are suspected of seeking to join them. . . .

In 1986 Israel's nuclear weapons program was detailed in a British newspaper using information and photographs provided by Mordechai Vanunu, a former technician at its Dimona nuclear complex. Vanunu claimed that Israel was manufacturing 40 kilograms of weapons-grade plutonium annually and had produced lithium deuteride, an ingredient necessary for the manufacture of thermonuclear bombs, and tritium, a radioactive gas used to boost the explosive power of fission bombs. . . .

Iran's Status

Iran is a signatory of the NPT. However, U.S. officials say that there are clear indications that it wants nuclear weapons. Iranian leaders have spoken openly of Iran's right to possess nuclear weapons and have suggested that Muslim nations should acquire nuclear weapons to match Israel's capabilities.

At present Iran lacks the industrial base to support a nuclear weapons effort. But it has been reported to be developing gas centrifuges for enriching uranium, to have agreed to purchase a small plutonium-production reactor from China, and to be seeking to buy a research reactor from India. China is also believed to have sold Iran technology for enriching uranium.

However, IAEA inspectors who visited Iran in February 1992 turned up no evidence of nuclear weapons development. So far U.S. officials, as well, have failed to identify any hidden facilities in Iran that might be part of a nuclear weapons program.

Iraq's nuclear weapons program was severely set back by the recent war and the continuing implementation of U.N. Security Council Resolution 687, which called upon the IAEA to assume custody of all weapons-usable nuclear materials in Iraq. Before the war Iraq was believed to be at least 5-10 years away from being able to make a nuclear weapon. Now IAEA inspectors estimate that it may have been less than 2 years away.

Iraq is a signatory of the NPT and concluded a full-scope safeguards agreement with the IAEA in 1972. Yet it was able to secretly violate the international nonproliferation system even while openly participating in it. The IAEA had inspected declared Iraqi nuclear facilities as late as November 1990 and found no evidence of misuse of nuclear materials.

After the war inspection teams uncovered a broad, multitrack program for nuclear weapons development through uranium enrichment. Iraq violated its IAEA inspection agreement by possessing undeclared nuclear material and extracting three grams of plutonium in its Tuwaitha research reactor from safeguarded fuel rods. Inspectors suspect that Iraq may still be hiding an undeclared plutonium reactor and some enriched uranium. . . .

The Koreas

The CIA has accused North Korea of building a plutonium reprocessing plant that will enable it to produce a nuclear bomb within "a few months to as much as a couple of years" once the plant is completed. Stung by its failure to detect the extent of Iraq's program, however, the CIA may be erring on the side of caution. Its estimate has been disputed by officials within the State Department.

Intelligence sources estimate that the plant will be capable of producing 18-50 kilograms of plutonium annually, enough for 2-7 atomic weapons. North Korea is also believed to have constructed a research reactor between 1980 and 1987 capable of producing 7 kilograms of plutonium yearly, perhaps enough for a single bomb.

Lately, however, there have been some encouraging political developments. In December 1991 the two Koreas signed a joint declaration that would transform the Korean peninsula into a nuclear weapon-free zone. The pact commits each side not to "test, produce, receive, possess, store, deploy, or use" nuclear weapons, prohibits possession of facilities for plutonium reprocessing and uranium enrichment, and provides for the establishment of a joint monitoring body to verify compliance.

Six years after it signed the NPT, North Korea has finally concluded and ratified a full-scope safeguards agreement with the IAEA. Reportedly President Bush has set a deadline of June 1992 by which time IAEA inspections must begin. There has been no indication of what the U.S. would do if the deadline is not met.

Supply

Except for North Korea, all of the aforementioned countries received help from profit-minded governments, businesses, and individuals from the industrialized world. France, for example, has provided nuclear-related assistance to India, Iraq, Israel, Pakistan, and South Africa. Germans have supplied nuclear technology to Argentina, Brazil, India, Iran, Iraq, Libya, and Pakistan. . . .

As for Iraq's push for nuclear weapons, according to David Kay, deputy leader of an IAEA inspection team in Iraq, there was "no area of the world that did not contribute." Most notably, German companies were found to have provided Iraq with key components for as many as 10,000 "gas centrifuges" needed to produce weapons-grade uranium.

The CIA has identified a potential "brain drain" to the Third World of scientists and technicians who worked in the former Soviet Union's nuclear weapons program as "the area that causes us the greatest concern. . . ." It estimates that "nearly a million Soviets were involved in nuclear weapons programs" of whom maybe "a thousand or two have the know-how to design nuclear weapons." Also of concern is the possibility that former Soviet nuclear weapons, technology, and an estimated 700-1,000 tons of weapons-grade fissile material might be sold or stolen. . . .

Countering Proliferation

The continued spread of nuclear weapons to additional countries is not inevitable. There are several steps which if taken can slow and perhaps even reverse this trend. First, it is important in the long run to seek resolution of the regional disputes and underlying tensions fueling the demand for nuclear weapons.

Second, because civil nuclear energy programs are a stepping stone to nuclear bombs, it is in the interest of nonproliferation to develop alternatives to nuclear power such as geothermal, wind, and solar energy.

Diplomacy and Nonproliferation

Non-proliferation should be given higher priority in our broader diplomacy. Many states that are now seeking or potentially seeking atomic or other mass-destruction weaponry—Iran, states of the former Soviet Union—are also seeking normalization of economic relations with the West. Strict adherence to non-proliferation standards should be one major price of admission to the Western economic community.

Patrick Glynn, *The National Interest*, Spring 1992.

Third, exports of sensitive nuclear materials must cease. Most industrialized countries have now agreed to limit nuclear exports only to countries that have accepted full-scope IAEA safeguards. But as traditional suppliers strengthen their export controls, emerging, or "second-tier," suppliers like Argentina, Brazil, China, and India must be discouraged from taking their place. Tough sanctions should be imposed against any individual, company, or country found to be contributing to the spread of nuclear weapons.

To keep former Soviet nuclear weapon scientists and technicians from selling their expertise to Third World bidders, their talents could be redirected to cleaning up the environmental and safety hazards left by four decades of nuclear bomb production, upgrading the safety of civilian nuclear power plants to prevent another Chernobyl disaster, dismantling and destroying nuclear weapons, and working as inspectors for the understaffed and overburdened IAEA.

It is also in the interest of nonproliferation that the U.S. and former Soviet nuclear arsenals be scaled back substantially more than is already planned. Short of eliminating them, the surest way to prevent nuclear weapons and related materials from turning up in the wrong hands is to use one of several available techniques to tag the weapons so that their whereabouts can be verified and to place all fissile material under IAEA safeguards. . . .

Beefing Up the IAEA

Given sufficient authority, resources, and backing, the safeguards system of the IAEA represents the best hope for preventing the further spread of nuclear weapons. In the past the IAEA has enjoyed very few rights. Acceptance of safeguards has been of a voluntary nature. Governments have insisted on the right to refuse inspections or to set conditions. Even the IAEA's own literature states that the safeguards system "is not designed in a way that would enable it to physically prevent a government from diverting nuclear material to the production of nuclear weapons."

The agency does possess, but has never exercised on its own initiative, the right to conduct mandatory, short-notice challenge inspections of undeclared facilities, referred to in full-scope safeguards agreements as "special inspections." It may request such inspections "if the Agency considers that information made available by the safeguarded country . . . is not adequate for the Agency to fulfill its responsibilities under the agreement."

To enable the IAEA to implement challenge inspections and inspect newly-declared fissile material in Argentina, Brazil, North Korea, South Africa, and former Soviet republics, it is essential that it be better funded. For several years the agency has operated on a zero-growth budget. Its FY [fiscal year] 1993 budget of about $207 million should be increased to at least $500 million. The assessed contribution of the U.S.—about $27 million—should also be increased and should be paid in January, not in October as is currently the practice. . . .

Other ways to improve the efficiency and effectiveness of the IAEA include doubling the number of full-time inspectors (at present about 200); increasing the frequency of inspections (Iraq was inspected only twice a year); sharing the intelligence information of the U.S. and other countries with the IAEA regarding suspect sites; and closing a current loophole by applying safeguards to fissile material used to fuel nuclear-powered ships and submarines. This highly enriched fuel potentially could be used in weapons.

Comprehensive Action

Finally, if India, Israel, Pakistan, and other countries that have not signed the NPT or accepted full-scope IAEA safeguards are to be persuaded to do so, it is important that the U.S. and other members of the nuclear club accept comprehensive IAEA monitoring of all of their nuclear activities, something they so far have been unwilling to do. There is still time to act.

Distinguishing Between Fact and Opinion

This activity is designed to help develop the basic reading and thinking skill of distinguishing between fact and opinion. Consider the following statement as an example: "The first atomic bomb was tested at Los Alamos, New Mexico, in 1945." This statement is a fact that can be verified by looking up *atomic bomb* in an encyclopedia. But the statement "Nuclear proliferation threatens global security" is clearly an opinion. Experts disagree about whether nuclear proliferation is a serious threat.

When investigating controversial issues it is important that one be able to distinguish between statements of fact and statements of opinion. It is also important to recognize that not all statements of fact are true. They may appear to be true, but some are based on inaccurate or false information. For this activity, however, we are concerned with understanding the difference between those statements that appear to be factual and those that appear to be based primarily on opinion.

Most of the following statements are taken from the viewpoints in this chapter. Consider each statement carefully. *Mark O for any statement you believe is an opinion or interpretation of facts. Mark F for any statement you believe is a fact. Mark I for any statement you believe is impossible to judge.*

If you are doing this activity as a member of a class or group, compare your answers with those of other class or group members. Be able to defend your answers. You may discover that others come to different conclusions than you do. Listening to the reasons others present for their answers may give you valuable insights into distinguishing between fact and opinion.

O = *opinion*
F = *fact*
I = *impossible to judge*

1. Plutonium is formed when uranium fuel is bombarded by neutrons inside a nuclear reactor.
2. The hardest part of building an atomic bomb is obtaining plutonium to fuel the explosive chain reaction.
3. North Korea is an inevitable nuclear threat to northeast Asia.
4. The first nuclear reactor was built in a university football stadium.
5. China exports nuclear technology only for peaceful purposes.
6. France and Great Britain would not cooperate with a global ban on producing plutonium.
7. Citizens of Taiwan, South Korea, and India account for more than twenty-six hundred of the science and engineering Ph.D.'s awarded annually by American universities.
8. Current conventional wisdom about nuclear proliferation is wrong.
9. Getting the bomb is much harder than most strategists believe.
10. South Africa has signed the Nonproliferation Treaty.
11. The list of nations with nuclear weapons includes India, Israel, and Pakistan.
12. The fatalistic assumption that proliferation will continue indefinitely to all regions of the world is not supported by either historical evidence or detailed analysis.
13. Doubling the number of full-time inspectors will improve the effectiveness of the International Atomic Energy Agency's monitoring program.
14. In 1939, German was the lingua franca of science—of physics in particular.
15. Nuclear proliferation cannot be controlled simply by preventing the duplication of existing technology.
16. In the 1980s, the technological capability of the former Soviet Union was more advanced than that of the United States.
17. UN monitors in Iraq found evidence of nuclear weapons technology.
18. Substituting military force for nonproliferation policy will not stop the spread of nuclear weapons.
19. The International Atomic Energy Agency was established in 1957 and is headquartered in Vienna, Austria.
20. Israel's nuclear capability was documented in 1986 by Mordechai Vanunu.

Periodical Bibliography

The following articles have been selected to supplement the diverse views presented in this chapter.

Graham Allison, Ashton B. Carter, and Philip Zelikov — "The Error of Caution on Disarming the Former Soviets," *The Washington Post National Weekly Edition*, April 13-19, 1992.

Marilyn Bechtel — "Disarmament—Progress and Problems," *People's Weekly World*, August 3, 1991. Available from 239 W. 23d St., New York, NY 10011.

John M. Broder — "Terrifying Quest for A-Arms," *Los Angeles Times*, January 19, 1992.

McGeorge Bundy — "Nuclear Weapons and the Gulf," *Foreign Affairs*, Fall 1991.

George J. Church — "Who Else Will Have the Bomb?" *Time*, December 16, 1991.

Richard A. Clarke — "A Multi-Faceted Approach to Nonproliferation," *U.S. Department of State Dispatch*, May 6, 1991. Available from the U.S. Government Printing Office, Superintendent of Documents, Washington, DC 20402.

Sidney Drell — "Abolishing Long-Range Nuclear Missiles," *Issues in Science and Technology*, Spring 1992.

Benjamin Frankel — "Explosive Matter: Nuclear Proliferation Policy," *The American Enterprise*, March/April 1990.

Patrick Glynn — "The Nuclear Proliferation Boom," *The New Republic*, October 28, 1991.

Joel Millman — "Weapons for the Masses," *Los Angeles Times Magazine*, May 10, 1992.

Michael Nacht — "Nuclear Proliferation in the Middle East," *The World & I*, December 1990.

The Nation — "A Soapbox Scandal: Henry Gonzalez and the Truths of War," June 1, 1992.

The National Interest — "An Exchange on Proliferation," Spring 1992. Available from 1112 16th St. NW, Suite 540, Washington, DC 20036.

C. James Novak — "Practicing for Armageddon," *Newsweek*, March 9, 1992.

George W. Rathjens and Marvin M. Miller — "Nuclear Proliferation After the Cold War," *Technology Review*, August/September 1991.

Carla Anne Robbins   "The X Factor in the Proliferation Game," *U.S. News & World Report*, March 16, 1992.

Eugene Robinson   "Brazil and Argentina Step Back from the Nuclear Brink," *The Washington Post National Weekly Edition*, February 3-9, 1992.

Steve Salerno   "The Nuclear Country Club," *The American Legion*, July 1991. Available from 700 N. Pennsylvania St., PO Box 1055, Indianapolis, IN 46206.

Raju G.C. Thomas   "Going Nuclear After the War," *Nuclear Times*, Autumn 1991. Available from 401 Commonwealth Ave., Boston, MA 02215.

Sheryl WuDunn   "China Backs Pact on Nuclear Spread," *The New York Times*, August 11, 1991.

2 CHAPTER

Are International Measures Effective Against Proliferation?

NUCLEAR
PROLIFERATION

Chapter Preface

Breakthroughs in the development of nuclear weapons caused many countries to fear the spread of these lethal armaments. Consequently, the United Nations called for a worldwide commitment to discontinue nuclear weapons development and manufacture. In 1968, the UN achieved its goal when the Nuclear Nonproliferation Treaty (NPT) was signed by eighty-two nations. Now, with more than 140 signatory members, the vast majority of which have adhered to it, the NPT is often hailed as the core of nonproliferation efforts.

Besides promising not to acquire nuclear weapons, NPT member nations with civilian nuclear programs also agree to inspections by the International Atomic Energy Agency, a UN-affiliated organization concerned with the safe use of nuclear energy. The IAEA designed such inspections to assure that a country is not using civilian nuclear technology to build weapons. The IAEA can penalize a nation by denying technical assistance to its civilian nuclear program. In addition, it can ask the UN Security Council to impose economic sanctions on NPT violators or even to order military action against more threatening nations.

However, many nuclear experts question the effectiveness of the IAEA. Critics argue that the IAEA is not aggressive enough in finding and punishing violators. For instance, although the IAEA is empowered to conduct "special inspections" without notification, it has done so only once, in 1991, when the UN ordered the destruction and removal of Iraq's prohibited nuclear facilities and supplies. Traditionally, the IAEA has acted in the spirit of cooperation, avoiding conflict with NPT members.

Critics also contend that it is too easy for suspect nations to inhibit inspections to protect their weapons programs. One glaring example of this is Iraq. In 1991, IAEA inspectors were shot at and detained by Iraqi soldiers for four days. North Korea is another example. The nation refused to allow inspections for years.

Many argue that the effectiveness of inspections to control proliferation can be summed up by Leslie Thorne, an IAEA inspector from Britain: "I'm not optimistic about inspections, but there's no other answer." The authors in the following viewpoints debate the effectiveness of the IAEA and other international measures to reduce nuclear proliferation.

"The Nuclear Non-Proliferation Treaty works. It makes an essential contribution to global peace and security."

The Nuclear Nonproliferation Treaty Is a Success

Lewis A. Dunn

Lewis A. Dunn headed the U.S. delegation to the 1985 Nuclear Nonproliferation Treaty (NPT) Review Conference. In the following viewpoint, Dunn argues that the NPT successfully prevents the spread of nuclear arms by encouraging treaty members to reject such weapons. Dunn maintains that the treaty helps build a commitment toward peace by obliging nations not to help other nations acquire nuclear arms. Dunn is an assistant vice president of Science Applications International, a defense contractor located in McLean, Virginia.

As you read, consider the following questions:

1. In Dunn's opinion, why have breakdowns in nuclear export controls failed to weaken treaty members' commitment to peace?
2. According to Dunn, why are some nations reluctant to seek nuclear weapons openly?
3. How would amendments to the NPT reduce the treaty's effectiveness, in the author's opinion?

Lewis A. Dunn, "It Ain't Broke—Don't Fix It." From the *Bulletin of the Atomic Scientists,* July/August 1990. Copyright © 1990 by the Educational Foundation for Nuclear Science, 6042 S. Kimbark Ave., Chicago, IL 60637, U.S.A. A one-year subscription is $30. Reprinted with permission.

In 1995, the parties to the Nuclear Non-Proliferation Treaty (NPT) will assemble to decide "whether the Treaty shall continue in force indefinitely, or shall be extended for an additional fixed period or periods." The prospect of this 1995 extension conference has led already to proposals to reform, strengthen, expand, or even abolish the NPT. . . .

The proposals for change need to be set against the treaty's record of substantial contributions to the security of its parties. Different schemes should also be evaluated in terms of the motives of their proponents as well as the high risks of attempting to amend the treaty. In other words, since the treaty isn't broken, don't fix it.

Nonproliferation Goals

The Nuclear Non-Proliferation Treaty has three goals: to prevent the further spread of nuclear weapons; to promote the peaceful uses of nuclear energy under safeguards against misuse; and to encourage nuclear disarmament, the cessation of the nuclear arms race, and general and complete disarmament. How well has it worked?

An essential nonproliferation bulwark. Under Article I of the treaty, the states that possess nuclear weapons have pledged not to assist other states to acquire them. Few doubt that this pledge has been met, despite occasional unintended breakdowns of nuclear export controls. Nor is there any reason to question the continued commitment of virtually all of the non-nuclear-weapons states which are party to the treaty not to manufacture or acquire nuclear weapons, as stipulated by Article II. This commitment has signaled their peaceful intentions and has helped to avert suspicions that could lead their neighbors to think about nuclear weapons. It has strengthened a global norm of nuclear nonproliferation.

The treaty has helped prevent the spread of nuclear weapons in other ways. Under Article III, parties which are nuclear suppliers promise to require safeguards on their nuclear exports, and implicitly, all treaty parties are obliged not to assist other countries to acquire nuclear weapons. This has been the primary legal foundation of international efforts to control nuclear exports. Despite occasional breakdowns, these obligations have been honored. The treaty has made it time-consuming, costly, and difficult to acquire the materials, facilities, and components needed to make nuclear weapons.

The NPT has indirectly restricted the political freedom of action even of non-party states that might be contemplating acquiring nuclear weapons. Above all, the treaty symbolizes international opposition to the further spread of nuclear weapons and a growing belief in the illegitimacy of these weapons. The acquisition of nuclear weapons is now likely to meet with condemnation, not praise. This changed milieu has contributed significantly to the reluctance of countries today—as opposed to two or three decades ago—to seek nuclear weapons openly. Since the treaty entered into force in 1970, not one additional country has openly acquired and deployed a nuclear arsenal. This has enhanced the security of all of the NPT's parties.

International Safeguards

A framework for peaceful nuclear use. Many developed countries have assisted developing countries which are party to the treaty to gain access to the benefits of the peaceful atom. The International Atomic Energy Agency (IAEA) has also provided extensive technical assistance, with support from NPT developed countries.

IAEA safeguards have not impeded peaceful nuclear cooperation. Instead, their widespread acceptance has been an essential precondition for cooperation, reassuring nuclear suppliers that exports would only be used for peaceful purposes and giving non-weapons states an effective means to demonstrate their peaceful intentions.

But not all NPT nuclear supplier states require their non-party customers to accept IAEA safeguards on all peaceful nuclear activities ("full-scope safeguards"). This has weakened the NPT regime and discriminates between NPT parties, whose nuclear imports are strictly controlled, and non-parties. The 1985 review conference called for "effective steps" toward agreement to require full-scope safeguards.

Commitment Against Nuclear Arms

NPT is probably the world's most successful arms control agreement. . . .

More than 140 non-nuclear-weapon states have committed themselves under the NPT to remain without nuclear weapons and to accept on-site verification by our inspectors to show that their word is kept. This has substantially reduced the risk of local and regional nuclear arms races.

Hans Blix, *World Monitor*, November 1991.

The arms control and disarmament imperative. It is not surprising that this was the most troublesome substantive issue at earlier review conferences. But with changing East-West political relations, the arms control logjam has finally begun to break up. The 1987 Intermediate-Range Nuclear Forces (INF) Treaty is being implemented. There is likely to be a framework START agreement beginning the reduction of U.S. and Soviet strategic offensive nuclear forces, and probably a treaty. An agreement markedly reducing conventional forces in Europe will be in sight. A multilateral ban on chemical weapons will be in the offing. Negotiated cuts of short-range nuclear forces are ahead as well. These accomplishments will be a substantial step toward meeting the NPT's arms control and disarmament goals, contributing to the security of the treaty's parties.

A comprehensive ban on nuclear testing is conspicuously absent from this set of important arms control and disarmament advances. The preamble to the NPT does recall the determination of the parties to the Partial Test Ban Treaty "to seek to achieve the discontinuance of all test explosions of nuclear weapons for all time and to continue negotiations to this end." But careful reading of the negotiating record of the Non-Proliferation Treaty does not support the view that a ban on all nuclear testing is the sole litmus test of progress in meeting the treaty's disarmament goals, or the key to its long-term vitality. Other measures—further nuclear force reductions and stability measures, a global chemical weapons ban, new arms control initiatives for conflict-prone regions—hold out much greater prospect of enhancing global peace and security.

Opposition to the NPT

Some states that are not party to the treaty are proposing not to extend the NPT in 1995 but to replace it with a new, nondiscriminatory system of comprehensive global nuclear and conventional disarmament. It is hard not to conclude that the disguised motive behind such proposals is to destroy the NPT. Given regional and global political realities, such a replacement system has no chance of coming into being. And without the NPT, non-party states could more easily pursue nuclear weapons ambitions.

Other proposals to amend the NPT seem motivated by a desire to use the treaty to pursue a particular disarmament goal, for example, a comprehensive nuclear test ban or a cutoff of nuclear materials production. Using the NPT to pull the disarmament cart, however, puts at risk the treaty's substantial contribution to global security. It is highly unlikely that the signatory nuclear weapons states will agree to amend the treaty and bind themselves to undertake specified nuclear disarmament steps, especially under duress.

Other proposals to amend or reform the NPT are said to be motivated by a desire to improve its effectiveness by closing loopholes, to tighten the obligations of nuclear weapons states, and to strengthen its appeal to non-party states. They range from requiring full-scope safeguards to delineating specific nuclear disarmament objectives.

Member Nations of the NPT

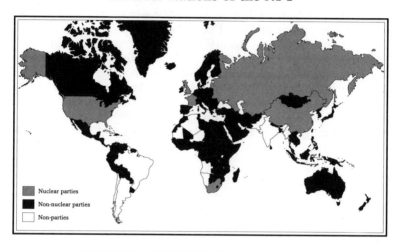

COUNTRIES THAT HAVE NOT SIGNED THE NPT

Algeria	Angola	Argentina	Brazil	Burma
Chile	Comoros	Cuba	Djibouti	Guyana
India	Israel	Mauritania	Monaco	Namibia
Niger	Oman	Pakistan	United Arab Emirates	

Note: Due to rapidly changing events in the former Soviet Union, the editors were unable to confirm if all Commonwealth states would adhere to the terms of the NPT.

But once the amendment process begins, it will be virtually impossible to stop until all of the treaty's basic provisions have been reopened. The NPT reflects a carefully negotiated balancing of obligations—between non-nuclear and nuclear weapons states, developing and developed countries, nuclear suppliers and recipients, and among the non-weapons states themselves. Attempting to amend the balance in all probability would undermine support for the old one but fail to reach a new consensus. As for critical non-parties—Pakistan, India, Israel, Argentina, and Brazil—the most important reason why they have not joined the NPT is that they want to retain the nuclear weapons option.

There are some problems with the treaty's implementation, and these will be addressed. North Korea's foot-dragging in bringing its nuclear research and reprocessing facilities under safeguards, and Iraq's apparent efforts to acquire nuclear-weapons-related materials and components are at odds with the spirit if not yet the letter of their treaty obligations. Other issues such as "negative security assurances" have a legitimate place on the agenda.

The Nuclear Non-Proliferation Treaty works. It makes an essential contribution to global peace and security. No single initiative is the key to the treaty's successful extension in 1995. Nor should we pursue possibly well-intentioned but no doubt dangerous proposals to fix the treaty. Instead, the United States and other parties to the treaty need to rededicate themselves to making even greater progress toward the treaty's basic goals: preventing nuclear proliferation, fostering the peaceful uses of nuclear energy, and negotiating arms control and disarmament. That is the best way to strengthen the NPT.

"The NPT has actually increased the likelihood of the proliferation of nuclear weapons."

The Nuclear Nonproliferation Treaty Is a Failure

Jennifer Scarlott

Many nations criticize those few countries with nuclear arms, such as the United States, for stockpiling nuclear weapons while simultaneously using the Nuclear Nonproliferation Treaty (NPT) to prevent others from acquiring them. In the following viewpoint, Jennifer Scarlott agrees and argues that this double standard weakens the NPT by discriminating against member nations without nuclear arms. Scarlott also contends that the treaty contributes to the proliferation problem by promoting nuclear energy, a by-product of which is plutonium, which can be used for nuclear weapons. Scarlott is a fellow at the World Policy Institute at the New School for Social Research and is on the staff of the Campaign for Peace and Democracy, both in New York City.

As you read, consider the following questions:

1. According to Scarlott, how has the flow of nuclear-bomb material and technology been facilitated?
2. In the author's opinion, how does the modernization of nuclear weapons weaken the treaty?
3. Why does Scarlott believe that the end of the Cold War has heightened regional tensions and weakened the NPT?

From Jennifer Scarlott, "Nuclear Proliferation After the Cold War," *World Policy Journal*, Fall 1991. Reprinted with permission.

It seems like an eternity since the halcyon days of 1989, when peace "broke out" in Europe and the rapprochement between the two leading nuclear powers seemed to bode the end of the threat of nuclear war. This optimistic expectation has given way to the sober realization that the nuclear genie has not yet returned to its bottle. The turbulent events of 1991, in particular, have underscored the likelihood that the long-neglected problem of the "horizontal" spread of nuclear weapons will pose an increasing threat to peace.

The nonproliferation regime—the network of treaties, export controls, safeguards, and inspections designed to prevent the spread of nuclear weapons—is in an advanced state of decay. At the 1990 Nonproliferation Treaty (NPT) Review Conference, a coalition of Third World countries asserted that they would not agree to extend the Treaty after its 1995 expiration unless the United States and the other nuclear-weapon states finally agree to a comprehensive ban on nuclear testing (CTB). The loss of patience of a large contingent of non-nuclear-weapon states over this issue signals serious trouble for the Treaty's continued existence. . . .

Weaknesses of the Nonproliferation Regime

The nonproliferation regime consists principally of the Nonproliferation Treaty, the International Atomic Energy Agency, and a variety of export controls designed to prevent the transfer of nuclear-weapons technology. The NPT requires non-nuclear-weapon signatories to forswear the manufacture of nuclear weapons and place their nuclear installations under the IAEA safeguards system. Countries that already possess nuclear weapons are obligated to share peaceful nuclear technology with the other signatories and to pursue disarmament. The U.N.-affiliated IAEA has a dual mandate to promote the peaceful uses of nuclear energy and to establish a global system of physical inventories, audits, and inspections, known collectively as safeguards, to prevent military applications of nuclear energy.

The nonproliferation regime has been in place long enough—the IAEA and the NPT date from 1957 and 1968, respectively, and export controls since the early 1970s—to be judged on its record. By any standard, the regime has failed to achieve its own purposes. Although the NPT roster boasted 142 signatories at last count, the sheer number of signatories is not as reassuring as it might seem, since many of these countries have had very little incentive to opt for nuclear weapons. A more accurate measure of the regime's success is its ability to deter determined countries from pursuit of the bomb, and here the record is disappointing. Since the mid-1960s, non-NPT members Israel, India, Pakistan, and South Africa have all joined the original nuclear club of five—the United States, the Soviet Union, Great Britain, France, and China. Brazil and Argentina reportedly came very close to a nuclear-weapons capability, but retreated from their programs in 1990. In addition, Iran, Libya, North Korea, and Taiwan, all parties to the NPT, are actively pursuing nuclear weapons, and Iraq may resume doing so at its earliest opportunity (if it has not done so already).

A Weak Regulatory Measure

The Nuclear Non-Proliferation Treaty is the Berlin Wall of nuclear affairs. Although its downfall is not imminent, the system of atomic apartheid embodied in the treaty has been unravelling for some time. In a modern and open world where walls are crumbling, the NPT is an anachronism. It is in force in a technical sense but without force as a regulatory regime among those determined to defy it. The regime works best where it is needed least, and it does not work at all where it is needed most.

Ashok Kapur, *The Bulletin of the Atomic Scientists*, July/August 1990.

The regime has also failed to prevent nations from acquiring the materials to abruptly opt for nuclear weapons at a time of their choosing. Belgium, Germany, Japan, and Switzerland are all stockpiling large quantities of plutonium and bomb-grade uranium, as well as the means to turn these materials into bombs. In the case of Japan and Germany, although there have been strong constraints on the countries' military programs since the end of World War II, both have active civilian nuclear programs with military overtones.

The ultimate indictment of the regime is that it has failed to stop the flow of nuclear-bomb material and technology. The past several decades are rife with examples of such material and technology transfers: the United States assisted France with its nuclear program; the United States, Canada, and Britain assisted India; Germany, Britain, the United States, and Israel assisted South Africa; France and the United States assisted Israel; France, West Germany, and the United States assisted Iran; the Soviet Union assisted Libya, Syria, Iraq, and Cuba.

Technical defects in the nonproliferation regime, stemming from loopholes in the NPT and the absence of a policing mechanism more effective than the IAEA's safeguards, have helped make these failures possible. The NPT allows adherents to come to the brink of assembling nuclear weapons and to withdraw from the Treaty at 90 days' notice. The regime cannot prevent a country from using its civilian nuclear program to manufacture nuclear bombs, ensure that illegal transfers of sensitive nuclear materials or know-how do not take place, or enforce sanctions. . . .

There are many examples of the nonproliferation regime lending itself to this kind of hypocrisy. Japan is considered faithful to the NPT although it plans to recover more plutonium from the waste of its nuclear reactors than it needs for its breeder reactor programs—plutonium that could be used to produce nuclear weapons. Although North Korea is a signatory to the NPT, it has refused to comply with the Treaty's requirement of full inspections of its nuclear plants. If it were to agree to IAEA oversight, North Korea would be legally entitled to stockpile weapons-grade plutonium, moving Pyongyang perilously close to possessing nuclear weapons.

The regime has been equally unsuccessful in inducing the nuclear-weapon states to substantially reduce or eliminate their arsenals. The United States and the Soviet Union claim they are abiding by the NPT by pursuing negotiations to reduce their nuclear stockpiles, despite the fact that both continue to modernize their arsenals—a process that poses a greater risk to peace and to nonproliferation efforts than the accumulation of sheer numbers of nuclear weapons.

The NPT May Force Proliferation

If technical defects in the NPT regime have made the flow of nuclear know-how possible, political shortcomings have made this flow likely. The regime's failure to address the political roots of proliferation has not only undermined its effectiveness, but could actually reinforce pressures for proliferation in the years to come. The problem stems from the nature of the three-part bargain on which the Nonproliferation Treaty rests. The Treaty is essentially an agreement to institutionalize the difference between states that have nuclear weapons and states that do not. The non-nuclear-weapon states, which also happen principally to be the world's less developed nations (a fact that does not escape them), give up their sovereign right to develop nuclear arms; in return, they are supposed to be compensated in three ways. First, the nuclear-weapon states agree to share civilian nuclear technology. Second, these states agree to work toward elimination of their own arsenals. Finally, it can be argued that in addition to these two explicit benefits, the bargain has always included a third, implicit element—the pledge that the nuclear states, especially the superpowers, would ensure a stable world order in which the nuclear "have-nots" would be protected and the nuclear "haves" restrained.

All three parts of the bargain have been met only partially. Indeed, the first part has always been counterproductive to the goal of nonproliferation, since distinctions between civilian and military nuclear technologies are spurious. In promoting the so-called peaceful uses of nuclear energy, the NPT has actually increased the likelihood of the proliferation of nuclear weapons. By the year 2000, commercial reprocessing of spent nuclear fuel will result in the creation of almost 400,000 kilograms of new, weapons-grade plutonium. The transportation of the spent fuel to reprocessing plants in Great Britain and France, and of the weapons-grade fuel back to the various countries of origin, will greatly increase the danger that plutonium will fall into the hands of terrorists or agents of a country tempted to cross the nuclear threshold. (A crude weapon can be made from as little as eight kilograms of plutonium.) The nuclear-weapons aspirations of states like Iraq, Taiwan, and the Koreas, to name just a few, have been significantly advanced by the transfer of civilian nuclear materials and know-how from the advanced countries.

The NPT Encourages Cheating

The treaty has cast a cloak of respectability over cheaters like Iraq (and probably North Korea). It's better than nothing, the argument used to run. But unless it is fixed, the NPT may be worse than nothing: if it is misleading about some countries, others will be tempted to cheat, or pull out.

The Economist, July 27, 1991.

In addition, now that nuclear power is out of favor in much of the world, assistance with civilian programs is no longer much of an incentive for adherence to the NPT. The cost of building and licensing reactors has risen astronomically as it has become clear that the atom is remarkably unsafe as an energy source. Thus the construction of nuclear power plants in many Third World countries has become next to impossible from an economic standpoint, as well as undesirable from a public safety standpoint.

As for the second part of the NPT bargain, the somewhat tepid moves toward nuclear disarmament, and in particular the failure to negotiate a comprehensive ban on nuclear testing, have undermined faith in the regime and angered the non-nuclear-weapon signatories. By continuing to modernize their strategic stockpiles, the superpowers and the other nuclear-weapon states have weakened the normative power of the NPT by signaling the importance of nuclear weapons while at the same time insisting that other countries should not have them. At the 1990 NPT Review Conference, a representative of Mexico sharply criticized U.S. intransigence on the CTB issue, asking, "How can the cessation of the nuclear arms race be attained without first closing the door on perfecting and qualitatively developing nuclear arsenals?"

The failure of the implicit third part of the bargain is evident in the growing international disorder and insecurity that has come with the end of Cold War bipolarity. This is not to say that we should be nostalgic for the Cold War. Despite the fact that the much-feared nuclear war between the superpowers never occurred, hundreds of thousands of people died in "conventional" struggles, the militarization of countries and regions proceeded at a rapid pace, and the underlying political and economic causes of violence were largely ignored or even exacerbated as the United States and the Soviet Union obsessively pursued their ideological competition. Abhorrent as it was, however, bipolarity provided a certain predictability in security arrangements. What now seems to be emerging is the worst of two worlds, in which the bloody-mindedness of the Cold War period is joined with an extreme political, economic, and social volatility. In this "new world order," many of the nuclear "have-nots" are threatened by internal fragmentation and regional challenges to their security, while the leading nuclear state—the United States—seems increasingly determined to exercise its prerogatives as the sole remaining superpower. As the war over Kuwait showed, this makes for a volatile combination.

A Climate of Instability

Because of the failure of the third part of the NPT bargain, the quid pro quo embodied in the Treaty is not only discredited, but increasingly irrelevant as well. By their very nature, regimes of international law tend to work best when relations among states are relatively stable and predictable. In a climate marked by growing suspicion and conflict, states may be likely to put their trust in weapons rather than in unenforceable laws.

In the Middle East, for example, the end of the Cold War seems to have weakened whatever effectiveness the NPT regime may once have had. Although tensions were frequently high in the region during the 1970s and 1980s, the two superpowers sought to restrain their clients because they feared that regional conflict would escalate into strategic conflict. Under these conditions, it made sense for Middle Eastern states to at least appear to abide by the NPT, so as not to alienate their superpower patrons. With the withdrawal of the Soviet military umbrella protecting Syria, Iraq, and other Arab states, the prospect of an increased and even permanent U.S. military presence in the region, and continuing hostility between the Arab states and a nuclear-armed Israel, there is considerably less incentive to adhere to the NPT.

"The International Atomic Energy Agency (IAEA) is a central component of the world's commitment to control the spread of nuclear weapons."

The International Atomic Energy Agency Deters Nuclear Proliferation

International Atomic Energy Agency

The International Atomic Energy Agency (IAEA) monitors civilian nuclear energy programs of many nations to ensure that such programs are not used to develop weapons. In the following viewpoint, the IAEA argues that its safeguards, including the surveillance and inspection of nuclear materials and facilities, have effectively controlled the spread of nuclear weapons. The IAEA maintains that the growing acceptance of nations to adhere to such safeguards provides assurance that nuclear programs will not be used for military purposes. The IAEA, an independent organization affiliated with the United Nations, is headquartered in Vienna, Austria.

As you read, consider the following questions:

1. According to the IAEA, why must inspections be agreed upon between the agency and nation involved?
2. In the agency's opinion, how have disarmament trends facilitated inspections of nuclear facilities?
3. How can surveillance techniques help control the use of nuclear materials, according to the IAEA?

From the 1990 International Atomic Energy Agency fact sheet *International Safeguards and the Peaceful Uses of Nuclear Energy*. Reprinted with permission.

In operation since the 1960s, the safeguards system of the International Atomic Energy Agency (IAEA) is a central component of the world's commitment to control the spread of nuclear weapons. Under agreements that States conclude with the IAEA, Agency inspectors regularly visit nuclear facilities to verify records that State authorities keep on the whereabouts of nuclear material under their control, check IAEA-installed instruments and surveillance equipment, and confirm physical inventories of nuclear materials. They then prepare detailed reports to the State concerned and to the IAEA. Taken together, these and other safeguards measures provide independent, international verification that governments are living up to their commitments to peaceful uses of nuclear technology.

An Increase in Safeguards

The rapid development of nuclear energy and the growing acceptance of IAEA safeguards are reflected in the volume of safeguarded nuclear facilities and materials. Safeguards are applied most intensively at facilities containing materials (namely, plutonium and highly enriched uranium) that could be used to manufacture nuclear explosives. Inspection goals, which take into account potential diversion paths and other technical criteria, are formulated accordingly and give top priority to safeguards at such facilities and to verify the whereabouts of these materials. Overall, the IAEA, within the limits of its authority and resources, has been able to improve attainment of inspection goals throughout the entire civilian nuclear fuel cycle. The levels provide assurance that no diversion for military purposes has occurred within safeguarded activities.

The system consists of three major components:

- Accountancy, i.e. reporting by States on the whereabouts of the fissionable material under their control, on stocks of fuel and of spent fuel, on the processing and reprocessing of nuclear materials, etc.;

- Containment and surveillance techniques, such as seals which allow conclusions that no material has disappeared, film and TV-cameras which record any action occurring in a particular area of a nuclear installation; and

- Inspection by Agency inspectors, checking instruments and seals installed, verifying books, confirming physical inventories of fuel or spent fuel.

A basic feature of safeguards is that verification can take place only on the basis of an agreement with the State in which the inspection is to occur. The IAEA is not a supernational organization with powers to impose its inspection on any State. Acceptance of safeguards is a voluntary act. The State is not giving up anything. It is issuing an invitation to inspection that it finds to be in its own interest.

A great many IAEA agreements on safeguards envisage Agency verification of all present and future fissionable material in a given State. They are referred to as "full-scope" safeguards agreements. Under the NPT, and the Tlatelolco and Rarotonga Treaties, contracting States are obliged to conclude agreements of this scope with the Agency. Other safeguards agreements are concluded to cover individual nuclear installations or individual quantities of fissionable material normally as a result of an agreement between a supplier and a recipient State. Lastly, safeguards agreements have been worked out between the IAEA and all five nuclear-weapon States, under which the latter invite the Agency to apply safeguards to all or some of the peaceful nuclear installations in their territory.

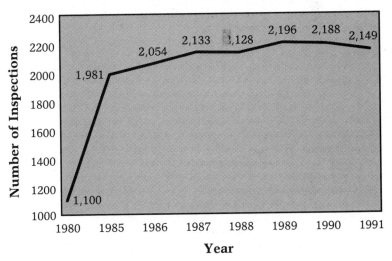

Number of IAEA Safeguards Inspections

Source: International Atomic Energy Agency, 1992.

To be credible, safeguards must be thorough and systematic. To operate the safeguards system is a major responsibility for the IAEA. Even after some 25 years of experience, new challenges arise. Complicated installations are built that handle large quantities of fissionable material which have to be safeguarded. Verification techniques which were once satisfactory become obsolete. Today the discussion of disarmament on any fronts has opened up a much greater general readiness to accept verification than existed at the time when safeguards were the first swallows in the air. IAEA safeguards will benefit both in cost efficiency and credibility if they are allowed to keep up with the advances made in other verification schemes.

Inspections and Surveillance

The most visible components of the IAEA's safeguards systems are the designated inspectors. Under agreed rights of access, they regularly visit nuclear installations to verify records, check instruments and surveillance equipment, and confirm physical inventories of nuclear materials; they later prepare detailed reports to the State concerned and to the IAEA. In Member States of the European Community (EC), IAEA inspectors work with those of the European Atomic Energy Commission (Euratom). In 1989, 211 IAEA inspectors performed nearly 2200 safeguards inspections worldwide.

At many nuclear installations the IAEA uses surveillance cameras and other electronic techniques to continuously and automatically record activities in key places. Also used are specially designed small metal seals which are fixed on the camera housings and other IAEA equipment to prevent undetected tampering, or at nuclear material storage areas or containers to safeguard the contents. Films and seals are regularly analyzed: In 1989, nearly 1860 films from 278 automatic cameras in the field were reviewed by the IAEA, and 13,500 affixed seals were checked and verified.

On a regular basis, the IAEA receives and analyzes reports from State authorities on the whereabouts of nuclear material under their control. Reports cover stocks of nuclear fuel and exports/imports of safeguarded materials and equipment. Annually, about one million data entries are processed and stored in IAEA computers. Systematic verification and analysis in 1988 found about 250 mostly minor irregularities and data discrepancies. Further investigation, evaluation, and inspections enabled the IAEA to conclude that none indicated the diversion or misuse of a significant amount of safeguarded nuclear material.

The fact that nuclear materials have distinctive radioactive characteristics makes it possible to detect and measure them; consequently, they can be accounted for with a high degree of accuracy. During inspections, IAEA inspectors conduct independent measurements for on-the-spot confirmation of the enrichment level and content of nuclear material. They also collect samples of certain types of safeguarded nuclear materials that are later tested and measured at the IAEA's Safeguards Analytical Laboratory (SAL) near Vienna, Austria, or at some national analytical laboratories. SAL and 18 laboratories in various parts of the world form a co-operative network.

Derailing Iraq's Nuclear Program

[The IAEA has] succeeded in unmasking major elements of the Iraqi nuclear program, including those secrets that I am personally convinced the Iraqis appear most determined to protect—that is, weapons design information and procurement information.

My conclusion is that we sit today with a substantial proven capacity to carry out inspections where at least three requirements are met. One is that there is information provided to the International Atomic Energy Agency about clandestine programs. I think it should be recognized today that, in fact, this is probably the first case in the U.N.'s history, certainly the first that I know of, where we have managed to couple national information with an inspection effort on the ground. I think it has benefited both tremendously.

Second, the inspectors have to have the right of unfettered access. In the case of Iraq, we have moved where we wanted to. We have pursued leads. We have given short notice, or recently even zero notice inspections.

Third, we have been backed by the united power of the Security Council, and the Iraqis have attempted to deny those rights of inspection.

If those three assumptions are filled, I think, in fact, that one can have confidence in an international inspection effort.

David A Kay, IAEA deputy inspector, statement to the Senate Foreign Relations Committee, October 17, 1991.

Legal agreements are the basis of IAEA safeguards. Many are popularly known as "full-scope" agreements because they extend to all peaceful nuclear activities and materials in the State. These mainly relate to the Treaty on the Non-Proliferation of Nuclear Weapons (NPT) and also to the Treaty for the Prohibition of Nuclear Weapons in Latin America (the Treaty of Tlatelolco) and to the South Pacific Nuclear-Free Zone Treaty (the Rarotonga Treaty). Other safeguards agreements cover individual nuclear installations or individual quantities of nuclear material. All told, 172 safeguards agreements were in force with 101 States (and Taiwan, [Republic of] China) at the end of 1989. In 57 States (and Taiwan, [Republic of] China) with significant nuclear activities, 922 installations and related facilities were under safeguards or contained safeguarded materials at year-end 1989, including the four Nuclear-Weapon States where safeguards were actually implemented in 10 nuclear installations. The greater part of the safeguards activities was in those States where safeguards were being applied pursuant to full-scope safeguards agreements. Safeguards were also being applied to facilities, equipment, and non-nuclear material, including 1457 tonnes of heavy water, under agreements covering individual facilities.

A Commitment Against Nuclear Arms

By the end of 1989, 137 Non-Nuclear Weapon States (NNWS) had adhered to the NPT—apart from the United Kingdom, United States and the USSR, the three Nuclear-Weapon States (NWS) party to the Treaty [China has since signed and France is expected to]—and have thus entered into an international legal commitment not to acquire nuclear weapons or other nuclear explosive devices in any manner whatsoever. Forty-five of these States have substantial nuclear activities which are safeguarded by the Agency pursuant to safeguards agreements. Nineteen of the twenty-three Latin American States party to the Treaty of Tlatelolco have concluded safeguards agreements with the IAEA pursuant to this Treaty, as have two States with territories in the zone of application of this Treaty. Safeguards agreements under the NPT have also been concluded with ten of the eleven signatories of the Rarotonga Treaty.

Some civilian nuclear facilities in four of the five NWS are safeguarded under so-called "voluntary offer" agreements concluded with the IAEA. Preparations for implementation of safeguards in the fifth State have been initiated. The entry into force of the agreements are: United Kingdom, August 1978; United States, December 1980; France, September 1981; USSR, June 1985; and China, September 1989. IAEA safeguards are applied in Nuclear-Weapon States in a limited number of facilities selected by the IAEA.

There are nine States not party to the NPT or the Treaty of Tlatelolco which have nuclear facilities in operation or under construction. In some of these States only some installations are under safeguards and there are unsafeguarded nuclear facilities known to be in operation or under construction.

"The IAEA's annual reports reveal that the agency frequently fails to inspect facilities as often as the agreements provide."

The International Atomic Energy Agency Is Ineffective

Leonard Weiss

Several countries, such as Iraq, have been accused of seeking nuclear arms despite legal agreements with the International Atomic Energy Agency (IAEA) not to do so. Leonard Weiss argues in the following viewpoint that these nations' progress in building bombs, however limited, proves the ineffectiveness of the IAEA. Weiss asserts that the agency must receive broader authority in conducting inspections, document transactions between nuclear material suppliers and nations, and strictly enforce its safeguard agreements. Weiss, chief architect of the Nuclear Nonproliferation Act of 1978, is the staff director of the Senate Committee on Governmental Affairs in Washington, D.C.

As you read, consider the following questions:

1. In Weiss's opinion, how can safeguards against proliferation be strengthened?
2. How can a nation's purchasing pattern of nuclear material signal plans to build a nuclear bomb, according to Weiss?
3. Why does the author believe it is important for the United Nations to detect nuclear weapons violations?

Leonard Weiss, "Tighten Up on Nuclear Cheaters." From the *Bulletin of the Atomic Scientists*, May 1991. Copyright © 1991 by the Educational Foundation for Nuclear Science, 6042 S. Kimbark Ave., Chicago, IL 60737, U.S.A. A one-year subscription is $30. Reprinted with permission.

When Israel attacked Iraq's Osirak reactor at Tuwaitha in 1981, the State Department denounced the raid. So did the International Atomic Energy Agency (IAEA), which passed a resolution condemning the action. The Israeli claim that Iraq planned to use the facility to produce nuclear weapons material was dismissed—the facility was under IAEA safeguards (international inspection), and Iraq was fulfilling its commitments to the Non-Proliferation Treaty (NPT) and its safeguards agreement with the IAEA. Still, the Israelis knew that the raid would deal a significant blow to Iraq's nuclear program, even if the reactor was used only for training and research purposes, not to produce plutonium.

During the Desert Shield buildup, when selective leaks to the press were used to heighten public concern about imminent Iraqi nuclear weapon capabilities (which, in retrospect, appear not to have had any basis in reality), I called a high-level official at the IAEA to inquire about Iraqi cooperation with the agency and asked whether the agency had any information suggesting that Iraq had violated its NPT commitments. I was told that Iraqi cooperation was "exemplary" and that no one had informed the agency of any Iraqi activities outside their treaty commitments.

Desert Storm Attack on Nuclear Facilities

Nonetheless, a few days after Desert Storm began, Iraq's nuclear facilities—a building housing two small research reactors and a plant where research on high-speed centrifuges was conducted—were attacked. The reactors had always operated under safeguards, and the centrifuge facility, since it contained no nuclear materials, was not subject to IAEA safeguards. But the Desert Storm raids, unlike the Israeli raid, were met by approval or silence, because of the realization that Iraq's nuclear program had been set back once again, even if the facilities destroyed were not directly used to produce weapons materials.

What had changed? Iraq's interest in a nuclear program that would lead to a weapons capability has been clear for many years. Intelligence analysts have watched Iraq's steady attempts—some successful, some not—to import needed components or facilities for both nuclear materials production (centrifuges) and ultimate weaponization (krytrons for nuclear triggers). But despite these activities, Iraq was no closer to being subject to a valid charge of violating its NPT/IAEA commitments in 1991 than it was in 1981.

This is, of course, a reflection on the international system, not on Iraq's innocence or the level of its nuclear progress. Iraq could have put into place every element of a nuclear weapons program, including production facilities, without violating a single provision of the NPT or of its safeguards arrangements with the IAEA. When Saddam Hussein was ready to produce the weapons, he could have invoked the NPT clause that allows a signatory to withdraw from the treaty after giving 90 days notice by declaring that "extraordinary events, related to the subject matter of this Treaty, have jeopardized" its "supreme interests."

Under these circumstances, what responsible leader is willing to base a nation's security on the slim reed of the NPT? Not Menachem Begin in 1981, and not George Bush in 1991. Even the activities of the Nuclear Suppliers Group, designed to supplement the safeguards system by encouraging restraint in nuclear exports, did not prevent Iraq from buying important components of a sophisticated nuclear weapons development and production program.

The Shattered Safeguards Myth

The allied raids on Iraq's nuclear facilities and infrastructure not only set back the Iraqi program but destroyed once and for all the fiction created in the public mind over many years by artful propaganda and obscuration that the safeguards regime and current international export controls provide an effective barrier to proliferation. It is to be regretted that this message about the regime's weakness, delivered by the Israelis in 1981, was buried at that time by an avalanche of criticism of Israel by the nations in the Desert Storm coalition. What changed their minds was evidently a reassessment of whose security was threatened.

IAEA Weaknesses Exposed

U.N. inspections of Iraq have dramatically exposed the inherent weaknesses of the IAEA system. Most obvious, inspections conducted by the Vienna-based international body charged with policing the Nonproliferation Treaty apply only to "declared" facilities involving special nuclear materials. Most, though not all, of Iraq's massive illicit bomb effort took place either at facilities outside the IAEA's legal jurisdiction or at potentially illegal, undeclared sites.

Patrick Glynn, *The New Republic*, October 28, 1991.

The NPT regime itself provides no early red flag indicating that one of its members has begun marching down the road toward weapon production, even if no treaty violations have yet occurred. Here is why. Under the provisions of its charter, the

IAEA safeguards *fissionable materials,* not facilities. When a facility contains or produces safeguarded materials, the facility is described as "safeguarded." In practice, this means that the IAEA negotiates an agreement on materials accounting and inspection at that facility. A laboratory that conducts research on machines or components for producing fissionable materials is not subject to safeguards if it has no such materials on its premises. And it is not clear when the agency must be informed about a production facility—how long before it becomes operational. "As soon as possible" after the decision is made to construct it is the operative phrase.

Basically, the object of the safeguards regime is the timely detection of any diversion of significant quantities of nuclear material and to deter diversion by creating the risk of early detection.

Timetable for Nuclear Weapons

What does "timely detection" or "early detection" mean? The IAEA has a set of informal technical rules of thumb for determining how long it would take a country with the appropriate industrial infrastructure and preassembly activities to convert a significant quantity of fissionable material into a nuclear explosive device. A significant quantity of plutonium (enough for a single, relatively simple nuclear device) is deemed to be eight kilograms; of enriched uranium, 25 kilograms. The estimated conversion time ranges from days to weeks for significant quantities of plutonium or uranium 235 metal or oxides, and from months to a year for spent fuel or low-enriched uranium. (The IAEA regards Iraq's stock of highly enriched uranium as less than a significant quantity, but it is disturbed by Iraq's failure to identify the location of the fuel following the Desert Storm raids.)

Although it would be logical to assume that these technical guidelines determine how the safeguards regime is implemented in a given situation (how frequently a nuclear facility is inspected), that is not the case in practice. Safeguards agreements—which are the result of negotiations between the IAEA and individual countries—almost never meet the technical objectives of the agency. If that isn't bad enough, the IAEA's annual reports reveal that the agency frequently fails to inspect facilities as often as the agreements provide. (Iraq has been an exception; after the Israeli raid, Iraq asked for increased inspections, presumably to bolster its claim of benign intentions.) In general, however, the agency must practice a form of triage as a result of an inadequate safeguards budget.

Insuring early detection in a classical diversion scenario is not the only problem. What if the "diversion" is not a clandestine spiriting away of fissionable materials, but simply a massive transfer out from under safeguards of a country's nuclear resources, using the ploy of "jeopardized supreme interests" legally provided by the NPT?

Strengthen the System

If the treaty is to be more effective in the struggle against proliferation, the system requires additional elements. These include:

First, a change in the NPT and IAEA charter should give the agency authority not only to apply safeguards to materials, but to inspect and report on facilities per se, including research facilities and plants that manufacture nuclear components or nuclear facilities. Regular access to these facilities should be required during and after their construction, and their design plans should be filed with the IAEA within a specific time after the plans are completed and before construction begins. Failure to declare design plans, facilities, or plants or to otherwise meet the above requirements should be considered a violation of safeguards. This broadening of the IAEA mandate would put NPT signatories in the position of having to open up nuclear design laboratories and factories that make special nuclear-related equipment. IAEA reports on such capabilities would make it much harder for a country to mount a clandestine program and would give the world earlier notice of worrisome activities.

An Inadequate Agency

The International Atomic Energy [Agency] is wholly ineffective in dealing with aggressive countries bent on acquiring nuclear weapons, such as Iraq.

Richard Perle, *After the Cold War: Questioning the Morality of Nuclear Deterrence,* 1991.

Second, in addition to establishing a more restrictive suppliers agreement on nuclear-related components and dual-use items, the IAEA or another appropriate U.N. body should maintain a registry of nuclear and specific dual-use items that have been sold or otherwise transferred by supplier nations belonging to the IAEA. The purchasing patterns of recipient nations might lead to earlier discovery and public revelation of their ultimate intention to make weapons or have the option to do so. This will require a concomitant agreement among suppliers to dispel the secrecy currently surrounding licensed exports, a move likely to engender opposition from various business communities.

Third, the IAEA must increase the credibility of the safeguards system. Safeguards agreements should meet the (now informal) technical objectives of the agency, and those agreements should be implemented to the letter whenever possible. This will require additional resources, but no one ever said credibility was a cheap commodity.

Problems Must Be Detected Earlier

Finally, even if all this is done, there is the question of what happens if a country that has been identified early as engaging in questionable nuclear activities or has committed a violation continues down that road, despite attempts to get it to reverse course. The U.N. Security Council is the ultimate arbiter of NPT disputes. The earlier a problem is identified and brought to the council's attention, the better the chances for peaceful resolution.

Suggestions for strengthening the NPT or IAEA are frequently met with an attitude of defeatism and cynicism based on an oft-quoted but unproven claim that, in its present form, the NPT could not be negotiated today. But any negotiation requires give and take; in the eyes of many parties, nuclear weapon states, despite significant progress in arms control, have still not satisfied their arms control obligations under Article VI of the NPT, particularly with respect to nuclear testing. If additional progress toward a test ban is necessary in order to obtain agreements that strengthen the treaty and charter, that is no threat to the security of the weapon states or to international security and peace.

*"NATO should do everything possible to
eliminate and reduce nuclear weapons."*

NATO's Nuclear Arsenal Encourages Nuclear Proliferation

Daniel Plesch

In the following viewpoint, Daniel Plesch argues that NATO should eliminate its nuclear weapons as a step against nuclear proliferation. Plesch asserts that disarmament by NATO would show that nuclear weapons have no worth and would set an example for other nations to reject them. Plesch contends that nuclear weapons should not be trusted to deter attack because they cannot prevent an enemy's accidental missile launch, nor should they be counted on to preserve peace. Plesch is the director of the British American Security Information Council, a Washington, D.C.-based international research organization specializing in European security issues.

As you read, consider the following questions:

1. Why does Plesch criticize attempts by the nuclear powers to prevent other nations from acquiring nuclear weapons?
2. Why does the author believe that the use of nuclear weapons is immoral?
3. In Plesch's opinion, how can nuclear nonproliferation be accomplished?

Daniel Plesch, "NATO and Proliferation," a position paper written expressly for inclusion in the present volume.

The possession of nuclear weapons by NATO is directly contradictory to the stated NATO goal of controlling the proliferation (spread) of nuclear weapons. NATO assumes that the nuclear powers have the right to retain their nuclear weapons indefinitely while preventing others from developing or acquiring nuclear weapons. This is a double standard. It is also a policy which invites other countries to acquire nuclear weapons. After all if NATO finds them so useful why should not other countries? NATO's desire to retain nuclear weapons leads it to do little about the spread of nuclear arms for fear that its justification for its own weapons will be called into question.

NATO's Nuclear Arsenal

Three NATO states have nuclear arms: the United States, Britain and France. In addition Belgium, Germany, Greece, Italy, Netherlands and Turkey all have fighter-bombers which in time of war could drop US nuclear bombs. The US has some 700 nuclear bombs for the use of its Air Force and the air forces of these allies. Any one of these weapons is ten times as powerful as the bomb dropped on Hiroshima. The total explosive power is equal to some ten million tons of TNT. In addition, US Trident missiles are assigned to NATO command for use in wartime and after the year 2000 the US will retain some 3,000 strategic nuclear missile warheads in its non-European forces. All of these weapons are under the control of the President. Britain has some 250 nuclear weapons on missile submarines and planes. It is planning to more than double this number by deploying a version of the US Trident missile submarine. France is carrying out a similar increase. At present there are no arms control talks aimed at reducing or eliminating these nuclear forces.

The advocates of retaining nuclear weapons argue that they have a unique value in preserving peace. They often point out that nuclear weapons were not used during the forty years of cold war and that nuclear weapons can be used to intimidate or destroy any third world country which may get nuclear weapons.

The argument that nuclear weapons have kept the peace is overconfident. The world came close to nuclear war in the Cuban missile crisis of 1961 and on other occasions which are only now being disclosed as the two sides talk to each other more openly. In the past, Western Europe has gone forty years without war without nuclear weapons. Before the first world war, for example, there was peace in the region from 1870-1914.

Implicit in the argument that nuclear weapons continue to be necessary is that they can keep the peace indefinitely. However, the one lesson of recent years is that we can expect the unexpected. Nuclear weapons are useless when supposedly deterring crazy leaders, events which run out of the control of Presidents and Prime Ministers, and, not least, people who believe that death in war is a sure passport to heaven.

As a general rule, the worse the nightmare nuclear weapons are supposed to protect us against, the less effective they are as a deterrent. That is, the crazier and more unstable the situation, the less deterrence works. It can be summed up in the question, "How do you deter an accident?" The author's view is that NATO should do everything possible to eliminate and reduce nuclear weapons and make it clear that it does not regard them as status symbols or useful political instruments.

Questioning First Use

Before moving on to consider the possibilities for reducing or eliminating nuclear weapons, the question of using nuclear weapons first to preempt an attack on NATO must be considered. NATO officially and clearly states that it would be prepared to start a nuclear war if it thought that this would mean that the war would be terminated on the Alliance's terms. This is the policy of "first use."

At first glance, a first use policy seems to make sense in some respects. Countries following such a policy could watch out for potential threats and attack those countries that threaten them or their allies with conventional and nuclear weapons before they themselves are attacked.

Eliminate All Tactical Nuclear Weapons

Critics point out that NATO plans to eliminate only land-based tactical nuclear weapons—those weapons in which the Soviet Union, a land-based power, predominates. But for the same reason that it is abandoning land-based weapons, goes the argument, NATO no longer needs its naval and air-based tactical nuclear weapons either.

Daniel Plesch, *The Bulletin of the Atomic Scientists*, November 1991.

However, there are a number of problems with a first use policy. First, it assumes that the US and the other nuclear powers of NATO have the right to crush other states that they consider a threat. This puts NATO in the role of aggressor. Second, many argue that a willingness to use nuclear weapons is immoral because of the massive suffering that would result and the likely global catastrophe resulting from delayed effects of using nuclear weapons. Others argue that the mere possession of nuclear weapons is immoral. This argument is based on the Nuremberg principles used to try the Nazis responsible for the Holocaust. Article 6 of these principles adopted by the United Nations makes it a "crime against humanity" to prepare to commit a war crime. Any use of nuclear weapons would potentially result in the massacre of millions of innocent people either directly or through radiation. As a result, it is argued that because any use of nuclear weapons would be a crime, even possession of the weapons is also a crime.

Even if we accept NATO's reasoning for possibly attacking countries which are building nuclear weapons, it is not clear that this is an effective policy, or the best policy choice available.

There are some circumstances in which preemptive attacks on a country which itself is preparing to attack can be extremely effective. The strongest recent example of this is the Israeli attack in the 1967 six day war.

Preemptive Air Attacks

Following the 1991 war with Iraq, some observers have suggested that preemptive air attacks would be an effective future method of controlling countries that seemed determined to be aggressors against their neighbors. However, the results of the war against Iraq indicate that air attack was not nearly as effective as commanders claimed. During the war US commanders assured the public that Iraq's nuclear capability had been completely destroyed. Afterwards many UN inspections were needed to find the extent of its capability and discover how much had been missed by air attack. Thus, preemptive attack on dispersed and concealed facilities may not be successful. First use of nuclear weapons against a proliferating state might require using large numbers of weapons against such targets. In addition, first use would likely alienate many allied nations inside NATO and beyond. If the weapons and factories being targeted for destruction were in or close to cities, then nuclear use would probably be politically unacceptable because of the likely civilian casualties. Thus, while such macho statements as "nuke the sand into glass and go skateboarding" may sound good over a beer they are hard to implement.

If one accepts the argument that nuclear use is an uncertain and barbaric instrument of policy and nuclear deterrence hard to make work, what is the likelihood that nuclear arms can be controlled, limited, and eventually eliminated? Many people assume that NATO and the US are working hard to control nuclear proliferation and reduce nuclear arms. In fact, while the NATO governments have often spoken about the need to reduce nuclear arsenals, they have accomplished little. At present NATO members are getting straight Fs for proliferation control, as is explained below.

Two NATO members (the United States and Germany) allowed their companies to actively assist the build up of Iraq's nuclear and chemical weapons industry. The Bush Administration has continued to back the Pakistani government and support the US-Pakistani foreign assistance program despite clear evidence of its nuclear program. Congress has passed legislation that requires the Administration to cut off foreign assistance to Pakistan if their nuclear program is continuing; President Bush continues to press for a waiver of this requirement.

An Outdated Strategy

Continuing to deploy nuclear weapons in Europe for NATO purposes is militarily unnecessary and politically dangerous. Since the threat of a massive Warsaw Pact invasion of Western Europe is gone, there is no military rationale for retaining this nuclear stockpile. Any remaining nuclear bombs are bound to complicate America's relations with Germany. America's NATO allies have no need for this outdated nuclear security blanket.

Council on Economic Priorities Research Report, December 1991.

After Russian President Boris Yeltsin came to power, the Russians continued to talk about eliminating nuclear arms and creating an international agency to assist with nuclear disarmament. These calls were ignored by NATO. No proposals for international control of nuclear weapons were made by the West and a very small portion of the $400,000,000 voted by Congress to help with the destruction of former Soviet nuclear arms has been spent by the Administration. At a NATO meeting in December 1991, US Secretary of State James Baker went so far as to reject the idea that making the whole former Soviet Union nuclear free would be unequivocally in the West's security interest—because it would undermine the United States' deterrent. In the nuclear arms talks in June 1992, the United States persuaded Russia to keep 3,000 to 3,500 nuclear weapons rather than the 2,000 to 2,500 that Yeltsin proposed. Suggesting that the Russians keep an arsenal significantly larger than they themselves proposed is bizarre indeed. The cause of this policy is that the US is more concerned about preserving its own arsenal than about seeing others' arsenals reduced. The same is true of the UK and France, NATO's other nuclear powers.

The Problem Requires Money

NATO countries have also given little support to the institutions that could aid the global control of proliferation. The organization charged with controlling proliferation and supervising the nuclear non-proliferation regime is the International Atomic Energy Agency. The IAEA budget for this work in 1992 was just $65 million, a third of its total budget. In comparison the US defence budget is close to $300 billion. If the United States and NATO want to be believed when they express their concern about proliferation, they need to devote hard cash to deal with the problem.

In conclusion, NATO's reliance on nuclear weapons to deter and preempt attack ignores the real risks that that policy may fail. In addition there is no worthwhile non-proliferation policy. This failure is partly the result of a concern not to see NATO's own right to possess nuclear weapons challenged. NATO would be better served by a strong non-proliferation policy which accepts that we would be best served by the global elimination of nuclear arms.

"The possibility of threats and risks . . . argues for the maintenance of a credible NATO nuclear strategy with as wide a range of options as possible."

NATO Must Maintain a Nuclear Arsenal to Counteract Aggression

Thomas-Durell Young

Many defense analysts state that the reduced military threat from the former Soviet Union warrants reductions in NATO's nuclear forces. Thomas-Durell Young disagrees and argues in the following viewpoint that NATO must retain a strong nuclear arsenal to guarantee Europe's security and deter aggression from unstable successor states of the Soviet Union. Young also asserts that NATO's nuclear weapons will deter potentially hostile Middle Eastern and North African nations from attacking NATO members. Young is an associate research professor of national security affairs at the U.S. Army War College in Carlisle, Pennsylvania.

As you read, consider the following questions:

1. How could dire economic conditions in North Africa eventually threaten Europe, according to Young?
2. Why does the author discount NATO's sophisticated conventional weapons as its primary means of deterrence?
3. In Young's opinion, why should NATO reconsider its concept of deterrence that was based on a U.S.-Soviet rivalry?

Excerpted from Thomas-Durell Young, "The Need for NATO-Europe's Substrategic Nuclear Weapons." This article originally appeared in the Spring 1992 issue of *Orbis: A Journal of World Affairs,* published by the Foreign Policy Research Institute, and is reprinted with permission.

President George Bush's speech of September 27, 1991, in which he announced massive unilateral reductions in the U.S. tactical nuclear weapons arsenal, brought home the magnitude of the changes that have taken place in the European security environment. The Bush announcement, which was dutifully endorsed at the 50th NATO Nuclear Planning Group meeting in Taormina, Italy, in October 1991, envisages substantial reductions in alliance nuclear forces by mid-decade, with no modernization of residual substrategic nuclear systems planned, although that option remains open. (The substrategic nuclear systems under analysis here are nonstrategic weapons systems with ranges under 5,500 kilometers, exclusive of ground-based short-range nuclear forces [SNF]).

Bush's move was politically well-timed; it came just as German foreign minister Hans Dietrich Genscher, who had been surprisingly quiet on SNF, was launching a new public campaign to press for the withdrawal of SNF from Europe. Unfortunately, Bush's move has not answered the underlying question of the future role for nuclear forces in a transformed Europe, where threats will be ambiguous but risks abundant.

NATO Needs a Nuclear Deterrent

The problem associated with the future role for nuclear weapons in NATO strategy is two-fold. First, the absolute number of nuclear forces available to NATO will diminish as SNF are withdrawn from service. Bush's announcement of the dismantling or withdrawal of all U.S. SNF and sea-launched tactical nuclear forces, and the cancellation of the program for a new short-range air-launched tactical missile (SRAM-T), can be interpreted as a continuation of one part of a NATO policy dating back to the Montebello decision of 1983, which set out the objective of modernizing SNF, while reducing their absolute numbers. Since that decision was reached, however, the alliance's zeal to reduce SNF has not been matched by a political commitment to modernize substrategic capabilities. The result will be to limit, by mid-decade, the alliance's substrategic nuclear forces to gravity nuclear bombs delivered by dual-capable aircraft (that is, aircraft capable of delivering nuclear as well as conventional weapons). Thus, NATO's on-call substrategic nuclear capabilities have been defined prior to a full review of future security requirements.

Secondly, this fundamental change in NATO nuclear forces is taking place as the break-up of the Soviet Union increases the likelihood of nuclear proliferation, particularly of tactical systems, in the East. Further, the acquisition of long-range weapons of mass destruction—and possibly even nuclear weapons at some future date—by anti-Western, fundamentalist

Muslim, and nationalist Arab regimes to Europe's south suggests that the alliance ought to be reassessing its substrategic nuclear requirements. In brief, even if SNF have served their purpose and can be dismantled with every confidence that their future use to West European security is negligible, the potential security threats emanating from a disintegrating Soviet Union and certain North African and Middle Eastern states suggest that the alliance must maintain a substrategic capability sufficient to deter potential aggressors. Unless the alliance is willing to face the politically delicate fact that nuclear forces will not automatically become irrelevant with the disintegration of the Warsaw Pact and the Soviet Union, then Western Europe may be left exposed to intimidation and blackmail.

Essential Weapons

We can't dis-invent nuclear weapons. . . . We believe that nuclear weapons are an essential instrument to prevent any kind of war simply by keeping the risks high enough. I do not see a situation in which we would de-nuclearize Europe.

Manfred Woerner, *Los Angeles Times*, October 19, 1991.

NATO, therefore, continues to have a need for nuclear forces that serve political ends—that is, "political weapons" for deterrence, as opposed to warfighting systems. Such weapons give the alliance a wide range of options in crises or conflicts. While it may indeed be the case, as stated at the end of the November 7, 1991, NATO summit in Rome, that "the circumstances in which any use of nuclear weapons might have to be contemplated . . . are . . . even more remote [than in the past]," the threat of nuclear proliferation in the East and the South warrants a serious re-evaluation of NATO nuclear strategy and force requirements. If the alliance continues in the future to adhere to its current practice of reducing numbers and capabilities of nuclear weapons, eschewing modernization (out of fear of the political consequences), and avoiding alliance-sponsored war games involving nuclear scenarios, NATO could find itself ill-prepared to meet future security challenges to its European members. . . .

European Security After the Cold War

Despite the end of the cold war, compelling reasons remain for maintaining NATO's ability to deploy modernized U.S. substrategic nuclear forces throughout the region, particularly to protect Western and Central Europe from acts of nuclear intimidation. U.S. substrategic forces will remain essential to European security at least until Western Europe develops its own integrated level of deterrence, and possibly even beyond that, as a further element of assurance.

First, and most obviously, many years may pass before stability returns to whatever amalgamation of states replaces the USSR. The question of the disposition of Soviet SNF—let alone strategic forces—in a number of former Soviet republics needs to be addressed in alliance strategy.

Despite assurances from Marshal of Artillery V. Mikhalkin, chief of Soviet Ground Forces Missile and Artillery Troops, at least some Soviet SNF could possibly fall under the control of independent republics, owing to the large numbers of these forces and their distribution throughout most of the Soviet Union. Most disconcerting has been the ambiguity or wavering of some republics' policies toward retaining nuclear forces on their territory, Ukraine not least among them. Even if the successors to the defunct Soviet central government have every intention of collecting and destroying the Soviet stock of SNF, press reports have estimated that such an effort could take ten years and cost the equivalent of $2 billion. Whether a commonwealth or Russian government can maintain control over all its warheads in the interim and find the financial resources to destroy them should be of more than passing interest to NATO. Little wonder that Washington has become increasingly concerned with the possibility of nuclear proliferation. This anxiety resulted in a November 1991 plan passed by the Senate to fund (to the tune of $400 million) the destruction of Soviet nuclear warheads.

Secondly, the favorable alteration in European regional security conditions, which has had such a profound impact upon NATO strategy and forces in the Central Region, has not been accompanied by improved security conditions in the South. Population growth that far outstrips economic expansion has sent a surge of Arabs to Europe in search of jobs also sought by equally desperate, but marginally more welcome East Europeans. At the same time, West European investment and aid is being directed eastward, leaving North Africa and other parts of the Middle East an increasingly destitute playground for hostile anti-Western regimes with increasing access to long-range weapons of mass destruction. The possibility of a direct threat to Turkish territory during the 1991 Gulf war is illustrative of such potential dangers. (According to one press report, NATO has already begun to plan for threats to Turkey from the South.)

Threats from the East and South

A number of Middle Eastern and North African states are known to be seeking intermediate-range ballistic missiles and nuclear weapons. The discovery by inspection teams from the

International Atomic Energy Agency of a nuclear weapons program of hitherto unsuspected dimensions in Iraq is an excellent case in point. Moreover, press reports suggest that certain Middle Eastern countries with nuclear ambitions have attempted to capitalize on the chaotic situation in the Soviet Union to recruit Soviet nuclear scientists. Retired Soviet general Dmitriy Volkogonov, a defense advisor to President Boris Yeltsin, acknowledged in November 1991 that desperate conditions in the Soviet Union could result in the emigration of Soviet experts, thereby constituting "a potential international disaster."

NATO Still Needs Nuclear Weapons

Nuclear weapons will continue to be needed by NATO to counterbalance the nuclear capabilities of any unpredictable, undemocratic, or hostile power. Quite apart from the military threat posed by nuclear arms in the hands of belligerent powers, the mere unilateral possession of such weapons creates the precondition for blackmail.

Beatrice Heuser, *Orbis*, Spring 1992.

Thus, the possibility of threats and risks from the East and South argues for the maintenance of a credible NATO nuclear strategy with as wide a range of options as possible, including substrategic nuclear forces stationed in Europe capable of functioning as a deterrent against escalation in a crisis. The argument that sophisticated conventional munitions can provide the alliance with a massive non-nuclear strike capability misses the point. The issue now, as it has been in the past, is one of deterrence, not warfighting. Even if one accepts the debatable proposition that modern precision-guided conventional munitions can produce a similar level of deterrence, financial exigencies in Europe will substantially limit the acquisition of these types of munitions in the years to come. Hence, as NATO has long recognized, nuclear forces are a cheap way of achieving effective deterrence.

To be sure, the previous concept of nuclear deterrence employed in NATO strategy may also require rethinking. For, as argued by Olivier Debouzy, the stability-enhancing "culture of deterrence" that evolved between the superpowers may not be shared by proliferating states. The new independent Soviet republics may not have the same interest in stability that was demonstrated by the superpowers, given the ethnic hostilities and irredentist ambitions at play there. Even more frightening would be the effect on stability of a radical nuclear-armed Islamic regime coming to power. In essence, it is too early to abdicate NATO's deterrence policy for one based on confidence. . . .

Collective Security for NATO

That Europe is not entering a new golden era of peace, tranquility, and stability is becoming increasingly apparent. Borders, which have been sacrosanct since 1945, are being disputed, and some are in the process of being altered, thereby establishing potentially dangerous precedents. States that have gained independence from the yoke of Soviet domination are already beginning to cast irredentist glances at their neighbors. Ominously, the first war in Europe since 1945 rages unabated in Yugoslavia. Finally, radical states in the Middle East demonstrate few signs of moderating their anti-Western views or abandoning their objective of obtaining nuclear weapons and long-range delivery systems.

The possession of limited substrategic nuclear forces by NATO will not in itself enable the alliance to confront successfully such potential threats to Europe's vital interests and stability. An active policy of dialogue and the eventual success of the Conference on Security and Cooperation in Europe are absolutely essential in this regard. East European states and ex-Soviet republics must be convinced that their security concerns will be heard in an institutionalized collective security forum. The civil war in Yugoslavia demonstrates that this nascent institution has a long way to go before it is able to provide even a minimal level of security to its participants. Whether such an institution will ever be able to address successfully the issue of extra-regional threats to Europe is uncertain.

NATO must, therefore, retain the nuclear element of its declared strategy if it is to provide for its European members' ultimate security in this quickly evolving and potentially unstable security environment. It would be futile to speculate at this point about the actual likelihood of potential future aggressors in the East or the South deciding that their interests could be furthered by intimidating or threatening the vital interests of NATO's European allies. What is crucial is that NATO must succeed in convincing all such regimes that the fates of the alliance members are inexorably linked. And, most important, if challenged, there can be no question that the alliance possesses, in theater and on call, the ultimate collective deterrent.

Evaluating Sources of Information

When historians study and interpret past events, they use two kinds of sources: primary and secondary. Primary sources are eyewitness accounts. For example, IAEA director Hans Blix's report regarding his personal inspection of North Korea's nuclear facilities is a primary source. An article in the *Washington Post* describing Blix's findings would be a secondary source. Primary and secondary sources may be decades or even hundreds of years old, and often historians find that the sources offer conflicting and contradictory information. To fully evaluate documents and assess their accuracy, historians analyze the credibility of the documents' authors and, in the case of secondary sources, analyze the credibility of the information the authors used.

Historians are not the only people who encounter conflicting information, however. Anyone who reads a daily newspaper, watches television, or just talks to different people will encounter many different views. Writers and speakers use sources of information to support their own statements. Thus, critical thinkers, just like historians, must question the writer's or speaker's sources of information as well as the writer or speaker.

While there are many criteria that can be applied to assess the accuracy of a primary or secondary source, for this activity you will be asked to apply three. For each source listed on the following page, ask yourself the following questions: First, did the person actually see or participate in the event he or she is reporting? This will help you determine the credibility of the information—an eyewitness to an event is an extremely valuable source. Second, does the person have a vested interest in the report? Assessing the person's social status, professional affiliations, nationality, and religious or political beliefs will be helpful in considering this question. By evaluating this you will be able to determine how objective the person's report may be. Third, how qualified is the author to be making the statements he or she is making? Consider what the person's profession is and how he or she might know about the event. Someone who has spent years being involved with or studying the issue may be able to offer more information than someone who simply is offering an uneducated opinion; for example, a politician or layperson.

Keeping the above criteria in mind, imagine you are writing a paper on international measures against nuclear proliferation. You decide to cite an equal number of primary and secondary sources. Listed below are several sources that may be useful for your research. *Place a P next to those descriptions you believe are primary sources. Place an S next to those descriptions you believe are secondary sources.* Next, based on the above criteria, *rank the primary sources, assigning the number 1 to what appears to be the most valuable, 2 to the source likely to be the second-most valuable, and so on, until all the primary sources are ranked. Then rank the secondary sources, again using the above criteria.*

P or S

Rank in Importance

_____ 1. A *New York Times* chronology of IAEA in- _____
spections of Iraqi nuclear facilities after the
Persian Gulf War.

_____ 2. IAEA videotape of activities inside an _____
Argentine nuclear research facility.

_____ 3. A Public Broadcasting Service summary of _____
an NPT review conference.

_____ 4. A *Los Angeles Times* article describing a _____
NATO plan to drastically reduce its nuclear
arsenal and revise its defense strategy in
Europe.

_____ 5. A document signed between North Korea _____
and the IAEA regarding the locations and
frequency of IAEA inspections.

_____ 6. A wire service report announcing NATO's _____
decision to eliminate all nuclear-armed missiles from Europe.

_____ 7. Transcript of a conference among NATO de- _____
fense ministers concerning the possession of
nuclear weapons as a deterrent against potentially hostile nations.

_____ 8. An IAEA inspection team leader's testimony _____
to a U.S. Senate committee concerning
Iraq's secret nuclear weapons program.

_____ 9. A *Newsweek* article describing the NPT and _____
listing nations that have refused to sign the
treaty.

_____ 10. A UN proposal to increase its role in future _____
on-site nuclear inspections.

Periodical Bibliography

The following articles have been selected to supplement the diverse views presented in this chapter.

David Albright and Mark Hibbs
"Iraq's Nuclear Hide and Seek," *The Bulletin of the Atomic Scientists*, September 1991.

Arms Control Today
"Keeping an Eye on a Nuclear World," interview with IAEA director Hans Blix, November 1991. Available from the Arms Control Association, 11 Dupont Circle NW, Washington, DC 20036.

Hans Blix
"The A-Bomb Squad," *World Monitor*, November 1991.

John M. Broder and Stanley Meisler
"U.N. Nuclear Inspection: Can It Really Work?" *Los Angeles Times*, January 20, 1992.

The Bulletin of the Atomic Scientists
Special issue on the Nuclear Nonproliferation Treaty, July/August 1990.

Louise Lief
"The Growing Nuclear Fold," *U.S. News & World Report*, November 25, 1991.

Gary Milhollin
"Building Saddam Hussein's Bomb," *The New York Times Magazine*, March 8, 1992.

Gary Milhollin
"North Korea's Bomb," *The New York Times*, June 4, 1992.

Joseph F. Pilat
"Iraq and the Future of Nuclear Nonproliferation: The Roles of Inspection and Treaties," *Science*, March 6, 1992.

John Simpson
"NPT Stronger After Iraq," *The Bulletin of the Atomic Scientists*, October 1991.

Lauren Tarshis
"The World's Nuclear Police," *Scholastic Update* (Teacher's edition), February 21, 1992.

Margaret Tutwiler
"Iraq: Weapons of Mass Destruction," *U.S. Department of State Dispatch*, July 1, 1991.

U.S. Department of State Dispatch
"Fact Sheet: Nuclear Nonproliferation Treaty," July 8, 1991.

Tom Wilkie
"A New Nuclear Age?" *World Press Review*, December 1991.

Jon Wolfsthal
"IAEA to Implement 'Suspect Site' Inspection Powers," *Arms Control Today*, March 1992.

Jim Wurst
"Arms Control: It's Not Bombing in Baghdad," *In These Times*, January 29–February 4, 1992.

Which Nations Contribute to Nuclear Proliferation?

NUCLEAR
PROLIFERATION

Chapter Preface

Nuclear proliferators can be divided into three categories: nations that possess nuclear weapons; suppliers of nuclear material for the manufacture of weapons; and countries that secretly seek nuclear arms.

World leaders are particularly concerned about this last category. Such would-be nuclear states, many of which are politically unstable or are ruled by dictators, could threaten Western nations or neighboring countries with nuclear attack. Perhaps no other nation illustrates this danger as vividly as does Iraq. During the late 1980s, under power-hungry Saddam Hussein's direction, Iraq spent billions of dollars acquiring the materials and technology needed to build a nuclear bomb. From sixteen sources as nearby as the former Soviet Union and as far away as South America, Iraq procured enough legal and illegal supplies to come dangerously close to creating a viable nuclear weapon. As Vladimir Isayev, who studies Arab affairs at Moscow's Academy of Sciences, states, "We can all share the blame: the U.S.S.R., France, Germany, even the U.S. We created a monster."

Exactly how close Iraq came is uncertain. UN inspectors estimate that Iraq needed as little as one more year to produce a crude, untested device. Fortunately, most experts feel, Iraq's defeat in the Persian Gulf War and a subsequent United Nations resolution ordering the elimination of Iraq's weapons of mass destruction virtually ended its nuclear weapon plan.

While Iraq's hopes were dashed, other nations continue to secretly seek nuclear weapons. Suspected nations include North Korea, Iran, and Libya, among others. Each has a working nuclear reactor, and North Korea and Iran possess reserves of uranium, an element whose U-235 isotope is ideal for nuclear weapons. Also, all three nations possess Scud-B ballistic missiles, which can be armed with nuclear warheads and targeted against nearby enemies.

These nations represent merely the demand side of an often complex and furtive relationship among nuclear proliferators. The authors in this chapter examine the tactics of several countries responsible for nuclear proliferation.

95

"U.S. policies continue to create pressures for the spread of nuclear weapons."

The United States Contributes to Nuclear Proliferation

Jennifer Scarlott

U.S. nuclear arms policies are often criticized for contributing to nuclear proliferation. In the following viewpoint, Jennifer Scarlott argues that by continuing to conduct nuclear tests and by condoning allies' nuclear weapons programs, the United States motivates other nations to obtain such weapons. Scarlott contends that the United States must stem the spread and possible use of nuclear weapons by making nuclear proliferation a foreign policy priority. Scarlott is a fellow at the World Policy Institute at the New School for Social Research in New York City.

As you read, consider the following questions:

1. In Scarlott's opinion, how do nuclear weapons influence the spread of chemical weapons and ballistic missiles?
2. How does the development of new U.S. nuclear weapons contribute to proliferation, according to the author?
3. Why does Scarlott believe that it is unfair to ban chemical weapons in the Middle East while allowing Israel to retain nuclear arms?

From Jennifer Scarlott, "Nuclear Proliferation After the Cold War," *World Policy Journal*, Fall 1991. Reprinted with permission.

By the end of the 1980s, it should have been clear that new thinking on the nonproliferation front was desperately needed. Already, the three parts of the original bargain embodied in the Nonproliferation Treaty—[agreement to share civilian nuclear technology; agreement to reduce nuclear arsenals; and a pledge against nuclear attack and for protection of nonnuclear states]—were under severe strain. After the Three Mile Island and Chernobyl accidents, nuclear power had lost much of its remaining cachet as a limitless, inexpensive, and safe energy source. Most major arms control efforts between the United States and the Soviet Union had stalled, and Third World countries were threatening to walk out on the NPT in droves if the nuclear-weapon states did not agree to a comprehensive test ban by 1995, when the future of the Treaty was due to be decided. Meanwhile, the fading of bipolarity, along with the growth of virulent strains of nationalism and the rising tide of highly advanced and deadly arsenals in volatile regions, had called into serious question the third part of the bargain.

America's Shortsightedness

The flip side of the coin, however, was that the end of Cold War hostilities and the obvious loss of relevance of the nonproliferation regime created an opportunity to rethink the traditional approach to nonproliferation. The United States was uniquely positioned to put the momentum of its improving relations with the Soviet Union behind strenuous efforts to breathe new life into nonproliferation policy. Yet the Bush administration, despite frequent professions of concern about the spread of nuclear weapons, has failed to take advantage of this opportunity. U.S. policy on nonproliferation remains just as inconsistent and counterproductive as it was during the Cold War. Worse yet, the administration does not seem to see the ways in which U.S. policies continue to create pressures for the spread of nuclear weapons.

The administration's shortsightedness on the proliferation issue is manifested in several different ways. First, despite the commendable decision to eliminate U.S. short-range nuclear weapons in Europe and Asia, the administration continues to avoid any explicit acknowledgment of the link between vertical and horizontal proliferation and to reject across-the-board cuts in U.S. nuclear programs that would support nonproliferation efforts. Second, the administration has failed to discard the Cold War ways of thinking and behaving that have traditionally made nonproliferation take a back seat to other, supposedly more important, security concerns. And third, the administration continues to ignore the critical link between nuclear proliferation and the spread of other kinds of weapons: conventional, chemical, and ballistic missiles.

Perhaps the most important disarmament failure where the future of nonproliferation is concerned is the U.S. refusal to support a comprehensive test ban. A CTB is viewed by a great number of Third World states as a sine qua non for preventing the emergence of additional nuclear weapons states, for spurring U.S. and Soviet nuclear disarmament, and for preserving the Nonproliferation Treaty. Nevertheless, the United States continues to drag its feet on this issue, as it has for decades.

Nonproliferation Comes Second

The extent of official U.S. opposition to a CTB was made explicit at the end of Reagan's second term when Kathleen Bailey, then assistant director for nuclear nonproliferation issues at the U.S. Arms Control and Disarmament Agency, made this revealing comment: "If the U.S. is forced to choose between its own national security and its nuclear testing program, versus the survival of the Nonproliferation Treaty . . . the U.S. would choose maintenance of its own national security, and therefore its own nuclear testing program." At an international conference on a partial test ban held in January 1991, the Bush administration stonewalled urgent requests from Third World countries for enactment of a test ban. In putting itself at odds with influential Third World countries on this issue, the administration is telling them, in effect, that it considers the maintenance and upgrading of its own nuclear forces to be more important than preventing the spread of nuclear weapons.

A Second-Fiddle Foreign Policy

Non-proliferation, in which we feign an earnest interest, has always played second fiddle in our foreign policy. Even with the Berlin Wall fallen, Cold War attitudes and reflexes mysteriously prevail. A case in point is China, which . . . sends nuclear equipment to Iran, builds a reactor in Algeria, and couldn't care less about North Korea's development of a nuclear bomb. Beijing just got a visit from Secretary of State James Baker and continues to enjoy most-favored-nation trading status.

Mary McGrory, *Liberal Opinion*, December 2, 1991.

Another disturbing development has been the administration's attempt to resuscitate the Strategic Defense Initiative (SDI). In his State of the Union address on January 29, 1991, President Bush cited the success of the Patriot antimissile system in the Gulf War and called for refocusing SDI on "providing protection from limited ballistic missile strikes—whatever their source." The Pentagon request for a "limited" SDI budget increase of $2.9 billion is worrisome from the point of view of nonproliferation because the program could complicate disarmament efforts far into the future. The erection of defenses will spur each state to respond by developing more sophisticated offensive weaponry, thus subverting nuclear arms cuts already achieved—and those yet to come.

Even recent progress toward disarmament does not go far enough. Despite the U.S. decision to eliminate tactical nuclear weapons in Europe and Asia and [the] signing of the Strategic Arms Reduction Treaty (START), which reduces the U.S. and Soviet strategic arsenals by roughly one-third, the administration retains the right to develop new nuclear weapons. Already, the Pentagon is devising future war scenarios that would make such weapons necessary. Chairman of the Joint Chiefs of Staff Gen. Colin Powell and Secretary of Defense Richard Cheney were arguing as late as September 1991 that the United States should be prepared to fight three wars simultaneously: a war like the one in the Persian Gulf, a smaller regional conflict, and, absurdly, a campaign against a resurgent Soviet threat. Such a scenario would require massive amounts of conventional weapons as well as strategic modernization. Modernization would introduce more effective and threatening weapons, thus spurring renewed arms races and undermining the prospects for nuclear disarmament.

Turning a Blind Eye

The second way in which the United States is endangering nonproliferation is by continuing to be inconsistent and selective in its approach to the problem. Carrying on in the Cold War tradition, the administration shows relatively little concern when a U.S. ally or client is known to be pursuing nuclear weapons, but is deeply concerned if an unfriendly country has such ambitions. Not only does this inconsistency damage the credibility of the NPT regime, but it overlooks the fact that nuclear weapons can create huge problems even when they are in friendly hands. A U.S. ally's nuclear program can spur nuclear efforts by neighboring rivals, eventually leading to a regional nuclear arms race. Even worse, a friendly regime can fall in a coup or revolution, leaving nuclear weapons suddenly in unfriendly hands.

In the fall of 1990, the Bush administration attempted to subvert the U.S. law requiring that yearly aid to Pakistan be conditioned on certification that it is not pursuing nuclear weapons. This time, however, it was the Gulf War, not the Cold War, that induced U.S. officials to look the other way. While acknowledging irrefutable evidence that Islamabad was continuing to enrich uranium and procure equipment for its nuclear program, the administration urged Congress to waive the certification requirement for six months to a year so that it could send Pakistan its annual military and economic aid package of $500 million. "This is not a particularly good time to bash the Pakistanis," an administration official explained, noting Pakistan's contribution of troops to the multinational force in the Gulf and the recent change in government in Pakistan.

The official's statement only underscored the selectivity and inconsistency of U.S. efforts to stem the tide of nuclear weapons. The administration, it should be recalled, was ordering the bombing of Iraq's nuclear facilities at about the same time as it was downplaying Pakistan's nuclear efforts. It is also revealing that the administration seems to believe that applying nonproliferation standards to friends is equivalent to "bashing" them. Despite the administration's efforts, Congress insisted on the certification, and Pakistan's annual aid package has been held up. In spring 1991, the Bush administration floated a proposal to eliminate once and for all the certification requirement, but was again rebuffed by Congress. In a refreshing turn of events, congressional determination on this issue bore fruit in the summer of 1991 when Pakistani Prime Minister Nawaz Sharif proposed that the United States, the Soviet Union, and China mediate talks between his country and India on controlling the spread of nuclear weapons in South Asia.

North and South Korea

On the Korean peninsula, the administration remains hostage to a narrow, Cold War-vintage conception of security despite evidence that its policies may be fueling nuclear proliferation. North Korea has pursued a nuclear-weapons capability for some time, largely in order to counter the security threat from the South. South Korea has a significant advantage in conventional weapons, and a military budget that is currently double that of the North. While the Gulf War has increased Seoul's confidence in its U.S. ally and in its American military equipment, Pyongyang relies heavily on Soviet weapons and is probably nervous about their poor performance in the war. While the South is prospering, the North has serious economic troubles. At the same time, the North is becoming increasingly isolated as relations with its Soviet patron have sunk to an all-time low, communism is collapsing worldwide, and both Moscow and Beijing are making economic overtures to Seoul.

In light of these imbalances, nuclear weapons would appear to offer a "potentially low-cost solution to the North's dilemmas," as Andrew Mack has argued. "The West should not find it surprising that such an option might appear attractive to the North. NATO deployed nuclear weapons as a low-cost strategic equalizer to the conventional military superiority of its enemy, the Warsaw Pact." Already, reports indicate that North Korea may soon begin to build one nuclear weapon per year.

Nonproliferation Pushed Aside

Our policies have failed because nonproliferation has always been pushed aside by other policy considerations. When confronted with the question of what to do about proliferation in isolated instances—Israel and Pakistan are good examples—American policymakers could argue with some justification that other U.S. policy objectives outweighed the goal of stopping the spread of nuclear weapons. But the United States may not be able to treat proliferation on a case-by-case basis for much longer. There is a difference between a world of five to eight nuclear countries and a world in which there are 20 or more nuclear powers.

Benjamin Frankel, *The American Enterprise*, March/April 1990.

The North seems prepared to abandon these efforts if its security fears can be allayed. For many years, North Korea has denounced the presence of U.S. nuclear weapons in South Korea and proposed a nuclear-free zone on the peninsula. It has also called for assurances from the nuclear-weapon states that they will not use their weapons against other states, and has made the case for a comprehensive test ban. The North has also offered to accept IAEA [International Atomic Energy Agency] safeguards and halt construction of its plutonium production program in return for a removal of U.S. nuclear weapons from the South—a quid pro quo that would begin to defuse the situation at little cost to perceived American security needs. Although the North Korean regime is highly repressive and militarized, its rhetoric about nonproliferation may well be sincere, given its security concerns.

President Bush's announcement of the removal of U.S. tactical nuclear weapons from the Korean peninsula and from ships offshore is the first sign of a more constructive U.S. approach to the Korea problem. This move will test North Korea's stated willingness to allow IAEA inspections of its nuclear facilities. The administration should now develop an overall disarmament and conflict-resolution policy for the peninsula, and terminate the annual U.S.-South Korea "Team Spirit" military exercise, which is "unambiguously intended as training for a major war with the North."

To date the Bush administration, while clearly concerned about North Korean interest in nuclear weapons, has rejected out of hand Pyongyang's proposals to dampen the incipient nuclear competition on the Korean peninsula. The stakes are high. A North Korean nuclear arsenal could result in the reactivation of South Korea's nuclear weapons program, dormant since the late 1970s, or induce Seoul to make a preemptive strike against the North's nuclear sites. In 1991, in the first such statement ever to come out of Seoul, South Korea's defense minister said that his country might be forced to mount such an attack against Pyongyang's bomb facilities. Perhaps most disturbing of all, a nuclear-armed North Korea could encourage Japan to reassess its nuclear-free and defensive security posture.

The Link to Nonnuclear Weapons

The third way in which the Bush administration is undermining nonproliferation is by continuing to ignore the inherent link between the spread of nuclear weapons and the proliferation of other kinds of armaments—conventional arms, chemical weapons, and ballistic missiles. For a brief time after the Gulf War, it seemed that the U.S. approach to weapons transfers might be changing. In May 1991, the United States proposed a disarmament package for the Middle East that included some promising elements. It would require Israel to cease production of material for nuclear weapons and agree to safeguards on its military reactor at Dimona; "prevent" Middle Eastern nations that do not have nuclear weapons from producing them; and ask all Middle Eastern states to sign a treaty requiring the elimination of chemical-weapon stockpiles over a 10-year period. . . .

This proposal provides some worthwhile building blocks for disarmament in the Middle East. It would impose limits on Israel's nuclear program for the first time in its long history. It seeks to address all kinds of weapons proliferation—nuclear, chemical, conventional, and ballistic-missile. Unfortunately, however, the proposal's negatives far outweigh its positives. It is militarily inequitable, and thus politically unsustainable as well. By leaving intact Israel's 100-200 weapon nuclear arsenal, while stripping the Arab countries of their ability to produce chemical weapons, the proposal would return to the status quo ante in which Israel held a monopoly on weapons of mass destruction. The proposal to "prevent" Middle Eastern states from developing their own nuclear arsenals is somewhat bemusing since most of the states in question are already parties to the Nonproliferation Treaty. . . .

While Cheney called for preventing the spread of what he termed "sophisticated technologies," such as ballistic missiles and chemical- , biological- , and nuclear-weapon capabilities, he pledged not to halt the flow of advanced conventional weaponry to U.S. allies in the Middle East. In a region that already has one nuclear power, Israel, and several nuclear aspirants, including Iran, Iraq, and Libya, this is a dangerous policy. The Bush administration's continued belief in the efficacy of conventional arms transfers as a means of promoting regional stability and preventing countries from pursuing nuclear weapons is particularly puzzling in the face of the Iraqi nuclear program, which was under way during the 1980s when Iraq was receiving large infusions of conventional armaments from the West.

By continuing to transfer large amounts of conventional weapons to troubled regions, the United States and other arms suppliers are also contributing to the spread of chemical weapons and ballistic missiles, as heavily armed Third World states seek a qualitative edge in rapidly escalating regional arms races. This trend is not only dangerous in itself, but may increase pressures for nuclear proliferation. . . .

Spurring South Asia's Arms Race

These trends are converging in a particularly deadly fashion in South Asia. The United States has positioned itself as the major conventional weapons supplier to Pakistan, India, and, until the Tiananmen Square massacre, China. The proposed program to provide loans to overseas customers seeking U.S. weapons, if extended to Pakistan, India, and perhaps at some point China, will worsen the arms race in South Asia. Pakistan and India are engaged in a heated ballistic-missile race, having successfully flight-tested surface-to-surface missiles capable of reaching each other's territory. If, as is likely, these tensions are exacerbated in the power vacuum created by the superpowers' withdrawal, the all-out nuclear arms race that has threatened the subcontinent for the better part of two decades may occur. Pakistani proposals for discussions among the United States, the Soviet Union, China, India, and Pakistan about creating a nuclear free zone in South Asia were dismissed by the Indian government in June 1991 as a "propaganda exercise."

The Bush administration's failure to make nuclear proliferation a foreign policy priority is a manifestation of its inability to learn from previous administrations' errors and to extricate itself from the mire of Cold War thinking. This double failure set the stage for a disastrous new approach to proliferation that is likely to have unforeseen, and highly counterproductive, consequences.

"China's arms sales . . . are furthering the spread of nuclear technology and nuclear-weapons capability to some of the world's most ruthless rulers."

China Contributes to Nuclear Proliferation

Shen Tong

Shen Tong is an exiled student leader of China's Tiananmen Square pro-democracy movement. In the following viewpoint, Shen argues that China is a major nuclear proliferator, selling nuclear supplies and production materials to many countries in the Middle East and Asia. Shen asserts that many family members of China's ruling elite act as arms sales merchants, helping China gain hard currency and strengthening its global influence. In order to stop China's proliferation, the author proposes that the United States maintain its preferential trade status with China, but only if China reduces its arms sales to other nations. Shen is the author of *Almost a Revolution* and chairman of the Democracy for China Fund in Newton, Massachusetts.

As you read, consider the following questions:

1. According to Shen, why is there a worldwide trend toward the acquisition of weapons for defensive purposes?
2. In Shen's opinion, how does a nation's purchase of inaccurate types of missiles signal a desire for nuclear arms?
3. How can Western nations limit China's arms sales, according to the author?

From Shen Tong, "China the Arms Merchant," *World Monitor*, June 1992. Reprinted with permission.

When Mao Zedong's "revolutionary" foreign policy gave way, during the 1980s, to Deng Xaioping's "nationalistic" foreign policy, China's "princes party"—the sons and daughters of the high-ranking ruling elite in Beijing—became deeply involved in China's arms sales around the world.

As most of their fathers are publicly condemning Western influence and the West's attempt to subvert China's socialist system through "peaceful evolution," the princelings secretly travel between China and the West, transferring money and, in some cases, getting permanent residential status abroad—perhaps preparing a comfortable place of exile for the post-Deng era. Some of the hard currency that is being transferred comes from the arms sale business.

It's no surprise that the Communist regime in Beijing is getting international attention yet again on a sensitive issue that worries the West deeply. The current government's involvement in the arms trade comes on top of its ruthless human-rights abuses, its poor record in international trade (violating copyright and exporting prison-labor products), and the killings in and around Tiananmen Square in Beijing and other cities in 1989.

Arming Third World Rivals

With the end of the Cold War, the strategic importance of international arms sales has diminished significantly. Weapons are needed mainly for scaled-down defensive purposes. At the same time, there is still active buying for use in some regional conflicts, most of which are in the third world. Many countries, including most of the major Western democracies, are on the list of important arms suppliers, with the US as No. 1, followed by Germany, France, and Britain.

The importance of China's arms sales goes beyond earning hard currency for Beijing and the dangerous side effect of stoking regional conflicts: In some cases the sales are furthering the spread of nuclear technology and nuclear-weapons capability to some of the world's most ruthless rulers.

China's arms sales—sometimes including missiles that can potentially deliver nuclear or chemical warheads—have played a role in many current regional military conflicts. And in every case, ironically, both sides of the conflict cut deals with China at the same time.

India and Pakistan: China in a significant way helped these two hostile countries in their obsessive drive to develop nuclear weapons.

Between 1982 and 1987, 130 to 150 tons of heavy water were sold to India through an ex-Nazi named Alfred Hempel, who ran a German company and acted as a broker for international arms deals. (Some secret aspects of his operation, including bribery, were discovered after his death in 1989.)

The heavy water is crucial for India's Madras-I reactor, which was short 60 to 70 tons of it in 1983. China reportedly transferred more than 60 tons in 1984, and the sale continued till 1987, enabling India to have at least one, maybe two reactors free of international control. India now can produce an estimated 40 atomic bombs or warheads per year.

© Tom Meyer/*San Francisco Chronicle*. Reprinted with permission.

China also sold Pakistan tritium, a key element for H-bomb-making. (Tritium doesn't come under International Atomic Energy Agency safeguards at present, and it has some medical and scientific uses besides the bomb, so in this case the buyer's intentions are crucial.)

Beijing also assisted Pakistan in developing its HATF-I and HATF-II surface-to-surface missiles, which are similar to Scud missiles. As such, they are bombardment missiles, usually ineffective unless they are fitted with a nuclear warhead. Pakistan has tested chemical explosive triggering mechanisms that would be needed for testing and then stockpiling atomic bombs.

In 1991 one of China's nuclear-capable M-11 missiles was prepared for sale to Pakistan. The M-11 is more sophisticated than its Soviet Scud prototype but less capable than US and NATO missiles, or other more advanced Soviet missiles. It has a range of 300 kilometers (185 miles), which could place India's Punjah region under threat. China is reportedly also training Pakistani Air Force technicians.

Arms Sales to the Middle East

Iran and Iraq: Both bought conventional arms as well as material relating to nuclear development from China during their lengthy war of the 1980s.

A reported $4.8 billion worth of Chinese arms was sold to Iran mainly through North Korea, including the much-watched Silkworm anti-ship missiles with 50-mile range and 1,000-pound warhead capacity that worried Western naval commanders escorting oil tankers to Iraqi and other Gulf ports during the Iran-Iraq war. China has reportedly been training Iranian technicians and acting as the principal source for Iran's fledgling nuclear effort, selling Tehran nuclear reactors. This could lead to an attempt to enrich uranium to weapons-grade quality. Beijing is also reportedly trying to sell Tehran its newer M-9 missile. The M-9 has a longer range—500 km (some 315 miles) and greater warhead capacity than the M-11.

Meanwhile, at least $3 billion in Chinese conventional arms was sold to Iraq mainly through Jordan.

In early 1991, when China was supposedly abiding by United Nations sanctions against Iraq, seven tons of lithium were transferred to Iraq. This chemical element may be used for producing nuclear weapons, missile fuel, and nerve gas—but also for civilian purposes.

Syria: 24 launchers of the same nuclear-capable missile that China has been trying to sell to Iran—the M-9—were spotted in 1991. It is not known whether the M-9s themselves are also there.

Saudi Arabia: In 1987 a multibillion deal was cut between Saudi Arabia and China for as many as 50 intermediate-range ballistic missiles (IRBMs), known as CSS-2 in the West (or DF-3 by the Chinese). Though both governments denied the possible use of nuclear warheads, the inaccuracy of the missile makes it unlikely to be used as just a conventional weapon. The Saudis don't have nuclear warheads. So it is presumed the Chinese were trying at the time to counter Soviet sales and influence in the area, and the Saudis were showing Iran that expansion of the Iran-Iraq war in the Saudi direction could send missiles to Tehran.

There are many other clients for China's conventional arms sales, including Algeria, South Africa, Zambia, Zimbabwe, Thailand, Bangladesh, Sri Lanka, Egypt, North Korea, Myanmar

(Burma), Brazil, and Argentina. Of these, only Argentina and South Africa may be buying items with any nuclear significance.

The question arises, what are the motives of China's arms sales and what are the foreign policy implications? In some cases, there seem to be obvious geopolitical considerations. China's sale of CSS-2 missiles offset rival Taiwan's influence with the Saudis—and apparently paid off. In July 1990, China established formal diplomatic relations with Saudi Arabia.

China's Nuclear Aid to Iran

China admitted that in the past it has arranged to sell nuclear technology to Iran. It said the equipment—a small reactor and a separator used to produce radioactive isotopes—was intended for peaceful purposes, including "medical diagnosis and nuclear-physics research." By itself, the equipment cannot produce nuclear material in sufficient quantities to make weapons, experts say. But if Iran wants to build bombs, all it has to do is reproduce the technology. U.S. officials now think Iran intends to make nuclear weapons.

Russell Watson, *Newsweek*, November 18, 1991.

In the case of Pakistan, the consideration would be balancing India's influence in Asia. Until recently there were also considerations of competing with the Soviets—as in dealings with North Korea and Egypt.

Some reasons for China's arms sales are quite clear and open—such as raising funds for the military, providing hard currency reserves for the Ministry of Finance, advancing military technology, and attempting to achieve real superpower status. Far less open—purposely—is the financial and power benefit to individuals of the ruling class in the form of sales commissions. This factor is believed to play an important role in the continuation of such sales in the face of intense international pressure, particularly pressure to stop the spread of nuclear technology and potential delivery systems. . . .

Controlling Arms Sales with Pressure

China is becoming the next great arms merchant to the world. This, of course, threatens not only international security, but also the well-being of the Chinese people. The arms sales benefit the current Beijing regime, which demonstrated its tough face to the Chinese people and the world when the tanks rolled into downtown Beijing in 1989. Despite the usual pride in technological achievements, this attempt to attain big-power status through

108

these arms sales is not approved of by most of the Chinese people. A powerful China will be good for the world and for the Chinese people only when it is also a democratic China.

Former US national security adviser Zbigniew Brzezinski once said China was "a key force for global peace simply by being China."

Well, times have changed. In the post-Cold War period, China cannot be of value to the US on international security issues simply by "being China."

There are a number of ways the West can impose pressure on China to regulate or limit its arms sales.

One way is to push China to adhere to various international treaties. The important ones are the Non-Proliferation Treaty (NPT) and the Missile Technology Control Regime (MTCR). The first treaty would supposedly put China's nuclear programs under international inspection; the second would prevent any sale of missiles that have a range of 300 km (185 miles) or more.

Another way for the West to bring pressure is to block the transfer of high technology to China. This would include powerful computers that are used for the production of missiles and nuclear weapons.

The US government so far hasn't imposed this sanction long enough to see any difference before lifting the ban. Even if the Bush administration were to reimpose and stick with a high-tech sanction, China could still receive transfers from other countries, like Israel. And in any case, such a ban would not immediately stop China's arms sales, because of the growing capability of China's own military technology.

Economic Sanctions

A third course of action would be more general economic sanctions. For the United States, the likely tool would be to attach conditions to the renewal of the nondiscriminatory tariff treatment for China (the so-called most-favored-nation trading status).

In 1990 China's trade surplus with the US topped $15 billion, almost equal to the profit of China's arms sales for the whole decade of the 1980s. Without MFN, China would hardly be able to conduct trade with the US.

But forcing a choice between trade with the US and restrictions on arms sales to the world is not a practical option. Attaching arms-sales conditions to MFN status is different from attaching human rights conditions.

In the latter case, the Communist regime has shown that it is willing to play the human rights card with the international community by once in a while releasing a few political prisoners. Imposing arms-sales conditions on MFN would, however, raise nationalistic emotions in China.

The Chinese government could point out—they have already done so—that the US and Russia are the biggest arms suppliers—so why should Beijing be singled out? (US arms sales in 1990 were worth $18.5 billion, almost the same as that for a whole decade of sales by China.) Moreover, such pressure does not reach the actual "princelings" who are running the arms sales companies.

Target the Elite

For a more practical solution one has to focus on the military industrial infrastructure, with sanctions that hit the people who are running the arms sales and benefiting from them—the princelings. These people, as already mentioned, are quietly moving money and themselves to the West. For example, Yang Li, the daughter of President Yang Shangkun and wife of Baoli's [an arms sales company] executive vice-president, travels often between China and the US.

The behavior of the princelings shows how much faith they have in the current regime in China. Deng has spoken some warm words for capitalism as being useful for China, but he also means useful for the Communist Party's control over China. A bigger test for China's rulers will be whether they can abide by international standards—be it for capitalist or socialist nations—on the transfer of technology and materials for weapons of mass destruction.

The West could, however, make clear that such transfers, and political refuge for the princelings in the future, when the current regime is overthrown, will not be allowed unless China stops such sales.

"A constant flow of West German exports has brought India and Pakistan to the brink of nuclear deployment. "

Germany Contributes to Nuclear Proliferation

Gary Milhollin

German companies play key roles in supplying India, Pakistan, and Iraq with nuclear-related supplies for use in weapons programs. In the following viewpoint, Gary Milhollin argues that such exports helped India and Pakistan build nuclear weapons and created a dangerous situation where a nuclear attack may occur if war between the two rivals arises. Milhollin contends that both nations should formulate mutual agreements promising not to use nuclear weapons or attack nuclear facilities. Milhollin, a professor at the University of Wisconsin School of Law in Madison, is director of the Wisconsin Project on Nuclear Arms Control, a Washington, D.C., organization concerned with nuclear proliferation.

As you read, consider the following questions:

1. According to Milhollin, how did India and Pakistan initially lack a clear nuclear strategy?
2. Why does the author doubt that India would launch a nuclear first strike against Pakistan?
3. Why does Milhollin believe that Germany should play a leading role in preventing a nuclear attack between India and Pakistan?

Gary Milhollin, "Nukes R Us: The West German Role in a Brewing Atomic War," *The Washington Post National Weekly Edition*, June 18-24, 1990. Reprinted with permission.

The risk of nuclear war is higher now than at any time in the past decade—but not between the superpowers. The Pentagon and State Department now believe that there is a real chance of war in South Asia over the disputed province of Kashmir. That outcome is not inevitable. But if fighting does erupt between India and Pakistan, each side must assume that the other will deploy and possibly use an atomic bomb. If such a thing happens, West Germany will be primarily to blame.

From Conflict to Nuclear War

A constant flow of West German exports has brought India and Pakistan to the brink of nuclear deployment. As I learned in meetings with senior officials in both countries, neither side has a clear nuclear strategy. And no one knows how to prevent the next Indo-Pakistani border conflict from going nuclear.

Pakistan took its first big step toward the bomb between 1977 and 1980. To convert natural uranium to gaseous form—an essential step in enriching it to weapons grade—Pakistan bought a giant, multi-million-dollar plant from West Germany. Sixty truckloads of parts, in broad daylight, rolled out of Freiburg in violation of German law. The exporter, Albrecht Migule, was fined $10,000 and allowed to stay in business.

A few years later, Pakistan needed the special steel, electronics and processing vessels to finally produce nuclear-weapon material. Pakistan made the crucial purchases from other German firms, including Arbed Staarstahl, Leybold-Heraeus, NTG and PTB.

To make the internals of the bomb, Pakistan imported high-precision milling machines and special "isostatic" presses—from still more West German firms. All this equipment was on the "international list" of export items that Germany, like Japan and most NATO countries, has agreed to restrict for strategic purposes.

"You never hear anything, you never see anything and you never block anything": That's the motto of Germany's export controllers, a member of the West German parliament told *Der Spiegel* [newsmagazine].

Not content to have mastered simple fission bombs, Pakistan decided to climb the nuclear ladder. To get tritium—a radioactive isotope of hydrogen used to produce fusion—Pakistan secretly bought the design for a tritium-making reactor from NTG. NTG and another German firm, PTB, even threw in the equipment for making the reactor fuel rods. To convert the reactor's tritium output to nuclear-weapon grade, NTG and PTB also supplied a giant tritium purification plant and some tritium to test it.

"A civilian use of the tritium gas produced by the plant," says the German prosecutor who investigated the NTG export, "is not plausible." In 1990, West Germany charged the former directors of NTG and PTB with violating export laws.

With tritium-induced fusion, Pakistan could make its bombs five to 10 times more powerful. All of the exports were secret, few had any civilian purpose, and most violated West German obligations under the Nuclear Non-Proliferation Treaty.

The Case of India

While Germany was supplying Pakistan, it was also supplying India. By 1982, India's nuclear effort had limped to a halt. It was paralyzed by a shortage of "heavy water," a rare form containing deuterium, a heavy isotope of hydrogen. It looks and even tastes like ordinary water but is used in reactors that convert uranium into plutonium—the fuel for nuclear weapons.

Fires and explosions at heavy-water production plants had cut India's output to a trickle. There was only one solution to India's problem: imports. That was easy if India agreed to international inspection, so that the plutonium its reactors made could not go into atomic bombs. The exporters of heavy water required such a pledge under the Nuclear Non-Proliferation Treaty.

But India wanted to import the water without the pledge, so it could keep the nuclear weapon option open. To do that, India needed a peculiar kind of supplier.

German Designs and Aid

Iraq's centrifuges are based on German designs and were built with German help. Iraq somehow got German blueprints in the 1980's. By 1988 it was already running experimental models. When one model developed a hitch in late 1988, Iraq summoned Bruno Stemmler, an ex-employee of M.A.N., the German company that makes centrifuges for the German national enrichment effort. After studying Iraq's illicit blueprints, Stemmler removed the hitch.

Gary Milhollin, *The New York Times Magazine*, March 8, 1992.

India found nuclear-materials broker Alfred Hempel, operating out of Dusseldorf. From 1983 to 1987, Hempel (an ex-Nazi who died in 1989) smuggled India enough heavy water to start three large reactors. Together, those facilities now make enough plutonium for 40 atomic bombs per year.

Hempel's secret heavy-water shipments, which totaled at least 250 tons, allowed Indian reactors to escape international controls for the first time. India could finally build a nuclear arsenal and change the strategic balance in Asia.

But Hempel too had a problem: He needed protection. U.S. intelligence had caught wind of him in early 1981. In secret cables, the State Department began alerting West German officials to Hempel's shipments. In one cable to the West German Foreign Office—which included flight plans and stopover points—American diplomats pleaded that "timely action by the Federal Republic is essential if the shipment is to be stopped."

But in an Economics Ministry internal memo, a German official observed that Hempel's firm had been "developed with Russian capital" and dismissed the American plea as "politically motivated."

Not until November 1983 did West German auditors open Hempel's books, in response to U.S. complaints. They found that for 46.5 million German marks, Hempel had already shipped 60 tons of Chinese-origin heavy water to Bombay in 1982 and 1983. This was exactly what India needed to start its first reactor free of inspection.

The German Economics Ministry did nothing. Its excuse was that, according to the audit, Hempel had made the deal through a Swiss subsidiary, beyond the scope of German law.

European Complaints to Germany

In 1985, the Swiss started complaining. Bonn's embassy in Berne cabled the German foreign office in July to report that Hempel had just smuggled a shipment of Soviet-origin heavy water through the Zurich airport. In a second cable, the embassy reported that the Swiss were "convinced that misdealings occurred."

German officials, however, still did not act. A bureaucrat at the Economics Ministry wrote in an internal memo that Hempel "is well known here," and that under German law "there is no leverage in this case." After Bonn did nothing, Berne cabled again in February 1986. Hempel had just tried to smuggle a second Soviet shipment through Zurich.

This time, another Economics Ministry official was more specific: Hempel's "consortium of firms enjoys extraordinarily good relations with the East (Soviet Bloc). In my opinion, this would constitute an additional reason not to subject his firms to a foreign trade audit." With the 1985 and 1986 shipments, India started its second and third reactors free of inspection.

By 1988, even Norway was complaining. In May 1988 Norway discovered that Hempel had diverted 15 tons of Norwegian heavy water that was supposed to go to Germany in 1983. Hempel had flown the water instead to Switzerland, where he combined it with 4.7 tons of Soviet water secretly trucked in from Kiev, and sent the whole lot to Bombay.

Norway complained that the deal violated pledges in German shipping papers it had received—documents that promised delivery to Frankfurt. West German officials agreed but explained in an Economics Ministry memo that Germany was blameless because the shipments "did not touch the national territory of the Federal Republic."

In fact, the Soviet shipment spent several days rolling across West Germany illegally in December 1983. If German officials had followed up their November 1983 audit of Hempel, which revealed the secret Chinese shipments, they would have found the illegal December shipment and could have arrested Hempel in early 1984.

Even under Germany's weak laws, this would have prevented the hundreds of tons of secret heavy-water shipments that Hempel made from 1984 to 1987. But German officials, it seems, weren't interested. Neither Hempel nor his agents were prosecuted.

What to Do with a Nuclear Bomb

India and Pakistan must now decide what to do with their German imports. One senior Indian official, describing his country's newest nuclear missile, told me that it "has no real strategic purpose." India and Pakistan now realize that they, like the United States in World War II, built the bomb without knowing what they would do with it.

America wanted only to get the bomb before Hitler did. No one thought of using it against Japan until events pushed that question forward. India and Pakistan also built the bomb defensively: India to counter China; Pakistan to counter India. But like the United States, India and Pakistan may find that the momentum of events can make the question of nuclear use very real.

In the most likely conflict scenario, India would try to destroy Pakistan's air force in the first hours or days—the standard opening of modern war. With two or three times as many planes as Pakistan, India could hope to succeed. India's superior army would also invade Pakistan's long, hard-to-defend border. Pakistan does not seem to have a reliable nuclear missile, so its dozen or so bombs will have to be delivered with aircraft. The rapid loss of airfields and planes, coupled with invasion, could pose the nuclear question quickly. Pakistan's leaders would have three choices: use the bomb, lose the bomb or move the bomb.

Using it would mean making a nuclear threat, and following through if the threat failed. This is a high-risk proposition that only a country being overwhelmed would entertain—meaning that Pakistan could entertain it. Pakistani leaders would have to communicate the threat in the chaos of combat, while reports of aircraft losses were pouring in—the worst time for reflection on either side.

The second option would be for Pakistan to watch the last

squadron of its planes succumb without making the nuclear threat. This would mean losing the bomb by losing the means to deliver it. The advantage would be the survival of millions of Pakistanis who could otherwise perish in the Indian response to option one.

Germany's Nuclear Pathway

For many developing nations, the path to the nuclear threshold led through the West German underground. Transnuklear, a German firm specializing in the transport of atomic wastes, has been at the heart of a number of scandals, allegedly for shipping weapons-grade atomic materials and bribing officials to look the other way. In 1989, the United States charged a second German company with selling beryllium to India. Still another German firm sent heavy water, a key atomic catalyst, to Dubai and Argentina by way of a stealthy, circuitous route across Scandinavia and the Orient. For sheer ingenuity, the clincher may have been a 1977 deal between a German firm and Pakistan. Investigators believe a plutonium processing plant was shipped piecemeal from Germany to Islamabad in 62 truck convoys during a three-year period.

Steve Salerno, *The American Legion*, July 1991.

Moving the bomb—probably to Pakistan's ally, China—would be a compromise. It would put the bomb where it was safe but couldn't be used. China would probably take in Pakistan's nuclear hardware but forbid its deployment from Chinese territory. The bomb, having failed to deter war, might someday return in peace to whatever was left of Pakistan after the conflict.

These alternatives are grim. To improve them, one needs to lengthen the time for decisions. Both sides would be better off if a quick nuclear showdown could be avoided. They would have a chance to stop fighting before one of them dragged the other over the brink. More time would also allow other countries to intervene and broker a ceasefire.

Indo-Pakistani Cooperation

There is one device that might buy a crucial amount of time. Pakistan and India have already signed an agreement not to attack each other's nuclear plants. They could extend this by granting each other a sanctuary that neither would attack by air, and from which neither would launch an attack by air.

As long as the parties observed the agreement, both sides' nuclear forces could be preserved. Each side could avoid forcing a hasty nuclear decision on the other; and if conflict ended early, or ended before either side's national existence were threatened, neither Pakistan nor India would necessarily have to decide whether to use a nuclear weapon.

The non-attack pledge would preserve the nuclear status quo in the early hours or days of war, when removal might seem less attractive or still have to be negotiated. Would India refuse to join, hoping to knock out Pakistan's whole air force at once? India could not count on doing that. If it failed, it would force Pakistan to weigh a nuclear threat—a risk that India should prefer to avoid.

Would Pakistan refuse to join, hoping to save a few planes by hiding them well? If Pakistan failed to hide them well enough, it would be worse off than with a sanctuary.

Would the agreement be too risky, because one side could break it without warning? Breaking it would be risky too, because neither side could be sure of getting all of the other's planes, which would take off with whatever they were carrying when attacked. Their load probably would not be conventional weapons.

All this assumes that neither side would launch a first strike. India doesn't need to because its vast army can handle Pakistan without the bomb. Pakistan wouldn't be able to because India's near-billion population (and larger nuclear force) could absorb a Pakistani attack and still retaliate. The greatest danger of a nuclear strike—absurd as it may sound—could be in a chaotic moment when the bomb itself was in danger of being lost.

West Germany's reckless acts have now brought two poor countries to the nuclear threshold. Because of a disputed border, India and Pakistan are about to learn whether nuclear deterrence really works. Germany should be condemned for producing this result . . . and [should] lead the effort to pull South Asia back from the brink.

"Every aspect of Iraq's nuclear weapons program shows signs of a patient, no-expense-spared search for help abroad."

Western Nations Contributed to Iraq's Weapons Program

David Albright and Mark Hibbs

Inspections in Iraq following the Persian Gulf War provided proof that Iraq imported nuclear-related items from Western nations to build weapons. In the following viewpoint, David Albright and Mark Hibbs argue that Western firms and governments, which sided with Iraq during its war with Iran, contributed to Iraq's nuclear arms program. The authors assert that while Iraq duped some firms into exporting nuclear-related equipment and material, others were well aware that their supplies would be used specifically for nuclear weapons. Albright is a senior scientist at Friends of the Earth, an environmental organization in Washington, D.C. Hibbs is a German-based editor for *Nuclear Fuel*, a biweekly newsletter.

As you read, consider the following questions:

1. Why were some firms' nuclear exports to Iraq kept secret, according to Albright and Hibbs?
2. Why do Albright and Hibbs believe that some exporting companies were ignorant of Iraq's motives?

From David Albright and Mark Hibbs, "Iraq's Shop-Till-You-Drop Nuclear Program." From the *Bulletin of the Atomic Scientists*, April 1992. Copyright © 1992 by the Educational Foundation for Nuclear Science, 6042 S. Kimbark Ave., Chicago, IL 60637, U.S.A. A one-year subscription is $30. Reprinted with permission.

In a series of articles [in the *Bulletin of the Atomic Scientists*] that began in March 1991, we have tried to separate fact from fiction about Iraq's ability to build nuclear weapons and to produce material to fuel them. After exposing Iraq's efforts to enrich uranium and design an atomic bomb, U.N. and IAEA experts zeroed in on how Iraq put its program together. The basic answer is that along with determination and persistence, Iraq had a great deal of foreign help.

Iraq's "Petrochemical Three," the secret nuclear program conducted under the authority of its Atomic Energy Commission with links to the Defense Ministry and the Ministry of Industry and Military Industrialization, received massive infusions of money and resources. Like the Manhattan Project that built the first atomic bombs in the United States, Iraq's program simultaneously pursued a number of different technical avenues to the bomb. Not knowing which efforts would succeed, Iraq poured billions of dollars into its multifaceted quest.

An Elaborate Network

Providing for these programs required the establishment of elaborate procurement networks in Europe, North America, and Asia. Like the technical quest, the procurement effort was carried out on many fronts at once. Diplomacy and secrecy were required, because few companies would knowingly supply a nuclear weapons program, or even a secret nuclear program that was ostensibly for civil purposes. Iraq showed great ingenuity in hiding its purchases behind such innocuous pursuits as automobile manufacturing, dairy production, and oil refining.

Some of the basic infrastructure Iraq needed for the program—factories, electrical supply, and power equipment—was easy to obtain from abroad. But the more specific the equipment Iraq sought, the more other countries' export controls began to bite. Crucial transfers of components were blocked.

To evade export controls, Iraqi officials divided equipment orders into innocuous subcomponents. They also tried to buy machines to make sensitive components in Iraq. They used middlemen to disguise the destination of equipment and materials they were importing and to assure Western suppliers that the products the suppliers were exporting would be used for peaceful purposes. And the Iraqis seized opportunities to obtain any uncontrolled equipment and material that was available, often in enormous quantities, regardless of whether they were ready to use it. That practice generated the impression that Baghdad was closer to having a nuclear bomb than it in fact was.

Inspections after the Gulf War revealed that in some cases, export controls did not suffice. Iraq's calutron program was successful largely because few of the materials or components were controlled. On the other hand, in its centrifuge program, Iraq blatantly circumvented Western controls on sensitive centrifuge design information and components. The failure to prevent the spread of this know-how—which is highly classified in all Western countries—partly explains why Baghdad's procurement effort remains the most sensitive aspect of its secret nuclear program.

Origin and Design of the Iraqi Bomb

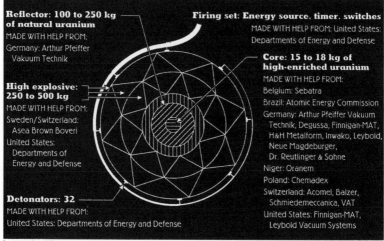

Reflector: 100 to 250 kg of natural uranium
MADE WITH HELP FROM:
Germany: Arthur Pfeiffer Vakuum Technik

High explosive: 250 to 500 kg
MADE WITH HELP FROM:
Sweden/Switzerland: Asea Brown Boveri
United States: Departments of Energy and Defense

Detonators: 32
MADE WITH HELP FROM:
United States: Departments of Energy and Defense

Firing set: Energy source, timer, switches
MADE WITH HELP FROM: United States: Departments of Energy and Defense

Core: 15 to 18 kg of high-enriched uranium
MADE WITH HELP FROM:
Belgium: Sebatra
Brazil: Atomic Energy Commission
Germany: Arthur Pfeiffer Vakuum Technik, Degussa, Finnigan-MAT, H&H Metalform, Inwako, Leybold, Neue Magdeburger, Dr. Reutlinger & Sohne
Niger: Oranem
Poland: Chemadex
Switzerland: Acomel, Balzer, Schmiedemeccanica, VAT
United States: Finnigan-MAT, Leybold Vacuum Systems

Western companies and governments, particularly Germany, do not want to be embarrassed by public revelations about their involvement with Iraq's nuclear program. Firms fear that commercial secrets will leak out. But exposing the way Iraq tried to buy itself a nuclear weapons program is critical to determining where export controls failed—or worked—and what improvements are needed if the Iraqi experience is not to be repeated. . . .

The Proliferation Food Chain

Lewis Dunn, a U.S. nonproliferation expert, said at a public meeting in mid-1991 that the history of efforts to tighten nuclear export controls is like working down a "proliferation food chain." That is, the more important an item is for producing plutonium or highly enriched uranium or for making a nuclear weapon, the earlier it was covered by export controls. Currently, tight controls cover export of completed nuclear facilities or their basic units, such as gas centrifuges and their major components. Subcomponents and equipment and technology to manufacture major components are less regulated. These often have many uses and are officially referred to as "dual-use" items.

Iraq had only limited success in acquiring tightly controlled items. It was more successful in obtaining dual-use equipment. Iraq's export permit applications almost always listed civilian industrial uses for such equipment.

Some of the exports never made it to Iraq. In July 1990, German and Swiss customs officials stopped a shipment of special computer numerically controlled (CNC) machines for making endcaps and baffles of centrifuges. CNC machines are highly sophisticated, modern machine tools, which can be programmed on-line to perform complicated and precise machining of metal parts. Also confiscated were 888 forgings for endcaps and baffles that would be finished on the CNC machines. Earlier that year, U.S. and British customs officials caught Iraq trying to smuggle detonation capacitors from CSI Technologies in California. These capacitors, which were of military standard and specification, would have been ideal for developing the implosion mechanism for a nuclear weapon.

The embargo imposed on Iraq after it invaded Kuwait in August 1990 kept a shipment of aluminum piping from leaving Switzerland. The material might have served to connect gas centrifuges in a "cascade" or assembly. There was enough piping to connect 500–1,000 centrifuges.

Siding with Iraq

But a great deal of technology, equipment, and materials got through before the embargo was imposed. Most of it never raised eyebrows, as business with Iraq was considered legitimate. The West favored Iraq in its bloody, eight-year war with Iran. During the last half of the 1980s, the U.S. government approved the sale to Iraq of $1.5 billion worth of computers, electronic equipment, and machine tools that could be used in its nuclear, chemical, and ballistic missile program. Europe supplied even more. France sold Saddam Hussein $5 billion worth of aircraft, missiles, and armor during the war. A U.S. customs official involved in stopping the sale of the detonation capacitors to Iraq summed up the situation: "The enemy of my enemy is my customer."

In this climate, many Western companies and individuals felt justified in exporting their products to Iraq and rarely questioned Iraqi assertions that the goods were for peaceful use. That changed only after Iraq invaded Kuwait and Iraq's programs to build nuclear weapons and other weapons of mass destruction were exposed after the Gulf War. The exposure of

Iraq's military programs has stiffened the resolve of companies that contributed to Saddam's effort to deny that they ever had anything to do with Iraq's clandestine nuclear program. But the specific nature of some of the equipment exported should have aroused the suspicions of companies and export control authorities. According to the eighth IAEA report, in some cases "the presence of application-specific fixtures removes most doubt as to intended use." Some of the companies supplying this equipment might not have known that Iraq's nuclear program was the final customer. But according to the report, the intermediaries who dealt with Iraq "must have known (or could reasonably have inferred) the intended uses." One inspector said that Iraqi officials insisted on successful demonstrations of centrifuge component manufacturing equipment before they accepted shipment. In these cases, one IAEA official asks, "How could they not have known?". . .

Iraq's Quest for Foreign Help

Every aspect of Iraq's nuclear weapons program shows signs of a patient, no-expense-spared search for help abroad.

Far less is known about Iraq's procurement of calutron components than about the centrifuge program, although the calutron program, too, depended heavily on foreign help. The difference was that export controls rarely hindered Iraq's attempts to buy calutron components. Iraq's success in hiding its calutron program from Western intelligence agencies can also be traced in part to a lack of export controls and the monitoring that accompanies them. Until 1991, calutron technology was thought to be too expensive, cumbersome, and outdated for any would-be nuclear weapons state to pursue.

One of the few cases about which some details are known involves the massive iron pieces used in calutron magnets and in connecting several magnets into a "racetrack." Iraq contracted with foreign foundries to cast and rough-machine the large iron components for calutrons being installed at Tarmiya. Final machining was done in Iraq at the Al Radwan facility.

Voest-Alpine AG, an Austrian foundry, has been identified by Western officials as one of several foundries where calutron parts were cast, although the officials do not believe the company knew that the parts were for calutrons. The first order to this foundry came directly from the Iraqi State Electric Establishment. A second order for 28 pieces, six of them identical to the first order, came from a German company. According to the eighth inspection report, the foundry's management has said that the company would have received a larger order from an intermediary if it could have met a required deadline. IAEA officials believe that other contracts must have been placed with other foundries, since the number of pieces found in Iraq is larger than the number the identified foundry supplied.

Much of the infrastructure at Tarmiya, the main calutron site, was built by foreign companies. A Yugoslavian firm, Federal Directorate of Supply and Procurement (FDSP), may have been the main contractor for the project. Electrical installation was provided by a Yugoslavian company, EMO. One inspector said that Siemens AG of Germany provided some of the electrical distribution equipment that connected transformers to ion sources at Tarmiya.

Building a Weapon

Tightening export controls did slow Iraq's effort to develop a deliverable nuclear bomb, as a 1990 Iraqi progress report made clear. Nevertheless, Iraq tried to obtain components illegally and exploited loopholes to acquire raw materials and manufacturing equipment when components were blocked. The main site at Al Atheer was being outfitted mainly as a materials research facility. Iraq was therefore purchasing a great variety of state-of-the-art equipment for this facility.

Iraq's Nuclear Supply List

On December 12, 1991, the IAEA, which is responsible for destroying Iraq's nuclear infrastructure under U.N. resolution 687, released the first list of companies whose equipment Iraq used in its nuclear weapon development program in the report of the eighth nuclear inspection team. The list of companies included one U.S. firm (Dupont); eight German companies (Acomel GmbH & Co., KG; Arthur Pfeiffer Vakuum Technic GmbH; Balzer AG; Degussa; H & H Metalform Maschinebau und Vertriebs GmbH; Leybold Hergens AG; Neue Maddeburger Werkzeugmaschinefabrik GmbH; and VAT AG); one Swiss firm (Dr. Reutlinger & Sohne, KG); one Swedish company (Asea Brown Boveri); and one Japanese firm (Hamamatsu). The IAEA report stressed, however, that the manufacturers of the equipment may not have supplied the equipment directly to Iraq, and may not have known either the intended use or the final destination of the items found in Iraq.

Jon B. Wolfsthal, *Arms Control Today*, January/February 1992.

Iraq imported hundreds of tons of HMX high explosives, the most desirable conventional explosive for nuclear weapons. Western intelligence believes that Chilean explosives expert Carlos Cardoen exported most of the HMX to Iraq. Cardoen, who set up a cluster bomb factory near Baghdad, is under investigation by the U.S. Justice Department. Who made the explosive and how it got to Iraq is unknown, although Eastern Europe is suspected.

Streak cameras are capable of taking high-speed photographs useful in a nuclear weapons development program. A Japanese firm, Hamamatsu Photonics KK, legally exported two streak video cameras and support equipment to Iraq's Ministry of Industry and Minerals in September 1989. The declared use was for experimental automobile engine research at the University of Technology, Baghdad. According to the eighth inspection report, the cameras had a speed and resolution suitable for weapons development.

Iraq acquired from the Swiss firm Asea Brown Boveri a large cold isostatic press that could be used to shape explosive charges, but the press was found in a location without adequate safety equipment for high explosives work. It also obtained a vacuum induction furnace (a very high-temperature furnace) manufactured by the German firm Arthur Pfeiffer Vakuum Tecknik GmbH, which might have been useful in making uranium metal components.

An effort of the magnitude of Iraq's nuclear weapons program requires the ability to transfer large amounts of money internationally. Iraq used bank letters of credit to purchase what it needed, and few questions were asked by the European and American banks—including the scandal-ridden Bank of Credit and Commerce International—that arranged Iraq's commercial transactions.

An Atlanta-based branch of Italy's Banco Nationale da Lavore (BNL) came under investigation by the U.S. Department of Justice for conspiracy, wire fraud, and mail fraud related to financing Iraq's global procurement effort. The U.S. government obtained evidence that BNL provided nearly $1.6 billion to Iraq's Ministry of Industry and Military Industrialization to buy petroleum interests, the investment proceeds from which were allegedly to be used for the procurement effort. These interests were to be managed by the brother and the son of Jaffar Dhia Jaffar—a deputy minister of the ministry as well as vice chairman of the Iraqi Atomic Energy Commission. Who headed Iraq's nuclear weapons program is still unknown, but Jaffar is a leading suspect.

How Iraqi Efforts Succeeded

The IAEA inspection effort in Iraq provides a snapshot of one country's success in attempting to procure equipment and know-how for a nuclear weapons program. Iraq spent 10 years and billions of dollars, but the evidence shows that Iraq got as far as it did because of political circumstances, suppliers' ignorance, commercial deception and greed, and even scientific curiosity.

Western governments that backed Iraq against Iran looked the other way when firms sent dual-use items to Baghdad, and companies have justified their behavior on the basis that Saddam Hussein was battling Teheran's bearded mullahs. But there is no reason to believe these firms would not have supplied Iran had their governments made another choice.

There is, however, little reason to doubt that many firms were victims of Iraqi deception regarding the end uses of their products. That is particularly the case for many common items, like small iron magnets, aluminum motor housings, and bolts of copper wire. Records seized by the IAEA testify that most of the items Iraq ordered from abroad were ordinary.

But not all. Some items used to manufacture centrifuge rotor assemblies—flow-forming machines, CNC-machine tools, and specialized welding gear—were critical to the success of the program. Lax export controls, particularly in Germany and Switzerland, gave Iraq easy access to this equipment.

Iraq's access to Western centrifuge enrichment know-how was even more critical. Key components in Iraqi centrifuges clearly show the fingerprints of Urenco [the European centrifuge enrichment consortium] designs. While the suspicion that Iraq obtained classified Urenco blueprints has not been confirmed, design details of Iraqi components have since prompted an even more worrisome proliferation scenario: On the basis of early Urenco centrifuges, yet-unknown freelance experts have been improving them. Unless the IAEA and the U.N. Special Commission find the source of this assistance, the roots of Iraq's clandestine nuclear program may still bear fruit.

"Israel possesses a potent nuclear force."

Israel Introduced Nuclear Weapons to the Middle East

Leonard S. Spector

Leonard S. Spector is one of the foremost experts of nuclear weapons programs. In the following viewpoint, Spector argues that Israel has a strong nuclear arsenal and may possess advanced nuclear weapons. Spector contends that Israel's nuclear capabilities have prompted a bloc of Arab nations to consider acquiring missiles, chemical weapons, and nuclear arms, as a defense against Israeli attack. The situation may trigger Middle East hostilities. Spector is the director of the Nonproliferation Project of the Carnegie Endowment for International Peace, located in Washington, D.C.

As you read, consider the following questions:

1. Why does Spector consider an Israeli-South African nuclear weapons connection significant?
2. What evidence leads the author to believe that Israel has advanced nuclear weapons?
3. According to the author, how does Israel's advanced missile technology threaten relations with Arab neighbors?

Reprinted from *Nuclear Ambitions* by Leonard S. Spector, 1990, by permission of Westview Press, Boulder, Colorado.

The revelations in late 1986 by former Israeli nuclear technician Mordechai Vanunu, now widely accepted as genuine, have confirmed the existence of Israel's nuclear arsenal, which probably consists of 60 to 100 devices. Some of these are of an advanced design that could make them many times more powerful than the atomic weapons used in World War II. During 1989 and the first half of 1990, it must be presumed that Israel added several more nuclear weapons to its preexisting arsenal.

Also in 1989, British scientist Frank Barnaby—the only nuclear expert to speak with Mordechai Vanunu—disclosed that Vanunu had told him that, in addition to producing sizable quantities of plutonium, Israel has been producing enriched uranium since 1979 or 1980, initially using centrifuges for this purpose, and then, beginning in 1981, also using advanced lasers. Since highly enriched uranium—like plutonium—can be used as the core of a nuclear weapon, this capability may have allowed Israel to expand its nuclear arsenal beyond the size estimated above. . . .

Israel's Nuclear Capabilities

Estimates of the size of the Israeli nuclear arsenal vary significantly. Based on the data supplied by Mordechai Vanunu, the *Sunday Times* projected that Israel might have as many as 200 devices. The consensus among U.S. officials who have attempted to harmonize Vanunu's testimony with other relevant information, however, is that Israel's nuclear armory probably contains fewer than 100 weapons, and perhaps no more than 50 or 60. Even such a smaller stockpile, however, would permit Israel to use a number of its nuclear weapons tactically, *i.e.*, against military targets, during any conflict with its neighbors, while keeping a number of weapons in reserve to threaten enemy cities and thereby deter actions that might imperil Israel's existence.

The key piece of information provided by Vanunu was that the plutonium extraction plant where he worked [at Dimona] produced a total of about 88 pounds (40 kilograms) of plutonium per year—possibly enough for ten weapons, if former U.S. weapons designer Theodore Taylor is correct that Israel has the sophistication to build weapons using only 8.8 pounds (4 kilograms) of plutonium per device. During the eight years that Vanunu worked at the plutonium facility (1977-1985), enough plutonium for 80 weapons could have been produced.

In his book on the Israeli nuclear program, published in 1989, Frank Barnaby states that the plutonium plant began operating in 1966 and reached full capacity in 1972; Barnaby also assumes that the plant continued to operate at this rate after Vanunu left in 1985. Thus by 1990, the facility would have operated at full capacity for eighteen years, producing ten weapons' worth of plutonium per year, or enough plutonium for about 180 weapons.

If the Dimona reactor was only 24 megawatts, the power level announced by Israel in 1960, it could irradiate only enough fuel to produce plutonium sufficient for two devices per year, however, not for the ten bombs suggested by Vanunu's data. This discrepancy led the *Sunday Times* to hypothesize that the reactor had been enlarged nearly six-fold, possibly to 150 megawatts.

Targeting Israel's Arab Neighbors

Israeli field commanders have accepted nuclear artillery shells and land mines as battlefield necessities: another means to an end. The basic target of Israel's nuclear arsenal has been and will continue to be its Arab neighbors. Should war break out in the Middle East again and should the Syrians and the Egyptians break through again as they did in 1973, or should any Arab nation fire missiles again at Israel, as Iraq did, a nuclear escalation, once unthinkable except as a last resort, would now be a strong probability.

Seymour M. Hersh, *The Samson Option*, 1991.

Barnaby agrees that a 150-megawatt reactor would be required for the larger plutonium-output capacity. According to Barnaby, Vanunu told him that the reactor's output was increased twice before his arrival at Dimona, the first time to 70 megawatts. Barnaby concludes that the second upgrade "presumably" raised the unit's power to the needed 150 megawatts, and adds, "To disperse the extra heat produced, a new large cooling unit was added to the reactor." Barnaby does not indicate whether this is his own speculation or a detail provided by Vanunu.

American Experts' View

U.S. government specialists, however, doubt that the Dimona reactor was enlarged so dramatically because, they claim, there is no evidence to suggest that the needed additional cooling units have been built. They believe that the reactor operated initially at 40 megawatts, because of the cooling efficiencies permitted by the desert climate, and, based on Vanunu's statements, concede that the reactor may have been enlarged to 70 megawatts before his arrival in 1977. If the reactor had been enlarged to this level in the early 1970s—perhaps, in 1972—and had operated through 1989 at the higher level, total plutonium output might amount to enough for about 90 weapons, altogether; if it was not enlarged, only enough plutonium for 50 to 60 weapons could have been produced.

To explain why the throughput of the plutonium plant was so high during Vanunu's tenure, U.S. analysts speculate that Israel had trouble running the plutonium plant for a number of years, which would have created a large backlog of spent fuel from the Dimona reactor for processing. Vanunu was hired as part of a large group of technicians in 1977 and was part of a 1985 lay-off that involved 180 workers at the Dimona site. An increase and sudden reduction in staff would be consistent with the hypothesis that extra manpower was needed for a number of years while a backlog was being worked off.

Israel's Arsenal Exceeds Previous Estimates

For now, the matter cannot be resolved. French journalist Pierre Péan's assertions that the reactor has always been larger than publicly described and that the Americans who visited the complex in the 1960s were deceived on this point may be correct. Alternatively, the reactor could have been enlarged secretly, eluding U.S. intelligence analysts, as Vanunu claimed. Or, as U.S. analysts suggest, the reactor may never have operated at 150 megawatts, but only at an intermediate power level, while operating difficulties in the plutonium plant led to a backlog and the subsequent periods of high throughput described by Vanunu. All of these estimates would suggest, however, that Israel possesses a nuclear armory larger than previous U.S. estimates of 50 or so weapons, which assumed that the reactor was never enlarged, but still somewhat short of the highest alternative projections of 200 weapons. (Moreover, to these various estimates of plutonium-based weapons should be added any weapons that Israel may have produced with highly enriched uranium cores, using either material obtained from the U.S. NUMEC [Nuclear Materials and Equipment Corporation] plant in the 1960s or from Israel's own enrichment facility.)

In November 1989, the Natural Resources Defense Council, a private environmental group that monitors nuclear issues, released a U.S. Defense Intelligence Agency document entitled, "Surface-to-Surface Missile Handbook—Free World," which it had obtained under the Freedom of Information Act. One page of the document is headed, "Jericho I," and under the column for type of warhead "nuclear, chemical, or HE [high-explosive]" are listed. The document also states that the system is "deployed on a wheeled TEL [transporter/erector/launcher] vehicle." The document is one of the few explicit indications of the U.S. view that Israel possesses nuclear arms and has deployed missiles to carry them. (It also represents the first published indication that the United States believes Israel has missiles equipped with chemical warheads.) Israel's missile program is discussed below.

As mentioned earlier, Mordechai Vanunu revealed to Frank

129

Barnaby that in addition to producing sizable quantities of plutonium for nuclear weapons, Israel has been producing enriched
uranium with centrifuges since 1979 or 1980 and with advanced
lasers since 1981. This capability may have allowed Israel to expand its nuclear arsenal further. Barnaby does not, however,
state whether Israel is enriching uranium to weapons grade or
only to lower levels. Nor does Barnaby indicate how large the
Israeli enrichment capability might be. Finally, testifying before
Congress in early 1989, CIA Director William Webster confirmed that Israel has been pursuing research on the use of
lasers for enriching uranium, but he indicated that the program
had only limited funding. He did not comment on whether
Israel also has a centrifuge enrichment capability.

Israel's Early Nuclear Program

The real test of U.S. concern with nuclear proliferation is the
case of Israel. As early as 1968 the CIA had concluded that Israel
had manufactured atomic weapons. Israel did so with a combination of early U.S. assistance to its "peaceful" atomic energy program, secret French assistance, and theft. The CIA believes that
Israel stole 200 pounds of enriched uranium from a plant in
Pennsylvania (with the connivance of the company president)
and that Israeli agents diverted 200 tons of processed uranium
ore at sea.

Whenever Washington found out about advances in Israel's nuclear program—in 1968, 1974, or 1976—there was no negative
U.S. reaction. In fact, U.S. aid to Israel increased. And U.S. laws
calling for the cutoff of aid to states producing nuclear weapons
were carefully written in such a way as not to include Israel.

Stephen R. Shalom, *Z Magazine*, February 1991.

Vanunu's claim that Israel had produced tritium and lithium
deuteride suggests that the Israeli arsenal consists, at least in
part, of advanced nuclear weapons. Presumably, the tritium is
used by Israel in the manufacture of "boosted" nuclear
weapons. These are nuclear devices that rely principally on the
fissioning of plutonium or highly enriched uranium for their
yield, but in which this reaction is enhanced by the presence of
tritium. The tritium undergoes an atomic fusion reaction when
the device is detonated, releasing a stream of neutrons that
greatly improves the efficiency of the fission reaction. Boosting
thus allows weapon designers to achieve a greater nuclear yield
than could otherwise be obtained from a given quantity of plutonium or highly enriched uranium. In practice, this means that

some Israeli nuclear weapons may have yields several times greater than the 20-kilotons nominally assumed to be the size of developing country nuclear devices.

In addition, former U.S. nuclear weapons designer Theodore Taylor, after examining Vanunu's photo of an unusually configured nuclear weapon component made from lithium deuteride, suggested that Israel also may be building "super-boosted" weapons—a term he coined to characterize the Israeli design— with a yield of perhaps 100 kilotons, the size of some warheads on U.S. strategic missiles. Presumably, the manufacture of full-fledged, multistage thermonuclear "hydrogen" bombs with megaton yields would require an extensive nuclear testing program and thus remains beyond Israeli abilities, since Israel is not known to have conducted the necessary tests.

According to Frank Barnaby, in 1977, Israel apparently began producing small quantities of lithium-6, a key precursor for the production both of tritium and of lithium deuteride. Full-scale production of lithium-6 began in 1984, and continued for two years; tritium production (and presumably lithium deuteride production) also began the same year. Altogether Israel produced approximately 375 pounds of lithium-6, which Barnaby estimated would have allowed Israel to produce enough lithium deuteride for 35 fusion weapons—presumably of the super-boosted type identified by Taylor. Or, Israel could have used some of the lithium-6 to produce tritium for boosted weapons. The proportion of lithium-6 that may have been used for each purpose is not known.

The foregoing analysis suggests that Israel probably has at least 60 to 100 nuclear weapons. These weapons most likely use plutonium, but some may rely on highly enriched uranium. Of these 60 to 100 devices, a number probably are boosted with tritium to increase their yield to perhaps 40 or 50 kilotons, while other weapons have been "superboosted" using lithium deuteride to give them a yield in the 100-kiloton range. . . .

Collaboration with South Africa

Israel has had close political ties to South Africa and the two states have cooperated extensively in the area of conventional arms. It also has been alleged for many years that Israel and South Africa have collaborated in the development of nuclear arms and that Israel may have used South African facilities to conduct a nuclear test in the South Atlantic in September 1979. Although a nuclear relationship has not been conclusively established, circumstantial evidence to support its existence has slowly accumulated over time. Allegations of an Israeli-South African nuclear connection deserve to be taken seriously, even if its precise contours remain unknown.

In late 1989, a major investigation by an American television news team reported that the two countries were collaborating on the development of long-range missiles. The report, by NBC News, stated that Israel had provided missile technology to South Africa in return for a supply of enriched uranium for nuclear weapons and access to long-range missile test facilities on the South African mainland at Overberg and on the Prince Edward Islands in the Antarctic. The report stated that the two countries had conducted a test of a missile from the Overberg site on July 5,1989, to a range of 900 miles—a range that suggests the system tested was one version of the Jericho Follow-on. An important benefit to Israel of gaining access to a test site in South Africa is that this would permit it to test missiles to a considerably longer range than is feasible from Israel.

Israel's Program Draws Attention

Both Israel and South Africa denied the charges in the NBC report, although some Israeli statements left open the possibility that collaboration in the missile field might be continuing under contracts signed by the two states some years ago. Moreover, as the story unfolded, additional press reports, quoting unnamed U.S. officials, basically confirmed the existence of joint missile activities between the two states. There appeared to be no additional support, however, for the view that Israel had received a nuclear *quid pro quo* for providing missile technology to Pretoria, and even NBC News began to downplay this aspect of the story.

The reported missile links to South Africa exposed Israel's missile and nuclear activities to public scrutiny in the United States for the first time in many years. Bush Administration officials, for example, publicized the fact that President Bush had raised Israel's transfers of missile technology with Israeli Prime Minister Yitzhak Shamir, during the latter's mid-November 1989 visit to Washington shortly after the story broke. Moreover, during the visit, Shamir was repeatedly questioned by the press about the matter and about Israel's nuclear program, issues which had traditionally been treated as off-limits. In addition, during late 1989, Israel's missile ties to South Africa augmented opposition to the sale of U.S. supercomputers to Jerusalem. Supercomputers can simulate nuclear explosions and ballistic missile reentry in order to reduce the need for costly and politically controversial full-scale tests. Concerns that Israel might have transferred U.S.-origin missile technology to South Africa, and Israel's possible involvement in a scheme to smuggle advanced U.S. missile gyroscopes to that country, added to the controversy. . . .

Vanunu's revelations—and the added details concerning them published by Frank Barnaby—together with the confirmation in authoritative U.S. government documents that Israel had deployed nuclear-capable missiles and nuclear warheads, have persuasively established that Israel possesses a potent nuclear force. Moreover, with its launch of the Offeq I and Offeq II satellites, Israel publicly demonstrated its considerable capabilities in the missile field, in effect partly removing the veil of ambiguity it had placed around its overall nuclear capability for some 20 years.

Israel's potential adversaries fully recognize Israel's nuclear might. Indeed, at the January 1989 Paris Conference on Chemical Weapons, a bloc of Arab states publicly opposed measures to slow the spread of chemical weapons because of Israel's continued possession of nuclear arms. . . .

The combination of Israel's nuclear capability and the chemical, missile, and emerging nuclear threat to that country promises to be extremely dangerous. Dampening the risk that these capabilities might become the trigger for serious hostilities in the region must be an urgent priority for international diplomacy.

"Pyongyang may become an exporter of nuclear weapons as well as ballistic missiles."

North Korea Could Acquire Nuclear Weapons

Andrew Mack

Many nations suspect that North Korea is conducting a secret nuclear weapons program. In the following viewpoint, Andrew Mack agrees and argues that North Korea allegedly built a re-processing plant and a testing facility necessary to build nuclear arms. Mack asserts that North Korea has several incentives for seeking nuclear weapons and that the nation could increase nuclear proliferation in Asia. Mack is director of the Peace Research Centre at the Australian National University in Canberra.

As you read, consider the following questions:

1. According to Mack, how may the collapse of Soviet-North Korean relations have increased the North's interest in nuclear arms?
2. Why does the author doubt that North Korea could match South Korea's military strength?
3. How could a North Korean nuclear arms program threaten global nonproliferation efforts, according to Mack?

A nuclear arms race may be developing in Northeast Asia. Washington, Seoul, and Moscow view with growing alarm the possibility that North Korea is building a nuclear weapons facility. If North Korea acquires nuclear weapons, the repercussions in South Korea and Japan will be severe.

Although public information remains circumstantial, fragmentary, contested, and often contradictory, international concern centers on a large (20 to 30 megawatt) research reactor at the nuclear complex at Yongbyon, some 100 kilometers north of the North Korean capital of Pyongyang. The reactor has been described as "very crude in quality . . . [but] suitable for the production of plutonium." Construction of the controversial reactor is said to have commenced in 1980. Initial U.S. trepidation lessened considerably when the North Koreans—apparently under Soviet pressure—acceded to the Treaty on the Non-Proliferation of Nuclear Weapons (NPT) in 1985. In so doing, Pyongyang pledged not to build or otherwise acquire nuclear weapons. However, new evidence about a possible nuclear-weapons role for the controversial facility has emerged. . . .

Evidence of Nuclear Weapons

In May 1989 a South Korean newspaper, *Chungang Ilbo*, reported that the CIA had obtained "crucial evidence proving North Korea's capability of developing nuclear weapons on its own." The evidence in question related to the construction of a nuclear reprocessing plant at Yongbyon that had been photographed by U.S. reconnaissance satellites. In order to make nuclear weapons, plutonium must be extracted from spent reactor fuel in a reprocessing plant like the one the North was allegedly building. Yongbyon's plutonium would almost certainly be utilized for nuclear weapons.

By July 1989 another component necessary for a nuclear weapons program, a testing facility, was allegedly detected. An article in the *Korea Times* noted: "North Korea is believed to have come closer to producing nuclear weapons as latest intelligence reports revealed the construction of a high-explosive testing site near what is known to be a nuclear reprocessing plant." The Yongbyon reactor is fueled by natural uranium mined in Pyongsan, some 100 kilometers southeast of Pyongyang. North Korean uranium reserves are said to exceed several million tons.

Somewhat surprisingly in view of the Yongbyon controversy, the IAEA has been assisting Pyongyang with its uranium mining program. Because the North has two small, long-established, and noncontroversial nuclear research facilities under IAEA safeguards, it is entitled to IAEA assistance for its civil nuclear program. It would be sadly ironic, however, if the uranium the IAEA helped Pyongyang mine turned up as fuel in the unsafeguarded reactor at Yongbyon, providing fissile material for nuclear weapons.

In July 1989, in a long and detailed article in the South Korean journal *Hoguk*, So Yong-ha, a researcher at the South Korean National Defense Intelligence Headquarters, wrote that

> Our estimate is that the time frame for potential North Korean production of a nuclear weapon will be the mid-1990s. This seems reasonable since we believe that North Korea at present has the ability to develop nuclear weapons, but it will take 3 years to produce 20kg of plutonium from the second [Yongbyon] reactor completed in 1987, 1 to 2 years to process it, and then 1 year to build a nuclear bomb for testing.

From 1986 until late in 1990, the public stance of the Democratic People's Republic of Korea (DPRK) on nuclear weapons changed little. According to a 1986 DPRK Foreign Ministry statement, the government would "refrain from the testing, production, stockpiling and introduction of nuclear weapons." Variations on this formulation recur frequently—usually coupled with denunciations of the presence of U.S. nuclear weapons in the Republic of Korea (ROK). The North Koreans have not, however, categorically renounced nuclear weapons research.

Threats to Seek Nuclear Arms

Surprisingly, in September 1990 the North came close to admitting its intent to manufacture nuclear weapons. Responding to news of the impending Soviet recognition of South Korea, a furious DPRK Foreign Ministry released a memorandum stating that Soviet recognition of the ROK "will leave us no other choice but to take measures to provide . . . for ourselves some weapons for which we have so far relied on the alliance." The weapons mentioned could only be nuclear weapons. During a stormy September 1990 meeting in Pyongyang between DPRK Foreign Minister Kim Yong-nam and then Soviet Foreign Minister Eduard Shevardnadze, Kim reportedly warned that the North would push ahead with nuclear weapons development if the Soviets recognized the South. Ignoring those threats, Moscow and Seoul established formal diplomatic relations on September 30, 1990.

There have been reports that the North may have begun construction of a new and much larger reactor at Yongbyon. If so, the number of nuclear weapons that the North may eventually be able to produce will increase considerably. This sobering prospect has led some U.S. analysts to warn that Pyongyang may become an exporter of nuclear weapons as well as ballistic missiles.

A broad consensus exists within the Bush administration that the DPRK seeks to build nuclear weapons. According to one

U.S. expert, the debate within the government centers on *when* North Korea will get the bomb, rather than on *whether* it seeks to do so. The Pentagon and Defense Intelligence Agency believe that Pyongyang is three to five years away from a workable weapon; analysts in the Department of Energy's nuclear weapons laboratories feel that it will take several years more, while State Department experts take a middle position. Since the different agencies presumably have access to the same intelligence, their differing estimates suggest that the evidence is fragmentary and open to different interpretations.

Weapons Research Exposed by KGB

The former Soviet KGB has solid evidence that North Korea is committed to building nuclear weapons. So asserts the well-informed Russian weekly, *Argumenty i Fakty*, which has disclosed and published the complete text of a 1990 KGB report on North Korean atomic R&D. . . .

The 200-word document states that on the basis of what it calls "hard" Soviet intelligence information, "PDRK leaders, in particular Kim Il Sung, who is in personal charge of nuclear research, seek to achieve military supremacy over South Korea (via development of nuclear weapons). The leadership also wishes to join the prestigious ranks of those states that possess such weapons."

Albert L. Weeks, *Washington Inquirer*, May 29, 1992.

Within 18 months of signing the NPT, states must complete a safeguards agreement with the IAEA. The North failed to meet this deadline, partly because the IAEA sent Pyongyang the wrong agreement to sign. However, the correct document was sent to Pyongyang in June 1987, along with an 18-month extension. The new deadline, December 1988, passed without an agreement. The North's persistent failure to fulfill its treaty obligations has increased Western suspicions about the nature of the nuclear program at Yongbyon. Pyongyang, however, blames the United States for the delays. [North Korea signed an IAEA safeguards agreement in January 1992.] . . .

Incentives to Go Nuclear

There has been little analysis of the rational incentives the North may have *for* acquiring nuclear weapons. This is particularly true in the United States and the ROK, where officials show little sensitivity to DPRK security concerns.

From the North Korean perspective, the reasons for *not* going nuclear may be outweighed by the perception of a growing strategic need for nuclear weapons. For instance, DPRK nuclear weapons targeted against the South could deter U.S. nuclear strikes on the North in any North-South conflict. A North Korea that sees itself as abandoned by its major nuclear ally may perceive a need for such a deterrent.

By the end of 1990, relations between Pyongyang and Moscow had sunk to an all-time low, primarily as a consequence of the USSR's decision to recognize the ROK. The annual Soviet-North Korean joint military exercises were canceled, the sale of Soviet nuclear power reactors was suspended, the offices of two Soviet newspapers in Pyongyang were shut down, and North Korean students were withdrawn from the USSR.

Consider then the shifting conventional military balance on the Korean peninsula. According to outside estimates, between 20 and 25 per cent of North Korean gross national product (GNP) is allocated to defense, compared with approximately 5 per cent of GNP in the South. Still, the military balance is moving inexorably in Seoul's favor—the South's current military budget is already approximately double that of the North. By the end of the decade the South may well have achieved conventional military superiority.

Additionally, the Gulf war has increased the confidence of the South, both in its U.S. ally and in its U.S. equipment. By contrast, North Korea, like Iraq, relies heavily on Soviet weapons and must be deeply concerned by the poor performance of those weapons in the Gulf. The North faces a no-win situation. Attempting to match the South militarily will be ruinously expensive for an economy already burdened with huge external debt and in deep economic crisis. The North cannot maintain, let alone increase, its current crippling rate of defense expenditure.

Pyongyang's economic problems are exacerbated by Soviet reductions in aid and by Moscow's policy since early 1991 of forcing the North to pay for Soviet goods, including the oil on which the DPRK depends heavily, at world market prices and in hard currency. The nation's external debt is currently estimated at $5 billion, economic growth is slowing, trade with fraternal socialist countries is declining, agriculture is in deep trouble, and, according to Soviet analysts, some 50 per cent of the North's industry may be idle because of energy shortages. These problems notwithstanding, failure to keep up with the South militarily would make the North vulnerable to its most deadly rival—an unthinkable prospect for Kim Il Sung.

A Low-Cost Option

Nuclear weapons offer a potentially low-cost solution to the North's dilemma. According to South Korean analyst Song Yong-son, the total estimated cost of the DPRK's nuclear program, excluding the cost of reactors, is $203 million—around 5 per cent of the annual defense budget. The West should not find it surprising that such an option might appear attractive to the North. NATO deployed nuclear weapons as a low-cost strategic equalizer to the conventional military superiority of its enemy, the Warsaw Pact. If the North had nuclear weapons, a conventional military balance favoring the South would be of far less consequence. Further, any future South Korean nuclear capability would not alter the deterrent value of Pyongyang's nuclear arsenal. Finally, the North's nuclear weapons would powerfully curb any U.S. temptation to use nuclear weapons against the North. . . .

An Effort to Conceal

North Korea now has enough nuclear-weapon material for six to eight atomic bombs.

This is the conclusion of U.S. intelligence analysts, who have watched a small reactor operate for four years at Yongbyon, 60 miles north of Pyongyang.

Each year, the analysts say, the reactor has created about two bombs' worth of plutonium. . . .

The North Koreans, who in April 1992 bent to U.S. and Japanese pressure to let the [IAEA] inspectors in, have told incredible stories about their nuclear past.

They say the small reactor didn't work when they started it up in 1987, so they have run it only sporadically.

This contradicts U.S. observations, which show continuous operation at high power.

Gary Milhollin, *The San Diego Union-Tribune*, June 14, 1992.

One major question remains: Why would the DPRK accede to the NPT in the first place if it intended to build a nuclear weapons capability? There are a number of possible reasons. Accession to the treaty may have been the price for continued Soviet assistance to the civilian nuclear power reactor program. In addition, in 1985 the North may have been less concerned about a possible shift in the conventional military balance, or its ability to bear the continuing burden of defense expenditure, than it is in 1991. The North also may have acceded to the NPT in order to assuage Western suspicions while simultaneously pursuing a clandestine nuclear program. As the Iraqi case indicates, signing the NPT and an IAEA safeguards agreement provides no watertight guarantee that a state is not developing nuclear weapons. . . .

What would happen if it became unambiguously evident that the North were building nuclear weapons? Some security analysts in Seoul have discussed the possibility of a preemptive strike against the Yongbyon reactor. The 1981 Israeli strike on Iraq's Osirak reactor provides one precedent for such an operation, while in April 1991 South Korean defense minister Lee Jong Koo suggested that an "Entebbe-style" commando raid was a possibility. Others contend that the South ought to build its own countervailing nuclear deterrent. One South Korean analyst suggested that, given suspicions that a DPRK bomb may be completed by 1995, the ROK would have to launch its own bomb program by 1993 at the latest. In fact, Seoul did have a nuclear weapons program in the 1970s, but abandoned it under U.S. pressure. In the early 1980s it sought to acquire nuclear fuel reprocessing facilities but was again dissuaded by the United States. The ROK, which relies on nuclear power for roughly half of its electricity and whose nuclear scientists have a high level of expertise, can build nuclear weapons quickly if it so decides. However, doing so openly would require that it withdraw from the NPT.

If nuclear proliferation becomes a reality on the peninsula, the first years of nuclear standoff would be extremely dangerous. When rival states have small and vulnerable nuclear inventories, the incentive to preempt in a crisis is high because disarming first strikes have a real chance of success and failing to strike first renders the hesitant state vulnerable to nuclear preemption by the other side. Strategic stability on a nuclearized Korean peninsula would be further undermined by the absence of sophisticated and reliable command, control, and communication capabilities, and by the lack of institutional measures, such as arms control, that have helped manage the nuclear competition between the superpowers. The prospect of a nuclearized Korean peninsula could also have a profoundly destabilizing impact on Japan, strengthening the hand of the so-called "Japanese Gaullists" who believe that Japan should have a nuclear weapons capability. Should Japan go nuclear, the global nonproliferation regime would be seriously damaged.

The United States and the ROK have no greater common security interest than preventing Pyongyang from going nuclear. The removal of U.S. nuclear weapons from the South may achieve that end.

"Conditions . . . are ripe for the emergence of a
nuclear black market."

Former Soviet Republics
May Contribute to
Nuclear Proliferation

William C. Potter

The breakup of the Soviet Union caused international apprehension concerning the command and control of Soviet nuclear weapons and the possible recruitment of nuclear scientists by other would-be nuclear nations. In the following viewpoint, William C. Potter argues that another equally important proliferation concern must be heeded: the end of stringent Soviet controls over nuclear materials and technology. Potter maintains that these weaker controls, combined with economic hardships in the former Soviet republics, create conditions under which valuable nuclear commodities could be sold illicitly to nations seeking nuclear weapons. Potter is the director of the Center for Russian and Soviet Studies at the Monterey Institute of International Studies, a graduate institute located in Monterey, California.

As you read, consider the following questions:

1. According to Potter, how could private nuclear-related companies in the new republics increase the risk of proliferation?
2. Why does the author believe that Soviet economic reforms contributed to the emergence of these firms?
3. How could the new republics' compliance to IAEA inspections bolster nonproliferation efforts, in Potter's opinion?

From William C. Potter, "Exports and Experts: Proliferation Risks from the New Commonwealth," *Arms Control Today*, January/February 1992. Copyright 1992 by the Arms Control Association. Reprinted with permission.

There is no equivalent in Russian for a "Going Out of Business Sale," but that is what we are now witnessing in the crumbling state sector of the former Soviet Union. Desperate for hard currency, the emerging Commonwealth's new "entrepreneurs" are selling everything from formerly classified KGB files to high performance military aircraft.

Particularly worrisome from the standpoint of nuclear nonproliferation is the danger that private firms may be able to acquire and sell some types of sensitive nuclear material, equipment, and technology with few effective export controls. Already, there are reports that private organizations have purchased zirconium, beryllium, and graphite at discount prices from state manufacturing firms and marketed them abroad, and that there have been similar uncontrolled exports of low-enriched uranium and plutonium. In October 1991, for example, Italian police seized a very small quantity of nearly pure weapon-grade plutonium in a black market sting operation, apparently being offered as a sample of what could be purchased in larger quantities. Although the evidence is inconclusive, there are indications that the plutonium may have been smuggled out of the Soviet Union after the failed August coup. The European press is filled with reports of similar black market activity allegedly involving nuclear material of Soviet origin.

There is no hard evidence that nuclear weapons, nuclear weapon components, or significant quantities of bomb-grade fissionable material have been smuggled out of the Soviet Union or its successor states. Conditions, however, are ripe for the emergence of a nuclear black market.

Soviet Nuclear Export Policies

Until recently, illicit nuclear exports from the Soviet Union were unlikely, due to the absence of private trading companies and the stringent Soviet controls over the production and sale of all commodities. The export monopoly in the nuclear sector belonged to Techsnabexport, a state-controlled company associated with the Ministry of Atomic Power and Industry (MAPI), and until recent years with the Ministry of Foreign Trade. Since Techsnabexport was the sole nuclear exporter and was operating under contracts and conditions approved by MAPI and the Ministry of Foreign Affairs, it was relatively easy for the central government to enforce stringent export controls. These regulations, in the form of decrees issued by the former Soviet Council of Ministers, eliminated any perceived need to enact comprehensive national legislation governing nuclear exports.

Despite substantial differences between the structure and process of Soviet and U.S. nuclear export policy, a remarkable degree of cooperation has existed between Washington and

Moscow in the nuclear export field. This cooperation, which continued even during the most troubled periods of superpower relations in the 1970s and 1980s, was promoted in regular bilateral consultations and in a variety of multilateral fora, including the International Atomic Energy Agency (IAEA), the Nuclear Suppliers Group, the Nuclear Exporters Committee (the so-called Zangger Committee), and the Nonproliferation Treaty (NPT) review conferences.

Proliferation Problems

Economic disorder within the former Soviet Union's nuclear weapon complex—comprising facilities and trained personnel for producing and storing special nuclear materials, and for designing and fabricating nuclear weapons and components—creates a potential source of nuclear proliferation outside the Commonwealth unlike any previously faced by the nonproliferation regime. Nuclear materials, sensitive non-nuclear components of nuclear weapons, the talents of skilled bomb builders, and even entire nuclear weapons could conceivably find their way onto world markets. Those markets have a demonstrated willingness to pay lavish prices for such materials and technologies, which could tempt Soviet enterprises and individuals strapped for hard currency. If systemic disintegration of the nuclear weapon production and custodial systems begins to take place, the world could see a diaspora of military technology not seen since the Nazi rocket scientists emigrated from Germany after World War II.

Ashton B. Carter, *Arms Control Today*, January/February 1992.

Notwithstanding the generally commendable Soviet record on nuclear exports since it cut off its nuclear cooperation with China in 1958, the former Soviet Union undertook a number of nuclear export initiatives even before the failed August 1991 coup that were reasons for concern. These initiatives include:
• a Soviet willingness to sell Pakistan a nuclear power plant in February 1990, soon after the United States had succeeded in persuading West Germany to withdraw its offer, but while France was promoting its nuclear reactor;
• Soviet contracts with India in 1989 to supply two pressurized water reactors, despite India's refusal to accept "full-scope" IAEA safeguards on all its nuclear facilities, which the United States has long made a condition for nuclear exports. In 1991, Soviet and Indian officials also reportedly discussed the possible sale of fast breeder reactors, which produce large quantities of plutonium;
• Soviet sales of heavy water to Argentina in 1990, and the

conclusion in October 1990 of a nuclear cooperation agreement with Argentina in the field of breeder reactors;

• Soviet discussions with Israel in April 1991 about the possible sale of a Soviet nuclear reactor; and

• continued Soviet assistance to Cuba in the development of its first nuclear power plant, as well as the reported delivery to Cuba in 1991 of a 10-megawatt research reactor utilizing highly enriched uranium as fuel.

An Exports-for-Profit Attitude

These nuclear initiatives toward non-NPT parties, although not prohibited by the treaty, are worrisome, in part because they sent a troubling signal to nonadherents that few benefits are derived from membership in the NPT, and because they demonstrated that even vocal supporters of nonproliferation are, for the right price, willing to sell nuclear-related equipment and technology to potential proliferators.

A number of recent Soviet export activities involving countries that are parties to the NPT also point toward a more lax export posture than in the past, presumably designed to gain overseas markets. During former President Mikhail Gorbachev's April 1991 trip to South Korea, for example, the Soviet Union expressed a readiness to transfer sensitive nuclear technology, including uranium enrichment and fast breeder reactor processes. The Soviet Foreign Trade Publishing House even prepared an English-language brochure providing the specifications of at least one Soviet fast breeder reactor (the BN-800). Also of concern is the conclusion since June 1989 of Soviet-Iranian nuclear cooperation accords, and the possible sale of new Soviet light water reactors.

These nuclear initiatives coincided with the decline of the former Soviet Ministry of Foreign Affairs' influence on nuclear export decisions, and the corresponding rise in power of the Ministry of Atomic Power and Industry. According to senior Russian government officials, MAPI policy was driven by hard currency considerations, with little regard for the foreign or defense policy implications of exports of sensitive technology.

In light of this profits-first policy adopted by the former central government, it is little wonder that newly emergent private trading companies in the new Commonwealth of Independent States believe they can sell even sensitive nuclear-related commodities.

New Nuclear Entrepreneurs

The collapse of central authority in the Soviet Union in 1991, coupled with the virtual bankruptcy of the entire Soviet defense sector (including the nuclear weapon laboratories), created an environment in which private entrepreneurs scrambled to sign up weapon designers and to make overseas deals, in the absence of strong central government oversight. Bodies such as the Military-Industrial Stock Exchange and the Military-Industrial Investment Company sprang up overnight, as state defense factories were turned into private shareholders' companies.

Illustrative of the new breed of Soviet nuclear entrepreneurs is the International CHETEK Corporation. According to CHETEK promotional literature, available in English, the corporation provides "peaceful nuclear explosive" (PNE) services as an ostensibly ecologically desirable means to dispose of highly toxic chemical and industrial waste, decommissioned nuclear reactors, and retired nuclear and chemical weapons. For as little as $300 per kilogram, CHETEK promises to dispose of anyone's toxic waste and guarantees "total safety." A demonstration PNE test, the corporation claims, is scheduled for June 1992 at the Arctic nuclear weapon testing ground on Novaya Zemlya. CHETEK officials claim the current one-year Russian test moratorium does not apply to PNEs.

A Clear Commitment Needed

Each of the newly independent states needs to make a clear commitment to international non-proliferation norms and to put in place an effective export control system.

We urged Russia to reaffirm the NPT commitments of the former Soviet Union, and the others to adhere to the NPT as non-nuclear weapons states. . . .

We urged all four states to move rapidly to put into place the necessary legal basis for export controls, in view of the dissolution of the former Soviet control system and the incentives for exports created by the difficult transition now underway to a market economy. And we stressed the need for enforcement measures and to provide adequate resources to the export control administration.

Reginald Bartholomew, *U.S. Department of State Dispatch*, February 10, 1992.

In case one is not inclined to ship one's toxic waste to Russia, CHETEK is prepared to bring the PNE service to you. According to a letter to the deputy secretary general of the United Nations from CHETEK boosters in MAPI, the controlled application of PNE technology might fruitfully be deployed in Iraq to dispose of that country's chemical weapons. CHETEK even promoted the use of PNEs as a means to extinguish Kuwait's oil fires.

CHETEK derives its name from the Russian words for man (*chelovek*), technology (*tekhnologiya*), and capital (*kapital*). It was founded in December 1990, ostensibly as a private company

145

with 250 million rubles in working capital. In fact, CHETEK is the direct descendant of the Soviet nuclear weapons complex, spawned by Soviet nuclear scientists who faced layoffs in a post-Chernobyl, post-Cold War environment. More specifically, CHETEK is the child of MAPI and the All-Union Research Institute of Experimental Physics—better known as Arzamas-16, the Soviet nuclear weapon design center, equivalent to Los Alamos National Laboratory, where Andrei Sakharov worked on the hydrogen bomb. In return for the infusion of cash and company stock (valued at 12,000 rubles a share), MAPI has given CHETEK exclusive rights to its thermonuclear PNEs and access to its nuclear test sites, while Arzamas-16 has provided nuclear weapon designers and technical personnel. At least 10 nuclear weapon designers are reported to be on the CHETEK payroll. According to Viktor Mikhailov, a major promoter of CHETEK and also deputy minister of MAPI, the deal was the only way to preserve the nuclear weapon facilities' research programs and to avoid the layoff of large numbers of scientists.

Potential for Abuse

In addition to PNE services, CHETEK appears to be interested in marketing radiochemical expertise and reprocessing equipment and technology. It is reported, for example, to be financing scientists at an uncompleted plutonium reprocessing facility near Krasnoyarsk—the site of one of CHETEK's eight offices in the former Soviet Union. CHETEK representatives also have recently expressed interest in converting highly enriched uranium from dismantled nuclear warheads into low-enriched uranium and marketing the latter product for civilian nuclear power programs.

Despite CHETEK's support from MAPI, the idea of selling PNE services or shipping PNE devices abroad is controversial within the Russian government, major representatives of which have opposed the notion. The plan also suffers from serious technical flaws, and may never come to fruition. It also remains unclear whether or not CHETEK has actually sold any other nuclear services or products abroad. What is clear is the potential for export control abuse in an environment in which a cash-starved national ministry that is supposed to regulate nuclear exports is financially dependent upon an export-oriented private company with access to sensitive nuclear material, equipment, technology, and services.

Companies like CHETEK may be able to absorb some of the nuclear scientists who will lose their jobs as a consequence of the end of the Cold War and the inability of the Soviet defense establishment to convert promptly to production of needed civilian goods. Other disgruntled and unemployed nuclear weapon scientists, however, may find their way into the international black market. . . .

Clearly, the breakup of the Soviet Union and the creation of new independent states, some of which have nuclear weapons or sensitive nuclear facilities on their territories, poses a serious proliferation threat. Although strong political, economic, and security disincentives are likely to weigh against decisions to pursue independent nuclear forces in most of the former republics of the Soviet Union, the same cannot be said about the balance of factors affecting decisions to export nuclear technology and know-how.

Indeed, all of the problems which characterized recent Soviet nuclear export behavior are likely to become more acute as central authority further diminishes, governmental oversight responsibilities and jurisdiction become more diffuse, and the new political entities face increased economic difficulties and demands for hard currency.

Nuclear goods and services, along with other defense-related products, are apt to be among the few commodities from the former Soviet Union that are in demand abroad and are able to generate hard currency. Special action, therefore, must be undertaken to counter this export tendency and to foster responsible nuclear export behavior on the part of the new Commonwealth states.

Signing the Nonproliferation Treaty

The creation of new independent states provides an opportunity to add new members to the NPT, whose support may prove significant at the 1995 NPT extension conference—and to apply IAEA safeguards to additional nuclear facilities.

It is imperative that the potential nuclear supplier states emerging from the former Soviet Union sign the NPT. The Bush administration must continue to impress upon the newly independent states the importance of NPT membership and responsible nuclear policies, making it clear that such issues will be major factors in U.S. and Western decisions on key questions such as economic assistance. The sooner all the Commonwealth states formally accede to the NPT—with all but Russia acceding as non-nuclear-weapon states—the better off the world will be.

Although the former Soviet Union, as a nuclear-weapon state, is not obliged to submit to IAEA inspections, since 1985 it has voluntarily agreed to them at a small number of its civilian nuclear facilities. . . .

The states emerging from the former Soviet Union, as new parties to the NPT, may bolster U.S. efforts to persuade the IAEA to make greater use of its authority to undertake special inspections. Some of the new states, which have their own reasons for gaining assurance that all nuclear weapons have been removed from their territories and that all fissile material has been placed under international safeguards, might even volunteer to be the subject of special inspections. Such "trial" inspections under noncrisis conditions might prove very helpful in both defusing the issue of the discriminatory use of special inspections, and in developing and refining special inspection procedures. . . .

The West Must Act Now

The breakup of the Soviet Union and the nuclear inheritance of its successor states belatedly focused Western attention on the proliferation risks posed by the disintegration of central authority. Most concern to date, however, has continued to emphasize the problems of nuclear command and control. But the nonproliferation threats associated with the unregulated export of sensitive nuclear material, technology, and equipment may be equally great, and present problems that are already real. At the same time, the new nation-building process in the Soviet successor states presents opportunities for expanding the NPT and international safeguards, containing the nuclear brain drain, promoting the cleanup of hazardous nuclear waste, enhancing international capabilities for monitoring proliferation, and building new communities of nonproliferation specialists. A rare occasion now exists for Western policy-makers to have a direct impact on the long-term nuclear export and nonproliferation behavior of the successor states to the Soviet Union. The speed and seriousness with which the West undertakes this task will largely determine how much ground, if any, will be lost from its decades-long effort to stop the proliferation of nuclear weapons.

Recognizing Deceptive Arguments

People who feel strongly about an issue use many techniques to persuade others to agree with them. Some of these techniques appeal to the intellect, some to the emotions. Many of them distract the reader or listener from the real issues.

A few common examples of argumentation tactics are listed below. Most of them can be used either to advance an argument in an honest, reasonable way or to deceive or distract from the real issues. It is important for a critical reader to recognize these tactics in order to rationally evaluate an author's ideas.

a. *bandwagon*—the idea that "everybody" does this or believes this

b. *categorical statements*—stating something in a way that implies there can be no argument or disagreement on the issue

c. *personal attack*—criticizing an opponent *personally* instead of rationally debating his or her ideas

d. *testimonial*—quoting or paraphrasing an authority or celebrity to support one's own viewpoint

The following activity can help you sharpen your skills in recognizing deceptive reasoning. The statements below are derived from the viewpoints in this chapter. *Beside each one, mark the letter of the type of deceptive appeal being used. More than one type of tactic may be applicable. If you believe the statement is not any of the listed appeals, write N.*

149

1. Muammar Qaddafi is a lunatic dictator who will not hesitate to use nuclear weapons against his enemies.

2. The United States clearly discriminates against Third World nations by denying them nuclear weapons technology.

3. The whole world knows that China is the most prolific exporter of nuclear weapons material.

4. Individuals who sell nuclear weapons material and technology to other nations are traitors to their governments. They should be imprisoned for the rest of their lives.

5. Palestinian leader Yasir Arafat correctly believes that America's nonproliferation efforts are really a strategy to suppress Arab power and influence.

6. Nations which continue to conduct nuclear tests demonstrate no real desire to stop the spread of nuclear weapons.

7. IAEA director Hans Blix believes that weak international nuclear export controls undermined nonproliferation efforts.

8. Chinese arms dealers are immoral profiteers guilty of nuclear proliferation.

9. Every Western nation agrees that a nuclear-armed North Korea poses a grave threat to peace.

10. Israel will never allow its Arab neighbors to become advanced in nuclear technology.

11. Member nations of the NPT all support the idea of stricter sanctions against nuclear proliferators.

12. North Korea is a terrorist state that will use all means of deception to hide its nuclear weapons program.

13. One Arab nation or another will inevitably obtain or construct a nuclear weapon.

14. India and Pakistan show much confidence in the ability of treaties to prevent a nuclear strike.

Periodical Bibliography

The following articles have been selected to supplement the diverse views presented in this chapter.

Reginald Bartholomew	"U.S. Effort to Halt Weapons Proliferation in the Former Soviet Republics," *U.S. Department of State Dispatch*, February 10, 1992.
Barbara Crosette	"India Is Pressed on Atom Project," *The New York Times*, February 12, 1992.
Richard Fieldhouse	"China's Mixed Signals on Nuclear Weapons," *The Bulletin of the Atomic Scientists*, May 1991.
Martin Hill	"American Sting: Nailing the Iraqi A-Bomb," *Reader's Digest*, November 1990.
Martin Hill	"Made in the USA," *Mother Jones*, May/June 1991.
Mark Hosenball	"Blind Eye: Ignoring the Iraqi Bomb," *The New Republic*, November 25, 1991.
Jean Krasno	"Brazil, Argentina Make It Official," *The Bulletin of the Atomic Scientists*, April 1992.
Michael Ledeen	"Iraq's German Connection," *Commentary*, April 1991.
Flora Lewis	"Beijing's Subtle Nuclear Diplomacy," *The New York Times*, November 29, 1991.
Emily MacFarquhar	"Breaking a Chain Reaction," *U.S. News & World Report*, March 9, 1992.
Mary McGrory	"Ideal of Global Nonproliferation Is Bombing," *Liberal Opinion Week*, December 2, 1991. Available from PO Box 468, Vinton, IA 52349-0468.
Gary Milhollin	"North Korea's Bomb," *The New York Times*, June 4, 1992.
Igor Reichlin and Mark Maremont	"Iraq's Silent Allies in Its Quest for the Bomb," *Business Week*, January 14, 1991.
Elaine Sciolino	"Counting Iran's New Arms Is the Easy Part," *The New York Times*, April 26, 1992.
Stephen R. Shalom	"Bullets, Gas, and the Bomb," *Z Magazine*, February 1991.
Russell Watson	"Merchants of Death," *Newsweek*, November 18, 1991.

How Can Nuclear Proliferation Be Prevented?

NUCLEAR
PROLIFERATION

Chapter Preface

On July 31, 1991, five months before the breakup of the Soviet Union, George Bush and then-president of the USSR Mikhail Gorbachev signed the Strategic Arms Reduction Talks (START) treaty, which called for the dismantling of many nuclear weapons and the reduction of both sides' arsenals to equal levels. Two months later, Bush announced further reductions not mandated by START. Gorbachev subsequently promised even deeper cuts, while his successor, Russian president Boris Yeltsin, announced that nuclear warheads would no longer be aimed at American cities.

These measures highlight the potential of arms control to reduce the world's stockpile of nuclear weapons. Proponents hope the START treaty will send the message to the world and to regional rivals such as India and Pakistan that nuclear weapons are not worthwhile options and that rejecting them would improve international relations.

Some analysts, however, are skeptical about the power of treaties to end the nuclear threat. Treaties are often fragile and liable to be broken by one side or the other, these critics contend. For example, the United States and the Soviet Union often accused each other of breaking their bilateral arms control agreements. North Korea, too, violated the Nuclear Nonproliferation Treaty for more than six years before finally submitting to inspections of its nuclear facilities in 1992.

As the United States and Russia have proven, arms control agreements can foster trust and cooperation to produce effective nuclear disarmament measures. However, rival nations with deep-rooted suspicions of each other or with rigid ideological differences may find such progress much more difficult. Whether START succeeds and spurs similar treaties among present and future nuclear powers remains to be seen. The authors in the following chapter debate whether arms control and other measures can prevent nuclear proliferation.

"Regional arms control will undoubtedly remain the best long-term way to slow proliferation."

Arms Control Will Prevent Nuclear Proliferation

Jack Mendelsohn

Several nations in the Middle East and South Asia now have the potential to develop or acquire nuclear weapons. In the following viewpoint, Jack Mendelsohn argues that arms control measures such as treaties are the most effective way to slow nuclear proliferation in these regions. Mendelsohn cites the Nonproliferation Treaty of 1970 as an example of successful international cooperation against the development of nuclear arms. Mendelsohn, a former state department official and member of the U.S. arms control delegations, is deputy director of the Arms Control Association, a Washington, D.C.-based organization that advocates arms control and disarmament.

As you read, consider the following questions:

1. According to Mendelsohn, why are few nuclear weapons necessary to deter an enemy nuclear attack?
2. In Mendelsohn's opinion, how can the demand for nuclear arms among regional counterparts be reduced?
3. Why must the United States share its knowledge of other nations' nuclear programs, according to the author?

From Jack Mendelsohn, "Dismantling the Arsenals: Arms Control and the New World Agenda," *The Brookings Review*, Spring 1992. Reprinted with permission.

The collapse of communism and the promise of a more cooperative East-West relationship have transformed the world of arms control. Goals that were once unthinkable—making enormous cuts in strategic forces or actually destroying nuclear warheads—are now at the top of the agenda. Developments that were always dangerous but of only secondary concern because of the primary East-West confrontation—the widespread deployment of short-range nuclear weapons or the spread of conventional weapons to the developing world—have now become urgent issues. And verification measures, originally born of deep distrust between East and West and intended to inform adversaries about each other's military programs, are now available to help monitor agreements, build trust, and reduce tensions.

Understandably, the most immediate concern of both the United States and Europe is the future of nuclear weapons in a disintegrating Soviet empire. For now, at least, the goals of the United States and Russia seem to be congruent: to ensure the centralized command and control of the nuclear forces of the newly formed Commonwealth of Independent States (CIS), to encourage the safe and secure withdrawal of tactical (and, eventually, strategic) nuclear weapons from the outlying republics to Russia, and to prevent the spread of nuclear hardware and brainpower to third countries. Programs to address these problems are already under way or under consideration, although concern about their continued successful implementation will certainly persist.

Paring Nuclear Arsenals

In the longer term a different set of nuclear arms control issues will challenge policymakers. The end of the Cold War offers a unique opportunity to push the size of U.S. and Russian strategic nuclear forces down to considerably lower levels. As Soviet President Gorbachev suggested in October 1991, and as President Bush proposed in his State of the Union speech in January 1992, the United States and Russia could readily cut in half the number of strategic weapons permitted under the Strategic Arms Reduction Treaty (START).

How low strategic forces can ultimately be taken will depend on the actual role assigned to nuclear weapons. Most analysts agree that the United States can maintain its present "warfighting" strategy with as few as 3,000-4,000 nuclear weapons (see Table 1). If, on the other hand, the United States were prepared to abandon its current warfighting strategy, which targets thousands of military, political, and economic sites, in favor of a purely deterrent one involving a very limited set of military-industrial targets, it would facilitate even steeper reductions in strategic warheads. This is apparently the strategy that underlies Russian President Boris Yeltsin's offer to reduce strategic arsenals to 2,000-2,500 warheads.

Table I. Selected Proposals for Strategic Arms Reductions Below Warhead Levels in START

Number of Warheads	Proposal
600	Andrei Kokoshin, *Bulletin of the Atomic Scientists*, September 1988
1,000	Carl Kaysen, Robert S. McNamara, and George W. Rathjens, *Foreign Affairs*, Fall 1991
1,000–2,000	Committee on International Security and Arms Control, National Academy of Science, 1991 (second-stage cuts)
1,000–2,000	Jonathan Dean and Kurt Gottfried, Union of Concerned Scientists, 1991
Below 2,000	Harold A. Feiveson and Frank N. von Hippel, *International Security*, Summer 1990
2,000–2,500	Boris Yeltsin, United Nations, 1992
Below 3,000	Harold Brown, *Arms Control Today*, May 1990
3,000	John D. Steinbruner, Michael M. May, and George F. Bing, *International Security*, Summer 1988*
3,000–4,000	Committee on International Security and Arms Control, National Academy of Science, 1991 (first-stage cuts)
4,700	George Bush, State of the Union Speech, 1992
4,000–6,000	Reed Report, Strategic Air Command, 1991
6,000	START Treaty, 1991**

*Most proposals consider 3,000 warheads to be the level beneath which current targeting strategy must be revised and 2,000 to be the level beneath which third-country forces (United Kingdom, France, China) must become involved in negotiations.

** START permits 6,000 "accountable" strategic warheads on each side. Because of lenient counting rules on air-launched weapons, each side may in reality deploy several thousand additional warheads.

An essentially deterrent strategy would be based on the premise that relatively few warheads are required to dissuade an adversary from launching a deliberate nuclear attack.

According to former Secretary of Defense Robert McNamara, during the 1962 Cuban missile crisis, when the United States had approximately 5,000 strategic warheads to the Soviet Union's 300, "President Kennedy and I were deterred from even considering a nuclear attack on the USSR by the knowledge that, although such a strike would destroy the Soviet Union, *tens* of their weapons would survive to be launched against the United States" (emphasis added). Nothing in the past 30 years has invalidated that conclusion or diminished the deterrent value of even a few nuclear weapons.

Preventing Inadvertent Conflict

With the end of the adversarial relationship between the United States and Russia and the prospect of large-scale reductions in existing nuclear arsenals, longstanding fears of deliberate attack have yielded to a new concern about inadvertent conflict. To respond to this concern, the two nations will need to make it as difficult as possible to launch their nuclear weapons. They will have to ensure that all nuclear weapons are subject to both physical safeguards and chain-of-command arrangements that cannot be defeated or circumvented. To this end, all deployed and nondeployed nuclear weapons should have the latest technology electronic locks to prevent unauthorized use. Both arming and release codes for all nuclear weapons should be held by the national command authority (on-board commanders have access to the codes for U.S. ballistic missile submarines).

Another way to reduce the risk of inadvertent war is to increase the overall confidence of both sides in the survivability of their nuclear forces. This can be done by some relatively simple measures. For example, the president has proposed that land-based ballistic missile systems be limited by agreement to one warhead. That is one way to eliminate the concern that a small number of land-based multiple-warhead missiles on one side could be used early in a crisis and, in theory at least, destroy large numbers of similar systems on the other side. Alternatively, land-based systems could be made mobile or dispersed among multiple protective shelters. Finally, overall warhead reductions, on the scale discussed above, would by themselves decrease the number of multiple warhead systems and increase survivability by making it difficult, if not impossible, to undertake a disarming strike against the nuclear forces of the other side.

As one confidence-building measure, warheads could be removed from a portion of the land-based missile force and the systems taken off high state of alert. Ballistic missile submarines could patrol out of range of their targets, and aggressive antisubmarine warfare training activities could be strictly limited.

Strategic bombers should remain off alert and their weapons stored away from operational bases. The sides could also limit the size and frequency of large-scale exercises and enhance confidence by exchanging data and giving advance notice of strategic force tests or practice alerts.

Finally, the United States, Russia, and the relevant CIS countries should agree to destroy the existing stockpile of retired and surplus nuclear weapons, perhaps 15,000 to 18,000 warheads on each side. As the two sides reduce their tactical and strategic arsenals, the number of warheads in storage will increase dramatically—as will concern over their possible theft, sale, misappropriation, or rapid redeployment. The destruction of redundant warheads should be coupled with a ban on the further production of fissile material for weapons purposes, a monitored limit on the production of new warheads to replace existing systems, and the storage, under international safeguards, of fissile material withdrawn from retired weapons. . . .

Stemming the Spread of Weapons

As the enormous changes in Europe have eased concerns about East-West conflict, the United States and other developed nations have turned their attention to the challenges to international security posed by the spread of weapons in the developing world. Ironically, the problem is largely the result of the developed world's own policies during the Cold War, when arming the enemy of one's enemy was considered to be the height of sophisticated geopolitics. Meeting the proliferation challenge will require of the developed world a full and rare measure of political will and self-restraint.

To be sure, regimes to control several types of proliferation already exist or are under negotiation. The nuclear Non-Proliferation Treaty, with some 140 members, has been a highly successful example of international cooperation and common perspective for a quarter of a century. Negotiations on a Chemical Weapons Convention are far advanced and likely to be concluded in the not-too-distant future. And major supplier groups (to control nuclear technology, chemical and biological weapons, missile technology, and conventional arms transfers to the Middle East) have already been established and are expanding their scope.

Building on the existing nonproliferation structures, arms control can make several useful contributions. The first is to encourage stronger supplier restraint. Supplier states first must resist domestic political or economic pressures to sell arms, and then they will have to demonstrate a high level of political skill to balance the concerns of the developed world with objections from less advanced countries that nonproliferation regimes will spark. The nuclear supplier group clearly increased the time and cost of Iraq's nuclear weapons program. Nonetheless, the extent of Iraq's program surprised almost everyone, a fact that underscores the need to strengthen and expand nuclear export guidelines to include limits on "dual use" items—an effort already under way.

Campaign for Disarmament

The decision of the world's two nuclear megapowers to move away from nuclear readiness and slash their nuclear arsenals makes the world a safer place. The historic steps will not totally free us from the horrors of future nuclear war. The US and the former Soviet Union will still have vast, if vastly safer, nuclear arsenals. In former Soviet lands, the disintegration of central power could still bring nuclear threats into intercommunal bargaining.

Meanwhile, the seven other powers around the world who followed the megapowers into acquiring nuclear arsenals, and those who have plans to do so, will have reason to question the trend away from reliance on these weapons of doom. We will have to find a way to persuade these parties to join the campaign for a world free from nuclear dread.

Helena Cobban, *The Christian Science Monitor*, October 10, 1991.

The United States and the other major arms exporters will also have to make more explicit efforts to limit sales of conventional weapons to areas of tension. For example, in conjunction with a supplier regime, "caps" might be placed on the value of arms exports approved by the supplier group to any one country in any one year. That would require an international register of arms transfer and agreement among at least the "big five" exporters (the United States, the United Kingdom, France, the former Soviet Union, and China, which accounted for nearly 90 percent of the arms trade in 1990) to declare transfers and respect the cap. Pressure could also be applied to potential arms recipients by linking, directly or informally, U.S. aid, as well as aid from international lending institutions, to military spending levels.

Regional Arms Control

As important as supplier restraint may be, regional arms control will undoubtedly remain the best long-term way to slow proliferation. Models already exist: the Treaty of Tlatelolco (establishing a nuclear-free zone in Latin America) and the Conventional Forces in Europe treaty are examples. Rallying the political will and muscle to apply these models to regions of the world where the underlying tension has not been directly eased by the new cooperative spirit in Europe will be a challenge. But easing these regional concerns is the key to taking the pressure off the "demand" side of proliferation. In fact, supplier restraint should only be a tool to buy time for regional efforts to work.

Regional arms control in areas such as the Middle East, South Asia, and Korea will have to involve major outside players. The United States, Russia, France, or Britain, depending on the region involved, will have to take an active interest and leading role in bringing about even a modest reconciliation. This reconciliation process would involve, first, political dialogue (as between the two Koreas and at the Middle East peace talks), then transparency (as in the Sinai and on the Golan Heights), supplier restraint, confidence-building measures, and, eventually, explicit arms control measures to limit forces and disengage (or separate) threatening forces.

Improved verification and monitoring would also strengthen nonproliferation efforts. Confidence in arms control regimes and regional security arrangements can, in general, be buttressed by increased transparency and predictability. In the proliferation arena, where one is dealing, almost by definition, with countries trying to acquire military capabilities by clandestine means, comprehensive intelligence, monitoring, and verification regimes are critical. First, as the Iraq experience has demonstrated, all agreements dealing with weapons of mass destruction must permit the right to challenge inspections of suspect sites. Second, nations with sophisticated intelligence capabilities, the United States in particular, will have to begin to share intelligence more widely. Making information more generally accessible will increase the stake of other participating states in the nonproliferation regime, enhance their confidence in its viability, and strengthen any eventual case against violators.

Finally, arms control by example is an important adjunct to specific nonproliferation treaties and cooperative measures. Although it cannot by itself stop states or leaders determined to violate an international agreement or tacit understanding, it can enhance the moral authority of the major powers. Evidence of serious intent to implement supplier restraint, to pursue deeper nuclear force reductions, to destroy conventional weapons and nuclear warheads, to stop fissionable materials production, and to cease nuclear testing would bolster the case for "demand" reduction in the proliferation arena. It would also strengthen the hand of the major powers in making the case for taking collective action—whether export controls, political and economic sanctions, or military measures—against any state that violates international agreements or standards.

"States which decide . . . to acquire a nuclear capability are likely to be successful regardless of existing and future arms control efforts. "

Arms Control Will Not Prevent Nuclear Proliferation

James Fergusson

Among the criticisms of arms control is that it is ineffective at restricting nations determined to acquire nuclear weapons. In the following viewpoint, James Fergusson agrees and argues that for many nations, the security offered by nuclear weapons overrides the importance of arms control agreements. Consequently, these agreements do not slow nuclear proliferation, Fergusson concludes. Fergusson is a research associate at the Centre for Defence and Security Studies at the University of Manitoba in Winnipeg, Canada.

As you read, consider the following questions:

1. Why does Fergusson believe that Third World nations should hesitate before developing nuclear weapons?
2. According to the author, why do most countries show no interest in acquiring nuclear weapons?
3. In Fergusson's opinion, how do political changes affect a nation's decision to acquire nuclear weapons?

James Fergusson, "Arms Control Will Not Prevent Proliferation," a position paper written expressly for inclusion in the present volume, June 1992.

In the early 1960s many commentators were concerned about the rapid proliferation of nuclear weapons. They predicted that around twenty new nuclear powers would emerge in the near future unless something was done to prevent proliferation. Moreover, in the context of regional conflicts in the developing world, this rapid expansion of the nuclear club would be inherently de-stabilizing, increasing significantly the prospects of the use of nuclear weapons. In response to these concerns, what has become a pillar of seemingly successful arms control, the Nuclear Non-Proliferation Treaty (NPT) was negotiated and ratified by the overwhelming majority of states. Since then, the nuclear club has remained relatively closed.

Determined Nations Will Acquire Nuclear Arms

The NPT, as a form of arms control, is credited with playing a significant role in halting the proliferation of nuclear weapons. The treaty, along with its monitoring agency, the International Atomic Energy Agency (IAEA), and more informal arrangements, such as the London Suppliers Group, comprise what is frequently referred to as the Non-Proliferation Regime. Although the regime does act as a significant impediment to attempts by non-nuclear states to acquire nuclear weapons, particularly the London Suppliers Group and associated national export control policies, it cannot prevent proliferation. States which decide for a variety of reasons to acquire a nuclear capability are likely to be successful regardless of existing and future arms control efforts.

In order to understand the functional limitations of arms control as a means of preventing nuclear proliferation, it is important to consider the following factors. First, consideration must be given to the reasons which might lead states to obtain a nuclear weapons capability. Second, it is necessary to explain the apparent success of the Non-Proliferation Regime and the continued adherence to it by the majority of states in the international system. Finally, it is important to examine the actual role that the regime and arms control do play in terms of proliferation.

There are many reasons which might impel states to pay the costs associated with the acquisition of nuclear weapons. These include security, prestige, the hope of wider political benefits, and domestic political considerations. To begin, it is important to realize that the costs entailed in acquiring a nuclear weapons capability are extremely high. Although the technology necessary to build a nuclear bomb is not overly complex, at least theoretically, the requirements to engineer nuclear weapons, which includes acquiring the raw materials, the refining of weapons grade material, and building the triggering mechanisms, the delivery systems, and the command and control systems, are extremely complex and costly. The decision to acquire a nuclear capability entails a willingness to divert a significant amount of resources, both financial and human, to the project and away from other pressing needs. In addition, there are significant political costs. These range from verbal condemnation to potential political and economic sanctions from the international community. Thus, there must be significant perceived benefits from the acquisition of weapons to warrant the effort required.

Arms Control Causes a Nuclear Buildup

Masked behind the rhetoric of arms control drastically reducing weapons is the reality of arms control actually pushing a buildup of weapons. This is rather perverse, violating the raison d'être of arms control. As Florence Nightingale said, "Whatever else they do, hospitals should not spread disease."

I have come to believe that we have more nuclear weapons today because of the arms control process than we would have without it—not enormously more, especially given the astronomical numbers today, but more nonetheless. For arms control seems ideally tailored to boost military programs and with them defense spending.

Kenneth L. Adelman, *The Great Universal Embrace: Arms Summitry—A Skeptic's Account*, 1989.

Given the nature of this decision, security considerations are generally seen as the primary motive behind the decision to acquire a nuclear capability. In a situation where political elites perceive a significant threat to their security, nuclear weapons will be considered as a potential option. This may be a function of perceptions of conventional military inferiority, the presence of a nuclear capable adversary or an adversary seeking to develop nuclear weapons, and the lack of a credible nuclear ally. Although the costs of developing a nuclear capability are high, governments may also perceive that the long-term costs of nuclear weapons are less than the long-term costs of a conventional arms race with an adversary.

While security is perhaps the most important consideration in the decision to develop nuclear weapons, the desire for prestige and other political payoffs should not be discounted. Many see nuclear weapons as conferring status in the international system. The nuclear powers are seen as members of an elite club. They are also among the dominant political powers in the system. Moreover, membership in the club is also viewed as providing tangible political benefits. In addition to international prestige, a nation's voice and influence, particularly over security issues in the system, increases with membership. As a nuclear power, a state cannot be readily ignored by the other powers in security deliberations. In addition, the acquisition of nuclear weapons can have payoffs at the regional level. A regional nuclear power is likely to have more influence over other regional actors. In so doing, the state may be able to advance its other interests more readily.

Finally, domestic political considerations may also play a role. Authoritarian governments, either civilian or military, may be able to entertain the nuclear option because of the absence of any opposition to their rule. In addition, the civilian decision-makers may see the nuclear option as a means to appease a discontented military. Finally, the prestige element of nuclear weapons from both the civilian and military internal politics perspective should not be discounted.

Adherence to the Nonproliferation Regime

Despite the reasons which might lead governments to embark on a nuclear weapons programme, the overwhelming majority of states have not done so, and, thus, have remained faithful to the NPT. The nuclear club remains limited to the five powers—the United States, Russia, China, France, and Great Britain. Moreover, those states viewed as likely proliferators in the 1960s have remained relatively constant. Although their nuclear capabilities vary significantly among them, from a known capability to a technological one, none of these so-called threshold states has officially announced its nuclear status.

Adherence to the NPT by the majority of states is a function of several factors. First of all, adherence carries no costs for the majority of states. The conditions which would push towards consideration of the nuclear option are absent. The majority of states do not face significant external security threats. They confront internal threats in which nuclear weapons have no utility. Also, the majority of states lack the financial and technical resources to even consider the option. For many states, the simple provision of basic needs for its citizens is extremely problematic. Of the group of threshold states, one finds either a situation of external conflict or regional insecurity, as in the case of India-Pakistan, North-South Korea, and the Middle East, great power ambitions, such as India and/or the resources required to develop nuclear weapons, as in the case of Argentina and Brazil, prior to their public announcements to forgo the nuclear option.

Second, adherence produces certain benefits for states. Here, adherence to the treaty and the regime can act to re-assure others about national policy, thereby avoiding the negative consequences of a nuclear arms race. Furthermore, adherence provides potential access to nuclear energy technology which may be important for states seeking alternative energy sources. Finally, adherence has wider value in terms of political relations. These may translate into greater political and economic support from other states or at least the avoidance of political and economic sanctions which may result from the decision to develop nuclear weapons.

Dual Nature of the NPT

The preceding discussion is formulated from a rational perspective in which states weigh the costs and benefits of the nuclear option. At the same time, proliferation arms control is legitimized by an international norm which places a taboo on nuclear weapons. This norm has two components, which reflect the dual nature of the NPT itself. The first concerns the two major nuclear powers, the United States and the Soviet Union, which had a common interest in preventing proliferation, and undertook a general pledge to negotiate nuclear disarmament in order to gain support for the NPT. Whereas the United States was deeply concerned about the issue of non-proliferation in a global sense, the Soviet Union was initially concerned about the issue in the context of East-West relations. The NPT could be used to remove the fear of West German nuclearization, and gain support for direct strategic arms control negotiations with the United States as a means to advance a wide range of Soviet political and security interests in Europe. At the same time, both Superpowers had a common interest in avoiding wider proliferation because of its potential implications for managing the strategic nuclear relationship between them. Moreover, the Soviet Union could also politically benefit in the context of its escalating conflict with China by portraying China as a 'pariah' because of its unwillingness to support the NPT.

The national interests which drove the Superpowers to push for the NPT were naturally opposed by China and France which were in the process of developing and/or expanding their nuclear capabilities. They saw the NPT as an attempt by the United States and the Soviet Union to continue their dominant political position in the international system. In particular, China justified its nuclear weapons programme and refusal to sign the NPT in terms of breaking the Northern monopoly on nuclear weapons and China's leadership of the Third World. The announcements by both China and France of their intentions to sign the NPT reflect the changes which have occurred with the end of the Cold War and the success of their own nuclear programmes. France and China no longer perceive the NPT as affecting their political and security interests. In other words, adherence does not entail any political or security costs for both. In addition, their current nuclear capabilities have created common interest with the other nuclear powers in avoiding proliferation.

The Delusion of Arms Control

It is intentions, not treaties, that govern behavior. Arms control, as the editor of Commentary magazine, Norman Podhoretz, once put it, is "the single biggest collective delusion, or superstition, that the world has known at least since the Middle Ages." When one is faced with an aggressive adversary, such a delusion can lead to disaster.

The Washington Times, October 6, 1991.

The second component of the NPT, which entails the rejection of the nuclear option by non-nuclear states, was made possible by the agreement between the United States and the Soviet Union, and the fact that the majority of states had no intention of pursuing the nuclear option. The net result was twofold for non-nuclear states. First, states actively pursuing the nuclear option, such as Israel and India, refused to sign the treaty. Israel perceived nuclear weapons as the ultimate guarantee of its survival against its hostile neighbours. India confronted a potential security threat from a nuclear state, China. In addition, India, along with other states critical of the NPT, recognized it as a wider attempt by the North to dominate the South, and as a means to maintain the global status quo.

Second, even signatories of the NPT, such as Iraq, have not forsaken nuclear weapons programmes. Their willingness to sign the NPT, yet undertake nuclear weapons development, reflected the inadequacies of the monitoring and verification elements of the NPT embodied in the IAEA, and a desire to avoid outright international condemnation in the context of a national decision that the development of nuclear weapons was in their national interests. Even though the international community is aware of these programmes, other political and strategic considerations have lead the major powers to avoid acting against them.

The Limits of Arms Control

The political considerations which have led states to pursue the nuclear option, and have affected how states have reacted to the issue, indicate the limits of arms control as a means to prevent proliferation. The limits of current arms control efforts stem from the very complexity of the issue. East-West arms control evolved in the context of direct negotiations between adversarial equals, and even then failed to alter the fundamental hostile political relationship between them. The altering of this relationship resulted from the fundamental political changes in the Soviet Union, which became manifested in arms control. Arms control in terms of proliferation exists in a complex web of adversarial and cooperative relations among a wide range of states. Nonetheless, at the centre of this arms control effort is an adversarial relationship, distinct from the East-West case and one of gross inequality. It is not an adversarial relationship between two neighbouring or regional states, but one between the Northern tier of industrialized states, particularly the nuclear powers, and the Southern tier of developing states.

An Unequal Relationship

Arms control in this relationship is, in effect, one element of the wider political and economic dominance of the North over the South. In other words, arms control, particularly in its NPT manifestation, represents the institutionalization of an unequal relationship made possible by the inability of the majority of developing states to consider the nuclear option, and the ability of the North to offer political and economic rewards to non-proliferators and political and economic punishment to potential proliferators. Moreover, inequality is also evident in the treatment of certain threshold states. For example, the United States has attempted to punish Pakistan for its nuclear weapons programme, but has ignored the nuclear weapons programme of Israel. Given the inequality embodied within the NPT and practised by the nuclear powers, credence is given to the case that developing nuclear weapons represents the overthrowing of an unequal relationship in which the strong have dictated to the weak.

This argument should not be interpreted as blanket condemnation of arms control and the NPT, or support for proliferation. Rather, it serves to illustrate that arms control in the context of the proliferation issue is the product of political and security interests of states in the international system. Certainly, arms control does have a limited functional role to play. At a minimum, it does enable some states to re-assure others that they do not wish to develop nuclear weapons, even though the monitoring and verification mechanisms are significantly circumscribed by the limits of national acceptability, as evident in the Iraqi case. Even then, the ability to slow proliferation, in fact, is not a function of arms control and the NPT. Rather, it is a function of the relative Northern monopoly on nuclear materials and technology which are controlled through national export policies and the coordination of these policies by the major suppliers primarily through the London Suppliers Group. This is not arms control, but rather the ability of a small number of states to affect the behaviour of others on the basis of their limited common national interests.

Politics Decides the Course of Proliferation

Arms control in the form of the NPT is a function of the nature of political relations among states. Notwithstanding the ability of non-nuclear states to consider the nuclear option, decisions to develop nuclear weapons will occur out of national considerations of the utility of these weapons within a particular political context of threats to national security as well as desires to achieve greater political status and influence in the system. Arms control cannot significantly alter these national considerations. Rather, it is the behaviour of states in the wider context of the political and strategic environment which will affect considerations about nuclear weapons.

Arms control is dependent on a host of political considerations which dictate what is possible. Moreover, arms control itself is simply one of many vehicles in which states seek to advance their political interests. Changes in national policy with regard to proliferation result from changes in national calculations of the relative importance of nuclear weapons. The current changes which are underway in the proliferation area are not a function of arms control, but rather a function of the changing political climate. This is nowhere more clear than in the case of the willingness of France and China to sign the NPT, as noted above, and the changes in South Africa, Argentina, and Brazil. For South Africa, the internal political changes which are underway as they affect its regional security has removed the security incentive for nuclear weapons, leading to its support for the NPT. For both Argentina and Brazil, the emergence of civilian governments have led to their mutual agreements to halt their nuclear programmes. Thus, the decision to develop or not develop nuclear weapons will remain driven by national considerations, which will in turn impact on the nature of arms control.

"Export controls . . . have been useful in stopping or delaying certain [nuclear] capabilities in the past and will continue to do so."

Nuclear Export Controls Limit Proliferation

Henry D. Sokolski

The United States and many other nations work to prevent the export of technology and materials critical to the often clandestine production of nuclear weapons. In the following viewpoint, Henry D. Sokolski argues that these nuclear export controls have been, and continue to be, successful in preventing nuclear proliferation. Sokolski contends that strict measures such as corporate penalties and imprisonment for nuclear suppliers have halted or delayed illegal nuclear weapons programs. Sokolski is the deputy for nonproliferation policy for the U.S. Department of Defense in Alexandria, Virginia.

As you read, consider the following questions:

1. In Sokolski's opinion, how could the spread of nuclear weapons affect U.S. influence abroad?
2. Why have some nations chosen not to develop nuclear weapons, according to the author?
3. According to Sokolski, why should governments specify which nuclear exports to control?

Henry D. Sokolski, Statement to the U.S. Senate Committee on Governmental Affairs, October 9, 1990.

Since the Trinity Shot in 1945, the U.S. has made a conscious effort to stem the spread of dangerous weapons technology. In the late 1940s, our fear was that the Soviets might acquire nuclear weapons. This concern, much as our current worry about smaller powers getting such weapons today, turned on three points.

The first was the high-leverage character of these weapons: For far less than the cost of equipping a navy or army, our potential adversary could threaten us with enormous harm. The second was our lack of adequate or systematic defenses: We knew how to cope with conventional air, sea, and land offensives. But, until the mid-1950s, we lacked even the most basic continental air defenses against Soviet nuclear bombers; and, later, when intercontinental ballistic missiles were introduced, we had no active missile defenses at all.

Impact of Proliferation on U.S. Influence

Finally, and also related, the spread of such weapons could threaten our allies and, more generally, reduce U.S. influence abroad; with our own nuclear forces deterred, the Soviets might feel freer to act against our interests.

A good deal, of course, has changed since 1945. Where once our proliferation concerns were focused on the Soviets acquiring nuclear weapons, now our worries center on several smaller nations acquiring not just nuclear, but biological and chemical munitions, and the missiles to deliver them.

Even now, however, what drives our proliferation concerns are apprehensions similar to those we had in the late 1940s. We still worry about the spread of weapons that have an extremely high level of military effectiveness against which we or our friends abroad lack adequate defenses. And we still worry that their spread might significantly undermine our influence.

As I have already noted, the specific nations and technologies that are of proliferation concern have changed over the last forty-five years. The trick to coping with these proliferation problems is, first, to keep them from getting beyond our ability to deal with them diplomatically or militarily; and, second, to anticipate what new problems we are likely to face before it is too late to establish controls over them. . . .

The record of prediction on the spread of advanced weapons has been uneven. In the case of nuclear weapons, it has generally been tainted by premature fatalism that has ignored what can be done to affect the demand side of proliferation. One such prediction was made in 1960 by the prestigious Twentieth Century Fund. Sixteen nations, it argued, would explode nuclear devices by 1966.

Clearly, this did not happen. One of the reasons it did not is that nations that might otherwise feel insecure without nuclear weapons, chose not to acquire them because of the security they already had in existing security alliances. Thus, in Europe and the Far East, several nations had the technical capability to develop nuclear weapons but felt no need to do so because of NATO and U.S. security arrangements.

Stringent Export Controls

[A] key element of the nuclear non-proliferation system is the highly developed structure of measures designed to assure responsible control by nuclear suppliers over transfers of materials, equipment or technology which could assist the development of nuclear explosives. The United States has long administered a stringent system of domestic nuclear non-proliferation export controls.

Office of the U.S. President, *Activities to Prevent Nuclear Proliferation*, September 11, 1991.

As the threat posed by the Soviet Bloc declines, the importance of maintaining these security guarantees for nonproliferation purposes is likely to grow and may be a significant reason for maintaining them.

Also, many governments have clearly decided that it is too dangerous for them to go beyond certain stages in the development or deployment of certain weapons.

Export Controls

Export controls address the supply side of the proliferation problem. They have been useful in stopping or delaying certain capabilities in the past and will continue to do so. Export controls will be challenged as the relevant technologies become increasingly dual-purpose in character. Many of the technologies of proliferation concern have commercial counterparts. Technologies for making chemical and biological weapons can also be used to produce pesticides, pharmaceuticals, fertilizers, or food products. This duality presents very real problems in controlling these technologies' diffusion. The more uses a technology has, the more rapidly it is likely to spread. Thus, technologies for communications and navigation tend to spread more rapidly than those for nuclear explosives.

A good example of this is provided in GPS [Global Positioning Satellite Navigational System]. Another is high-performance computers, which are critical and legitimate tools for commercial and scientific use but can also help reduce the time and risk associated with missile and nuclear weapons design and testing or the development and cracking of codes.

Of course, in each of these cases, we exercise controls to help prevent illicit use. In the case of the most capable computational machines, supercomputers, special care is exercised.

This same problem is present in high relief with space launch vehicle technology exports. DoD [Department of Defense] backs current U.S. policy on SLV [space launch vehicle] exports, that is, to *hinder* the spread of nuclear-capable missile systems, *including* ostensibly civilian space launch vehicle programs. It is for this reason that the U.S. supports the Missile Technology Control Regime (MTCR).

As the U.S. government noted publicly when the MTCR was announced in April 1987, "The Regime aims at the control of all devices of this [nuclear] capability even if they are called 'peaceful' or are alleged to be for military purposes other than weapons delivery. Space launch vehicles, for instance, are virtually interchangeable with ballistic missiles." When President Kennedy was asked the difference between the Atlas rocket that put John Glenn into orbit and the Atlas rocket armed with a nuclear warhead, he replied with one word—"attitude."

Precisely because we cannot control for attitudes, U.S. policy and the MTCR control *capabilities* and treat space launch vehicle technology as restrictively as they do ballistic missile technology.

What we *can* provide, and what U.S. policy does support—as I noted before the House Foreign Affairs Committee—is provision of space launch services within the U.S. for any and all nations, including the Third World.

Maintain Strong Controls

Again, controls of this sort will require vigilance. At a minimum, we must be on guard not to lower existing nonproliferation controls as we lower controls over dual-use commodities that might be exported to the Soviet Union and Eastern Europe. As we streamline the COCOM [Coordinating Committee on Multilateral Export Controls] lists, [the Departments of] State and Commerce, in conjunction with DoD, are working to ensure that nuclear- and missile-related items being dropped from COCOM are placed under separate nonproliferation controls to maintain current restrictions.

Innovation, however, also has its place. For more than one year, DoD has made clear that it will debar or suspend foreign firms that violate their own nations' export control laws or regulations from business with the Defense Department. The significance of this announcement should not be underestimated. Each month, scores of European defense firms are consolidating under larger entities, many of which do business with DoD.

These firms now have an incentive to monitor the behavior of their subsidiaries.

DoD believes its initiative will also increase in significance as nonproliferation controls are strengthened abroad. This trend is underway. On 21 September 1990, both Houses of the then West German Parliament passed legislation entitled, "Improvement of the surveillance of external trade for the prohibition of nuclear, biological, and chemical weapons" as an amendment to the Weapons Export Control Law. The law requires a minimum two-year prison term for the "development, manufacture, sale, purchase, supply, import or export, of nuclear, chemical, or biological weapons." Additionally, the dissemination of knowledge associated with these activities is no longer considered "insignificant" by this law. In addition to Germany, Sweden and other European nations are reviewing their export controls to see if they cannot be extended and strengthened for nonproliferation purposes.

Prolonging Nuclear Weapons Programs

Export controls increase the time it takes to complete the construction of sensitive nuclear facilities capable of producing weapons grade materials, and often make a proliferating state vulnerable to external pressure. . . . Effectively implemented export controls—particularly if they are backed up with strong diplomatic pressure, counterintelligence initiatives, or media attention—can delay some proliferators for decades and might even keep a few nations from *ever* proliferating. This is especially true for less technically developed potential threshold countries.

Thomas W. Graham, *Arms Control Today*, September 1991.

What we want to do and what we are planning to do is to build on this trend to make sure that the items the U.S. controls for are the same as others control for in the nuclear, missile and chemical-biological weapons technologies areas. DoD is also chairing an effort to spell out more precisely what is meant by the categories of items on the MTCR annex and suggest what else might usefully be added to the annex.

Export Controls Thwart Nuclear Programs

It has sometimes been argued that because export controls do not always work in stopping proliferation, they are not worth implementing. I disagree. First, sometimes they do freeze programs. A good example here is the Condor missile project. Second, they generally do slow them down.

Here I speak from personal experience. A single missile system can require precise integration of over a quarter of a million different parts. If you want to keep a program from being completed, the key is to reduce the program manager's confidence, not build it. That's where effective export controls come in and I can assure you they do. Indeed, complaints from proliferant nations about export control efforts such as the MTCR come in on a regular basis.

Such confidence reduction efforts and the project slowdowns they induce are important to our security. Deterring and defending against these weapons of proliferation concern can be costly. In some instances, such as ballistic missiles, we lack active area defenses and their development will take time. The more time we buy by slowing proliferation, the easier it will be to develop military and diplomatic answers to the threat they pose. Also, sometimes even our adversaries can become friendlier, as we have witnessed with most of the Warsaw Pact. In the eyes of the Defense Department, then, buying additional time is worth some effort.

"The biggest problem facing nuclear export controls is . . . a nonproliferation regime that is too long on secrecy and too short on political will."

Nuclear Export Controls Do Not Limit Proliferation

Paul L. Leventhal

Several nations' lax nuclear export controls contribute to the growth of nuclear proliferation, Paul L. Leventhal argues in the following viewpoint. Leventhal asserts that these weak controls enable some nations to acquire uranium, plutonium, and other materials that can be used to build nuclear weapons. Leventhal also maintains that U.S. foreign policy interests often ignore other countries' nuclear material acquisitions in exchange for military or economic cooperation. Leventhal is president of the Nuclear Control Institute, a Washington, D.C., group concerned with the spread of nuclear weapons.

As you read, consider the following questions:

1. Why will an increase in nuclear export controls be useless, according to Leventhal?
2. In Leventhal's opinion, how does the United States justify weak nuclear export controls?
3. Why does the author believe that nuclear weapons are likely to be used in the future?

From Paul L. Leventhal, "Plugging the Leaks in Nuclear Export Controls: Why Bother?" a position paper given at the Conference on Supply-Side Control of Weapons Proliferation, Ottawa, Canada, June 20, 1991. Reprinted with permission.

The various items needed to manufacture nuclear weapons continue to find their way from a worldwide nuclear industry into the purportedly peaceful nuclear programs of a number of developing countries, despite the panoply of nuclear agreements, laws, and regulations that comprise present U.S. and international nuclear export controls. U.N. inspectors discovered a vast nuclear weapons program in Iraq, a party to the 1968 Treaty on the Non-Proliferation of Nuclear Weapons (NPT), and one whose cooperation under the treaty had been labelled "exemplary" by the International Atomic Energy Agency (IAEA)—indeed, Iraqi officials were deemed by the IAEA to "have made every effort to demonstrate that Iraq is a solid citizen." This discovery provides only the latest evidence of a growing, global nuclear bazaar that makes a mockery of the long-revered nuclear nonproliferation regime. The question therefore arises: Is it possible to plug the leaks in nuclear export controls? Perhaps more to the point, given the apparent lack of willpower among governments and industry to do so, should an attempt even be made?

The Nuclear Control Regime

The U.S. proposal on the peaceful uses of atomic energy was unveiled by President Dwight D. Eisenhower in a speech to the U.N. General Assembly in 1953. A series of "atoms-for-peace" conferences in Geneva followed, at which the United States and other countries possessing nuclear weaponry disclosed previously classified nuclear technology associated with production of materials for nuclear weapons, so that it might be applied for civilian research and the generation of electricity. The IAEA was then established in 1956 to safeguard as well as to promote peaceful uses of nuclear energy. Today, the nuclear control regime now includes the NPT, the IAEA (including the agency's Zangger Committee on nuclear export controls), the Nuclear Suppliers' Group ("London Club"), the Department of State Munitions List (Arms Export Control Act), the Coordinating Committee on Multilateral Export Controls (COCOM), the Department of Commerce COCOM List (Export Administration Act), and other U.S. agency and interagency nuclear-export controls pursuant to the Nuclear Non-Proliferation Act.

Casting a wider and a finer net than this one will be exceedingly difficult, and for all the effort, only a marginal or diminishing return is likely. A better net might prove successful in catching more items of importance to nuclear-bomb making, but most of the newly caught items would probably be dual-use components—computers, microchips, special alloys, pumps, valves, and the like—that are also important to industrial development in the Third World. The vast majority of developing countries can make no practical use of nuclear energy and have no interest in nuclear weapons.

At the same time, negotiating longer, more complex lists of sensitive dual-use items—however gratifying that might seem to nuclear bureaucrats and diplomats—will do little to restrict commerce in these items if they can continue to be exported (albeit subject to IAEA safeguards) to countries determined to develop nuclear weapons. The safeguards are weak in the face of determined would-be nuclear powers, and acquiring the technologies to produce bomb-grade materials enables these states to produce the weapons themselves. Thus, tightening controls over these items might well stir deep resentments and widen the North-South divide far out of proportion to any gain realized in further inhibiting nuclear development in the relatively few problem states for which the new restrictions would be intended.

Weak Controls for New Nuclear Exporters

The machinery governing export behavior in the emerging suppliers tends to be rudimentary. Most emerging supplier states have underdeveloped and understaffed domestic nuclear export control structures and lack well-defined procedures for regulating nuclear exports. In the absence of routine procedures to license and monitor exports and mechanisms to coordinate and to implement interagency decisions, declarations of support for prudence in nuclear exports, even if they are a sincere reflection of leadership beliefs, may well diverge from actual export behavior.

William C. Potter, *Orbis*, Spring 1992.

In addition, more comprehensive lists of controlled items will not end the secrecy and political machinations that undermine enforcement of the present nuclear export control regime. Though such list-writing is again underway within national bureaucracies and the international Nuclear Suppliers' Group, it is an exercise that will not mean much if the past decade's pattern of weak enforcement is allowed to persist, including weak or nonexistent controls over nuclear as well as dual-use items.

Démarches sent by the U.S. Government protesting the export of sensitive items to would-be nuclear states have been ignored by suppliers and have not been pursued aggressively by U.S. officials. If diplomacy continues to transform démarches into "demarshmallows" [a phrase coined by defense expert Richard Perle]—making it impossible to confront wayward exporters and importers—and if secrecy is still used to conceal illicit nuclear trade, what is the point of investing untold thousands of hours on drafting, negotiating, and ratifying yet more controlled items?

Nonproliferation Paralysis

The biggest problem facing nuclear export controls today is not a control list that is too short, but a nonproliferation regime that is too long on secrecy and too short on political will. Bluntly stated, current U.S. practice is to abstain from enforcing nuclear export controls whenever competing interests are deemed to take precedence—which is almost always. To date, almost any political, industrial, or diplomatic interest takes precedence over nuclear nonproliferation. The net result is nonproliferation paralysis, often with no one outside of classified circles being the wiser until the damage is done—that is, the offending export is sent, the uranium is enriched to weapons grade, the weapons-usable plutonium is recovered from spent reactor fuel, the weapons are built.

Competing interests explain the failure of the United States to respond effectively to the nuclear weapons programs of Israel, South Africa, India, Pakistan, and Iraq; to the renegade nuclear supplier roles played by China, France, and Germany; and to Japan's determination to recover vast stocks of unneeded, uneconomical plutonium from U.S.-supplied reactor fuel. In each instance, a case was made as to why immediate, specific interests had to take precedence over longer-term, nuclear proliferation concerns.

History will judge whether, for example, Pakistan's cooperation with U.S. military assistance to the anti-Soviet insurgents in Afghanistan warranted the United States finally turning a blind eye to Pakistan's nuclear weapons program. History will also judge whether pressing trade issues with Japan warranted a U.S. decision to enter into a nuclear trade agreement with the Japanese in 1988, clearing the way for Japan to recover from U.S.-supplied nuclear fuel more plutonium than in all U.S. and Soviet nuclear weapons combined.

The premise underlying these policy decisions has been that nuclear proliferation cannot be prevented, only managed, thereby justifying weak or flexible nuclear export controls that can give way to immediate industrial and diplomatic imperatives. The cumulative effect of these individual trade-offs, however, is to hasten both the spread of nuclear weapons and the industrial potential to build nuclear weapons with little or no warning. Whether this spread proves manageable remains to be seen. It would seem prudent, however, to place a higher priority on preventing today what might not prove manageable tomorrow.

One has only to read accounts of the 1988-89 Bundestag investigation of the West German nuclear export scandals to get the flavor of how weak the controls have been in the face of a determined industry backed by a sympathetic bureaucracy unmoved by proliferation concerns. German corporations and middlemen made unsafeguarded transfers of critical components, whole plants, and heavy water to Iraq, India, and Pakistan after the German government ignored or rebuffed well over one hundred démarches and other communications from the United States and Great Britain protesting the impending exports. Investigators found a memo in which a German export official reported that the notes "usually end up in my wastepaper basket." Only some of the export abuses involved dual-use items that lacked specific controls. Most involved nuclear items—components, equipment, technology, and materials—for which there were adequate controls but inadequate enforcement.

The Germans are not alone, of course; many are to blame for the presently weak export control regime. . . .

Iraq's Nuclear Weapons Program

Three principal lessons can be drawn from examining Iraq's secret nuclear weapons program. These lessons shed light on the feasibility of plugging the leaks in nuclear export controls and suggest priorities other than upgrading export controls that must be addressed.

Porous Export Controls

[Some] countries can pose a grave proliferation risk if they provide items otherwise unavailable to countries aspiring to possess nuclear weapons. Pakistan's and Iraq's experience in circumventing international nuclear export controls is especially relevant, and underlines the porous nature of existing international control arrangements. The entry of new vendors into the nuclear marketplace will undoubtedly provide new loopholes.

William C. Potter, *Orbis*, Spring 1992.

First, the NPT, the principal bulwark against the spread of the bomb, actually facilitated the supply of very sensitive items—research reactors, bomb-grade uranium fuel, and equipment for processing plutonium—to a rogue state. Iraq laid to rest a longstanding belief that a state will not join the NPT for the purpose of cheating. In this case, Iraq cheated on its treaty commitments, and the treaty did not inhibit Iraq's ability to go forward with a dedicated nuclear weapons program, including the acquisition of unsafeguarded equipment and technology for enriching uranium to weapons grade.

Secondly, IAEA safeguards proved incapable of detecting the vast, multi-billion-dollar weapons program that Iraq had concealed inside unsafeguarded facilities, even when these weapons facilities were located within nuclear installations where safeguards were being applied. Following the 1991 Gulf war, Iraq first tried to conceal and then grudgingly showed inspectors evidence of at least four technologies and several large plants for producing its own highly enriched bomb-grade uranium. IAEA safeguards also failed to provide timely detection of Iraq's removal of bomb-grade nuclear fuel from safeguarded facilities. Before the war, agency inspectors had been checking twice a year on safeguarded, highly enriched uranium fuel that the agency knew could be converted into weapons components in one to three weeks. . . .

Thirdly, Iraq is demonstrating that the potential to produce nuclear weapons, once acquired, cannot easily be eliminated. Iraq continues to play a cat-and-mouse game with the IAEA-U.N. Special Commission inspection team, despite being required under the U.N. Ceasefire Resolution to give up its weapons-grade nuclear materials and to allow its nuclear weapons facilities to be destroyed. . . .

Unless the lessons learned from Iraq and from the present industrial and bureaucratic mismanagement of atoms for peace are translated into a radically different approach to nuclear nonproliferation, it is anyone's guess as to when (not whether, but when) nuclear weapons will again be used.

Unfortunately, there are few signs, even after Iraq, that powerful nuclear industrial interests and their backers in national and international bureaucracies are prepared to embark on a straightforward, transparent, and unambiguous approach to bringing nuclear commerce under control.

*"All existing nuclear weapons should be
eliminated and their possession banned
throughout the world."*

Eliminating Nuclear Weapons Will Prevent Proliferation

Gerd Schmückle

A choice must be made between the profusion of nuclear arms and their complete elimination, Gerd Schmückle argues in the following viewpoint. Schmückle maintains that partial disarmament by the world's nuclear powers is unacceptable because ambitious nations seeking nuclear weapons will still strive to increase their arsenals. The author states that the elimination of all nuclear weapons and a ban on their possession is the only logical way to ensure a nuclear arms-free future. Schmückle is a former commander of the North Atlantic Treaty Organization (NATO), a military alliance of the United States, Western Europe, and other nations.

As you read, consider the following questions:

1. According to Schmückle, why is a nuclear attack on Europe unlikely?
2. In the author's opinion, how has the military significance of nuclear weapons diminished?
3. Why would it be difficult to achieve a nuclear arms-free world, according to Schmückle?

Gerd Schmückle, "Keeping the Peace Without the Weapons," *World Press Review*, May 1992. This article first appeared in *Die Zeit*, a weekly newspaper of Hamburg, Germany, and is reprinted by permission of World Press Review, 200 Madison Ave., New York, NY 10016.

Nuclear weapons once were a deterrent to nuclear war in Europe. They kept the cold war from turning hot, however corrosive the crises between East and West may have been. Does this still hold true? The answer is: no, at least for now. The old balance broke down with the collapse of the Soviet Union. It has given way to Western superiority. This is seldom heard, but NATO has lost its nuclear objective, too. A large-scale Eastern offensive has become less than unlikely. The nuclear weapons of the former Soviet Union now menace the West less than they do the cohesion of the collapsed empire itself.

When former Soviet President Mikhail Gorbachev ceremoniously passed to his successor the briefcase with the nuclear-weapon codes, as if he were passing on a scepter to the new emperor, the world was supposed to believe that Soviet weapons were under uninterrupted control. This is far from the truth. There is more to political control than codes. Political control of nuclear weapons is a farce unless backed by ingenious intelligence, guidance systems, and, above all, highly trained, expert personnel. Firing these extremely dangerous weapons requires commands to be critically analyzed and checked at every step before they are transmitted further.

Scattered Nukes

Such a command-and-control system no longer exists for the nuclear weapons of the former Soviet Union, scattered as they are among the numerous republics. It is an open question whether the system has ever functioned reliably.

Today, the strategic weapons are under the political control of the presidents of four republics. How can their decision process be coordinated? The technical prerequisites for such coordination cannot exist at the moment. Moreover, these presidents are occupied with such an array of political, economic, and social problems that they do not have time to master the difficult subject of nuclear weapons. For a rather long time, they will be dependent on military personnel, and that dependence requires that there be functional cooperation with the Commonwealth of Independent States (C.I.S.).

No one is consoled by the knowledge that these heads of government are dependent on military personnel. The military is more than dissatisfied with the emergence of the C.I.S., because the military has seen its very existence as a vocation downgraded. The army, once viewed as the backbone of the entire state, now watches this state coming apart at the seams, with some republics fighting one another. Heaven only knows who will emerge victorious. It is a mess.

The instabilities in the C.I.S. must be dealt with. The weapons that have been designated by treaty to be eliminated must be truly eliminated. Finally, the worldwide proliferation of nuclear weapons must be halted.

Such a large-scale program is a challenge to America and Europe. New approaches must be tried. The United States could provide the C.I.S. with the American control system. American security would not be undermined—just the opposite: The prerequisite for such an offer would require the C.I.S. to reveal its own control mechanisms. Next, a C.I.S. control system could be developed as a joint venture. Ultimately, everyone would know that everything humanly possible had been done to keep nuclear weapons under political control in peace, crisis, and war. At the same time, the C.I.S. would have to accept the American offers to provide technical assistance in the dismantling of nuclear weapons. Here, there is a lot of pride to be overcome. Many Russians still dislike the idea of letting foreigners poke around. The C.I.S. must get over this aversion.

© David Suter. Reprinted with permission.

The third step is the most difficult one: to guide the future of nuclear weapons. Sometimes it seems as if people are resigned to the idea that nuclear weapons will spread through a wide part of the globe. Politicians speak only rarely about this. Nuclear experts have been concerned about such possibilities for decades, yet they, too, have been mute, as if resigned. Whoever, like Cassandra, sounds an alarm is considered a

183

doomsayer. In fact, the situation today offers a greater opportunity than ever before of alerting the public to the issue of nuclear weapons.

Nuclear Newcomers

One might maintain that we cannot prevent other countries from going nuclear. Why should they not be able to develop a deterrent system as America, NATO, the U.S.S.R., and the Warsaw Pact all did? These nuclear dwarfs will harm only themselves if deterrence fails, while the great nuclear powers will not be dragged into a nuclear war.

Not so fast! A system like that of NATO required a formidable expenditure on science, technology, and personnel in order to make deterrence credible: "Whoever shoots first dies second." Nuclear dwarfs are not in such a position. Without a sure second-strike capability, their philosophy would go something like this: "Whoever shoots first has already won." Their systems would not have a deterrent effect but would actually foster war.

Even if the nuclear giants managed to keep out of the nuclear dwarfs' duel, they would eventually be affected. Chernobyl would send its regards. If the worldwide trend toward proliferation continues, we will be faced with a new world order based on a nuclear hierarchy: America at the top, countries such as England and France in the middle, and a growing number of nuclear dwarfs at the bottom, each gnawed by ambitions to become giants. In that case, it would be no help if America and the middle nuclear states were to disarm to a lower level. The nuclear dwarfs would only be encouraged to build up to those levels.

Ban All Nuclear Weapons

Such a new world order could not be more unstable. What might the alternative be? The answer sounds simple but remains difficult to implement: All existing nuclear weapons should be eliminated and their possession banned throughout the world.

Many people consider this to be mere dreaming. Yet the reality of modern weapons technology has changed. During the Persian Gulf war, precise conventional weaponry showed that targets could be hit accurately and without the catastrophic side effects of nuclear weapons. That war greatly diminished the military significance of nuclear weapons.

The political status of nuclear weapons is also being reduced. When French President François Mitterrand intimates that his nuclear missiles could be "Europeanized," this change of heart springs less from the vision of a united Europe than the recognized political and military downgrading of these weapons. In the end, one shares everything that has lost its value.

The United States would have to set the pace for the world-wide abolition of nuclear weapons. Such a program would answer that country's moral impulse. Nuclear weapons would have to be eliminated, further production banned, a global supervision system financed, and sanctions against violations formulated. Responsibility for this program, run under a specific timetable, should pass, step by step, to the United Nations.

There are plenty of objections to this plan. National egoism, faith in nuclear weapons, or political obsession will cause many to attempt to block any such plan. But the future provides no middle ground between a world full of nuclear weapons and one free of such weapons. Today, the great powers have the opportunity to take the first step toward a new world order—a better one.

"Deep cuts would increase the legitimacy of U.S. and Russian efforts to stop the international proliferation of nuclear weapons."

Drastically Reducing Nuclear Weapons Will Prevent Proliferation

Harold Feiveson and Frank von Hippel

An alternative to worldwide nuclear disarmament to reduce proliferation involves deep reductions of nuclear arsenals. In the following viewpoint, Harold Feiveson and Frank von Hippel argue that the United States and Russia should cut their nuclear arsenals to one thousand warheads each. The authors contend that this measure would assure the world that the two nuclear powers are genuinely committed to reducing nuclear proliferation. Feiveson is a senior research scholar and Frank von Hippel is a professor of public and international affairs at Princeton University in Princeton, New Jersey.

As you read, consider the following questions:

1. According to the authors, how can deep arms reductions by the United States and Russia limit other nations' nuclear weapons?
2. Why do Feiveson and von Hippel believe that reduced nuclear arsenals would still offer the United States and Russia effective protection?
3. Why do the authors oppose the acceptance of nuclear arms as a permanent part of military arsenals?

From Harold Feiveson and Frank von Hippel, "Dismantling the Doomsday Machine," *Technology Review*, May/June 1992. Reprinted with permission from *Technology Review*, copyright 1992.

The huge nuclear arsenals of the United States and Soviet Union were built on a fantastic illusion—that nuclear explosives could be used for military purposes by the thousands without destroying modern civilization. Only such an illusion can account for the accumulation of more than 10,000 long-range strategic nuclear warheads and 10,000 tactical nuclear warheads by each country, with a combined destructive power greater than that of 150,000 Hiroshima bombs.

The principal mission of these oversized strategic forces—to target each other—led to exaggerated fears about the possibility of surprise attacks. This in turn led both sides to place large numbers of nuclear weapons on hair-trigger alert and to disperse authority to launch attacks among large numbers of people, thus heightening the danger of accidental nuclear war. The superpowers' preoccupation with mutual nuclear threats also distracted them from the growing dangers of nuclear-weapons proliferation.

The end of the Cold War offers an unprecedented opportunity for the United States and the former Soviet republics, principally Russia, to begin to cooperatively dismantle the largest part of this Doomsday Machine. As a first step, the arsenals could be cut deeply and quickly to about 1,000 warheads on each side.

By making such deep cuts, the superpowers would acknowledge an important reality: that nuclear weapons are useless as war-fighting instruments. A 1,000-warhead arsenal would be plenty destructive enough to hold the other side hostage, but far too small to mount a large attack on the other's nuclear forces. If both sides cut their nuclear forces to such levels, therefore, neither will feel as much pressure to strike first if a conflict arises. It will become easier to move away from the hair-trigger, "use them or lose them" postures that undermine the stability of the present strategic balance.

Bolstering Nonproliferation Efforts

The deep cuts would increase the legitimacy of U.S. and Russian efforts to stop the international proliferation of nuclear weapons. They should make it easier to achieve a universal ban on the further production of fissile materials not subject to international safeguards. This ban could cap the arsenals of the middle nuclear powers (Britain, France, and China) and of the "threshold" nuclear-weapons states (Israel, India, and Pakistan). Deep cuts in Russia's nuclear forces, along with similar cuts in its conventional forces, would also help ensure that Kazakhstan and Ukraine stick to their decisions to become non-nuclear states.

A 1,000-warhead force would be consistent with the criteria offered in a study commissioned by Air Force Gen. Lee Butler, director of U.S. strategic targeting. The study concluded that in the post-Cold War era, the United States should retain a long-range nuclear force at least as large as that of the Commonwealth of Independent States (CIS) and larger than the forces of Britain, France, and China combined. Thus, for whatever it is worth, the United States would retain its "superpower" status. Finally, a study by the Congressional Budget Office shows that a 1,000-warhead force would cost billions of dollars per year less than the nuclear arsenal that would remain after the more modest reductions already agreed upon in the Strategic Arms Reductions Treaty (START).

The Minimum Deterrent Message

No nation has more to lose in a world of nuclear anarchy than the United States. Because this nation is the world's leading nuclear power, it retains considerable potential as a prime architect of a new security system. But that influence is waning fast, as weapons spread. Only a "minimum deterrent" force, ranging from dozens to about a hundred weapons, and a clear commitment never to use nuclear weapons except in retaliation for a nuclear attack, will send the message that the United States and the other nuclear powers are committed to a post-nuclear order.

Richard J. Barnet, *The American Prospect*, Winter 1992.

The reduction of the superpower nuclear arsenals has already begun. Since the failed Moscow coup in 1991, a series of reciprocated unilateral initiatives have added up to what Russian President Boris Yeltsin described as a "landslide of disarmament." Both countries have already agreed to either dismantle or place in storage almost all tactical nuclear weapons. START will cut their strategic arsenals by thousands of warheads each, and they are negotiating still deeper strategic reductions. . . .

A One Thousand-Warhead Arsenal

In designing the 1,000-warhead force, we have made two general assumptions: First, it is unlikely that either country will want to eliminate entirely any leg of the strategic triad. Submarines are able to hide under the ocean and survive a nuclear attack. ICBMs are more vulnerable but it would take a huge attack to even partially destroy a force of a few hundred silo-based missiles. Bomber forces are the most versatile—they can carry either conventional or nuclear weapons and, unlike missiles, can be called back.

Second, in making radical reductions in nuclear forces, both countries should cut the concentrations of warheads on missiles and bombers. The reasoning is that with only a few nuclear "eggs," it would be important not to have too many in any single "basket." Otherwise, a 1,000-warhead force might appear vulnerable to attack—and it is its ensured survivability that makes the small nuclear force work.

The ICBM component of the U.S. force, for example, could consist of 248 Minuteman III missiles "downloaded," as President Bush has already proposed, from three warheads apiece to one. The obvious candidate for the Russian ICBM is the single-warhead, mobile SS-25, of which approximately 300 were deployed as of the end of 1991. Roughly this number could remain in a 1,000-warhead force. However, mobile missiles depend upon dispersal for survivability, and such dispersal creates troubling security problems. A missile on a truck is not as safe from hijack as one in a silo. Russia may therefore wish to consider placing these single-warhead missiles in some of the silos that will be left empty as a result of the elimination of multiple-warhead ICBMs.

The Role of Subs and Bombers

The potential for too many eggs in a basket is even more pronounced with submarines than with land-based missiles. Just two Trident submarines, each equipped as today with two dozen, eight-warhead missiles, would carry almost 40 percent of a 1,000-warhead force. But two submarines cannot ensure robust survivability. If the United States wanted to keep all of its planned Trident submarines, it could download their missiles to a single warhead each, for a total force of 432 warheads. Or the same number of warheads could be carried on a smaller number of submarines with partially downloaded missiles. Russia could similarly download as many as 440 missiles on 25 of its most modern submarines.

To reduce concerns that the stripped-down missiles might be reloaded, the extra warheads should be destroyed in a verified manner. Also, the "buses" that currently direct the warheads of multiple-warhead missiles to their different targets should be eliminated, and tests simulating release of more than the reduced number of warheads banned, as stipulated in the START treaty.

The remaining 320 U.S. warheads could be carried by 40 long-range bombers, each carrying its maximum internal load of eight cruise missiles. The United States would presumably use B-1 bombers for this purpose and either retire its B-52s or convert them into conventional bombers. Russia could similarly complete its 1,000-warhead force with some of its long-range bombers carrying their maximum internal loads of six cruise missiles each. Surplus cruise missiles would be destroyed, as would pylons that would enable aircraft to carry cruise missiles externally. As today, the bombers would be kept off alert, with their nuclear weapons in storage nearby.

No plausible cheating or breakout from these 1,000-warhead limits could threaten either country's ability to retaliate. In the U.S. case, with current at-sea rates, two-thirds of the Trident submarines would be hidden in the sea at any one time. These subs would carry a total of 288 warheads, each with an average destructive power equal to seven Hiroshima bombs. In addition, at least 50 ICBMs, each carrying a warhead with eight times the destructive power of the Hiroshima bomb, could be expected to survive even a worst-case attack. These surviving warheads would contain a huge destructive potential and constitute a more than adequate deterrent.

An Impressive Plan

A ray of sunshine is appearing on the horizon. There will not be a totally nuclear-free world . . . but what was called 'East' and 'West' two years ago could now move and agree on a minimum deterrence, let us say 1000 nuclear weapons on each side.

Frankfurter Rundschau, September 29, 1991.

Critics of proposals like ours sometimes assert that a drastically pared-down nuclear force would be incapable of a large "counterforce" attack on the enemy's military. These critics maintain that this would leave a country with only one option for retaliation: the "immoral" one of attacking cities. But a small arsenal does not necessitate attacks on cities. Even after being hit by a nuclear attack, a country with a 1,000-warhead arsenal would still have hundreds of surviving warheads, and it would always have the option of retaliating with some of them against military targets. And in any case, massive attacks on military targets would kill so many civilians that distinctions between counterforce and counter-city attacks become nearly meaningless. The deterrent strategy associated with a 1,000-warhead force would therefore be no less moral than the counterforce strategies around which today's forces are designed.

The Bush administration has proposed deploying strategic defenses to protect against accidental launches of up to 200 CIS warheads and against Third World missile attacks. But any defensive shield that could guard against 200 warheads would also raise doubts about the effectiveness of the retaliatory attack by a 1,000-warhead force. Thus any strategic defense system could make deep cuts impossible to achieve.

Other ways to provide similar protection would not conflict with deep cuts. For example, "command-destruct" devices would make it possible to destroy accidentally launched missiles with a coded radio command. As for Third World nuclear threats, the principal focus should be on stopping nuclear proliferation—especially since such nations would probably use methods other than long-range ballistic missiles to deliver a warhead. . . .

How Much to Reduce?

How low should we go? One criterion suggested by Herbert York, a former director of Livermore [National Laboratory], is that nuclear forces should be cut to such a level that no single person or group could produce damage substantially worse than an all-out conventional war such as World War II. By this standard, the arsenals of the nuclear-weapon states might each retain up to about 100 strategic warheads, with Britain and France perhaps sharing a "European" force.

The nuclear forces of some or all of the members of the U.N. Security Council might then be placed under a joint command. Individual countries could reserve the right to unilateral action in response to a nuclear threat against itself—just as Britain now subordinates its nuclear submarines to NATO except in case of "supreme national emergency."

Further in the future, we hope it will be possible to eliminate nuclear weapons entirely. The alternative—accepting nuclear weapons as a permanent part of the military arsenals of certain nations—would in the long term fatally undermine the effort to control proliferation, since there is no universally acceptable prescription for dividing nations into nuclear-weapons haves and have nots.

The possibility of a nuclear-weapons-free world is just beginning to be taken seriously again. The resulting debate will be complex, challenging us to examine our deepest assumptions about international relations. The United States and Russia could take a major step by reducing their arsenals to 1,000 warheads without stretching too far the currently accepted standards on stability and verifiability. After they take such a step, all nuclear states will be better positioned to explore together how to proceed with further reductions.

"Keep[ing] highly experienced, well-educated weaponeers away from rogue-nation proliferators would be a valuable contribution to worldwide nonaggression."

Hiring Former Soviet Nuclear Scientists Can Reduce Proliferation

Richard A. Eisner and Stephen Rosen

Since the Soviet Union no longer exists, many people fear that some nonnuclear countries will recruit former Soviet scientists to help them build nuclear weapons. In the following viewpoint, Richard A. Eisner and Stephen Rosen argue that American corporations and institutions should hire these scientists to prevent nations seeking nuclear arms from using their expertise. Richard A. Eisner, C.P.A., is a managing partner of Richard A. Eisner and Co., Inc., a New York City accounting firm to high-technology firms. Stephen Rosen is chairman of the Science and Technology Advisory Board, an organization in New York that helps émigré scientists and engineers locate jobs and market products in the United States.

As you read, consider the following questions:

1. According to Eisner and Rosen, how can corporations benefit financially from hiring former Soviet scientists?
2. How has the United States previously helped foreign scientists emigrate, according to the authors?

For 28 years, Georgi worked in Moscow on research and development connected with electromagnetic rail guns, using stored high-energy pulses that can launch heavy projectiles. For 25 years, Sergei—in what was then Leningrad—labored to improve the design of compact, long-lived nuclear energy sources using thermionic converters to power space stations and spy satellites. Meanwhile, in the same city—now once again called St. Petersburg—Aleksandr for 28 years developed laser gyro and fiber-optic compasses with sophisticated inertial navigation instrument systems for use in the accurate guidance of missiles to their targets.

These individuals, and others like them, worked on classified military research. None favors nuclear proliferation, but each has the potential to make substantive scientific and engineering contributions to weapons programs in what have come to be known as the "rogue nations" of the world—Iraq, for example.

But they also have the potential to contribute to the United States gross national product. Fortunately, they are in the U.S. at the moment, seeking productive employment in the research and development, science, engineering, and technology communities. They are ambitious, energetic, and willing to accept entry-level positions to obtain U.S. experience, to build their professional contacts and reputations, and to start new lives.

A Step Toward Nonproliferation

They came here recently as refugees, immigrants, or those in search of political asylum. And they serve as examples of new talent available to the U.S. that can deter or prevent—at modest cost to American citizens—weapons proliferation, including nuclear weapons.

A U.S. foreign policy that keeps highly experienced, well-educated weaponeers away from rogue-nation proliferators would be a valuable contribution to worldwide nonaggression. A step in the right direction is the formation of a Western-financed "clearinghouse," aimed at helping nuclear scientists find jobs in the former Soviet Union. But as for émigré scientists, U.S. employers can hire Georgi, Sergei, Aleksandr—and thousands of others like them. It wouldn't be the first time the scientific resources of a former adversary were used to foster U.S. progress; remember "Operation Paperclip," which brought Wernher von Braun and his team of Nazi rocket scientists to America after World War II.

Corporate Incentives

Practically speaking, the U.S. could reduce the potential threat to peace with the adoption of incentives, a new tax policy or credit, that would encourage U.S. employers—including science and technology companies, engineering and manufacturing firms, academic and research institutions, and even the U.S. government—to hire selected weapons scientists from the former Soviet republics. Normally, U.S. corporations deduct 100 percent of their employees' wages. We propose a new incentive for the nation's corporations to hire ex-Soviet weapons scientists: Allow 200 percent of their salaries to be deductible. Here are some benefits:

• The employer would hire highly trained talent at great bargains. (For example, an entry-level scientist's salary of $25,000 would qualify for a tax deduction of $50,000; in the 40 percent corporate tax bracket, this would be an employer credit of $20,000.)

Mike Ramirez/Copley News Service. Reprinted with permission.

• Those ex-Soviet weapons scientists would be given the chance of a lifetime to work in the U.S., to eventually earn citizenship, and to build a new life.

• U.S. policy objectives are advanced. The machinery for resettling refugee scientists and engineers is in place. And the judgment of world opinion would be favorable: The U.S. does not merely talk about nonproliferation—it responds enthusiastically to clear opportunity.

Following are some inevitable objections to our proposals (along with our responses to them):

• "We must not use U.S. tax structure as a device in advancing national policy." (Why not? We already use tax incentives as an instrument of such policy; consider the tax-deductibility of charitable donations.)

• "We must not interfere with the internal affairs of foreign countries." (Why not? We are eager to see U.S. businesses develop in the new Commonwealth of Independent States, in Japan, in the European Community.)

Precedents for Aid

• "We must not entice foreigners into the U.S." (But isn't there abundant precedent? Indeed, for decades, thousands of the Soviet Union's best scientific personnel fled persecution to find refuge in America. Already, owing to the Immigration Act of 1990, we are positioned to accept some 700,000 individuals a year. What would happen if a few thousand more would seek safe harbor in the U.S.?)

• "There wouldn't be a way to screen out those who are not really scientifically qualified, the opportunists." (There are enough bureaucratic functionaries—experts in the U.S. military establishment, for example—who could be called upon to scrutinize candidates for inclusion in the program.)

• "Unemployed U.S. citizens will say that such a policy unfairly penalizes them." (This is a virtual emergency we're dealing with—and it calls for extraordinary, one-time relief.)

• "The costs of supporting the beneficiaries of these changes in American tax and immigration policy—once they have assumed residency in the U.S.—would be prohibitively high." (The experience of domestic resettlement programs with similar populations indicates that each new émigré from the former Soviet Union costs about $500 per month for their first five months, then drops to about $200 per month thereafter. With scientists like Georgi, Sergei, and Aleksandr, about five months, on average, will elapse before they find work in or near their narrow specialties. Total cost to the U.S. taxpayer is about $20 million to $50 million.)

"A CTB would limit proliferation."

Adopting a Comprehensive Test Ban Can Limit Proliferation

Tina Rosenberg

In the following viewpoint, Tina Rosenberg argues that a Comprehensive Test Ban (CTB) would reduce nuclear proliferation by ending the development of new nuclear weapons and promoting cooperation among regional adversaries. Rosenberg asserts that a CTB would strengthen and extend the multinational Nuclear Nonproliferation Treaty (NPT) and allow the enforcement of sanctions against violators. Rosenberg is a visiting fellow at the Overseas Development Council, a Washington, D.C.-based organization concerned with the social and economic problems of developing nations.

As you read, consider the following questions:

1. According to Rosenberg, why are nations without nuclear arms opposed to treaties that ban such weapons?
2. Why does the United States favor continued nuclear testing, according to the author?
3. Some types of nuclear weapons can be built without testing. What would prevent nations from building these weapons, in the author's opinion?

Tina Rosenberg, "Nuking the Nukes," *The New Republic*, January 28, 1991. Reprinted by permission of *The New Republic*, © 1991, The New Republic, Inc.

If we are permitted nostalgia for the cold war, let us mourn the passing of a time when we pursued nuclear destruction predictably and methodically, and could trust our enemy to do the same. Today the bomb that could threaten us might be built by a man who relishes telling the world to go to hell. It matters little if we have 5,216 ICBM warheads or the 3,456 mandated by START. Either number is both far too great and far too small against an Iraq with one crude bomb.

Nuclear Newcomers

Iraq isn't the only threat. To the list of declared nuclear powers (the United States, the Soviet Union, China, Britain, France) and the list of de facto ones (Israel, South Africa, India, Pakistan), we must now add those on the brink of nuclear capacity. . . . North Korea began running a large research reactor in 1987 and now seems to be building a reprocessing plant to turn the reactor's spent fuel into plutonium for weapons. The country could have a crude nuclear arsenal by 1996. Libya makes no secret of its nuclear envy and has bought technology from several countries. Iran, spurred by Iraq, has begun to devote more research to its weapons goals and might be able to build a bomb by 2001. These countries are hostile to U.S. interests and behave in ways that seem irrational in Western eyes.

But their desire for a bomb is easy to understand. Governments believe it makes them more secure. This accounts for the nukes of Israel and South Africa, both pariahs in their regions, and for those of rivals India and Pakistan. (According to the Carnegie Endowment's Leonard Spector, Israel has between sixty and 100 atom bombs, South Africa has the essentials for fifteen to twenty-five, India for forty to sixty, and Pakistan for five to ten.) For the same reason, many European countries that could have built nuclear weapons are nuke-free: their security was assured by the superpowers.

The bomb also confers less tangible benefits. "Nuclear weapons are the international currency of power," a leading Indian proponent of his country's weapons program says. It's the Third World's anti-imperialist revenge on the snooty nuclear club. It appeals to prestige-hungry despots. Argentina and Brazil began their nuclear programs under military dictatorships. Civilian presidents halted them. In 1990, while the heads of the three military branches watched and fidgeted, Brazil's President Fernando Collor de Mello threw the first shovel of cement into a 1,000-foot-deep hole the military had dug as a potential test site.

To control the spread of nuclear weapons, the world has relied on the 1963 Limited Test Ban Treaty, the 1968 Treaty on Nuclear Nonproliferation, and the safeguards of the International Atomic Energy Agency [IAEA]. This regime has put the brakes on many countries' nuclear weapons programs, and persuaded others—Taiwan, Egypt, and South Korea—not to start, or to abandon programs early on. The prediction often heard in the 1960s that some thirty nations would have the bomb by now has mercifully fallen short.

© Robert Neubecker. Reprinted with permission.

But with two or three new nations going nuclear each decade, we can hardly call the regime a success. Controls have been least effective where they are most needed: with outlaw states like Iraq. And the regulatory mechanisms are deeply flawed. The IAEA, a U.N.-sponsored agency based in Vienna created in 1957, started with a dual mission: to guard against the misuse of nuclear technology for armaments, and also to promote the peaceful use of nuclear power. This tension still exists. "I would prefer to think of all the agency's activities, including safeguards, as promotional," IAEA director Hans Blix said in 1983.

Nuclear Haves and Have-Nots

The Nonproliferation Treaty [NPT], signed in 1968, placed IAEA safeguards—cameras, seals, and regular inspections—on all the nuclear facilities of signatory countries that didn't already have nuclear weapons. Its flaw was that it divided the world into haves and have-nots, using the arbitrary criterion of nuclear capacity in 1967. The have-nots promised not to acquire nuclear weapons, while the haves promised, in Article 6 of the treaty, "to pursue negotiations in good faith on effective measures relating to the cessation of the nuclear arms race at an early date." The preamble also committed nuclear states to "the discontinuance of all test explosions of nuclear weapons."

The idea of forswearing the bomb in exchange for a vague future promise of arms control seemed a bad bargain to many have-nots. India, Pakistan, Israel, South Africa, Argentina, and Brazil, among others, refused to sign, citing discrimination. From the have-nots' point of view, the treaty continues to be a dud. Although none of the have-nots that signed the treaty has acquired the bomb, the superpowers have gone from about 3,000 strategic nuclear weapons at the time of the NPT's signing to 23,000 today. Bitterness about this failure to disarm has been the principal point of contention at each of the NPT review conferences held every five years. The treaty must be extended in 1995. If the NPT dies, the issue of "balanced compliance" will be the reason.

The third leg of the regime is the 1963 Limited Test Ban Treaty, which prohibits atmospheric nuclear tests but allows underground tests (which at the time were unverifiable) to continue. Because it treats all parties equally, even the NPT critics have signed it. Its main success has been environmental, cutting nuclear fallout. But underground nuclear tests continue.

What ensures that the parties live up to the treaties? Nothing. The IAEA's inspectors are reporters, not commandos. All they can do is alert the world when they spot a violation—and there are so many constraints on their work that they can't even always do that. IAEA inspectors must schedule visits well in advance, have the host country's approval, and can poke around only where the host country allows. . . . There are only 197 IAEA inspectors to cover the 934 nuclear facilities under safeguards. A determined proliferator can prepare a bomb before inspectors return to discover the diversion.

Proliferation Is Tolerated

The IAEA can ring the alarm. The world can choose to keep dozing. The truth is that the West has tolerated proliferation within the family. "Not all 'proliferation' is bad from our perspective," Jim Hinds, a deputy assistant secretary of defense for negotiations policy, testified before a Senate committee in 1989. "It may be very much in our interest to assist our friends and allies in developing the same kinds of [nuclear] technology for the purposes of stability." Nor is nonproliferation a national priority. State Department officials in the Nonproliferation Bureau rarely win battles with other regional bureaus at State. No single congressional committee exists with authority to act on proliferation.

Pakistan's weapons program, for example, was widely known and widely ignored, because we needed Pakistan to help the Afghan *mujaheddin*. In 1985 Congress passed a requirement that for Pakistan to qualify for U.S. aid, the president had to certify each year that Pakistan does not possess a nuclear device and that renewed aid will "reduce significantly" the risk of its getting the bomb. Only in 1990 did a president refuse to certify. And the same day aid to Pakistan stopped, the administration went to Congress to ask for its reinstatement. It's the same story with Germany's blindness to its companies' nuclear commerce with Iraq, Pakistan, and India, among others. President Jimmy Carter nagged Germany to tighten up, but pressure stopped when German cooperation for the Euromissile program took precedence.

The current regime for stopping the bomb's spread depends on political will that has never existed. The North has overlooked proliferation when it conflicted with other strategic interests. The South has overlooked it out of regional solidarity against the North's arms buildup. But both these factors may be starting to change. The superpowers are more concerned about proliferation now that they are less concerned about each other. The cold war thaw may in turn reassure the South that real disarmament is possible.

A Comprehensive Test Ban

The catalyst for turning these trends into a new era is a simple act: a *complete* ban on all nuclear testing. . . . The United States and Britain—which carries out its nuclear tests in Nevada—are the only nations in the world that oppose a Comprehensive Test Ban. As nuclear powers, they can both veto the CTB. Every nuclear-age U.S. president until Reagan favored it. Yet the Bush administration opposes the conference and relegates the CTB to a long-term goal.

What would a CTB do to the U.S. nuclear weapons program? To start with, it would end the development of a few new weapons, such as the ballistic earth penetrator. Scientists would be able to keep designing and testing new delivery systems for existing warheads, but the CTB's blockage of new third-generation nuclear weapons probably explains opposition by the laboratories and among those who still see a use for the Strategic Defense Initiative.

The administration can no longer argue that the Soviets could get away with hiding a significant nuclear test; almost everyone agrees that the old problems in verification have been solved. The new argument is that we need to keep testing for reliability. Reagan and Bush administration officials continually cite Roger Batzel, who while director of Lawrence Livermore National Laboratory testified before Congress that problems had developed in many weapons after deployment that were caught only through tests. But a classified report by Livermore senior physicist Ray Kidder said Batzel was talking about problems that occurred decades ago in aspects of bomb design that are no longer used. Weapons must be thoroughly tested before deployment, of course. But scientists check deployed weapons by dismantling and measuring them to see if they still meet original specifications, not by nuclear tests.

Eliminate Underground Testing

The spread of nuclear weapons throughout the world will bring to naught all efforts to reduce this type of weapon, will drive us into a new arms race over the creation of means of defense from nuclear attack, and will destabilize the military-political situation in the world. To erect barriers to the spread of nuclear weapons is very complicated. But first and foremost, we must successfully complete that which we failed to finish in 1963, when we left open the possibility for conducting underground nuclear tests.

Eduard A. Shevardnadze, *The PSR Quarterly*, December 1991.

The administration also argues that only testing can assure that a nuclear explosion will not occur by accident. (It's never happened.) In December 1990 a group of prominent scientists reported to Congress that some weapons would be safer with design modifications, including some, such as the use of less volatile conventional explosives, that could have been done decades ago. The United States could test a few weapons after making these modifications before a test ban kicks in, to assure our weapons are safe.

Mikhail Gorbachev, looking surprisingly relaxed, reiterated Soviet support for the CTB during a fifty-minute meeting with some U.S., British, and Soviet legislators sponsored by Parliamentarians for Global Action in November 1990. (PGA paid my airfare.) The Soviets halted their tests for nineteen months back in 1985, and in 1990 did only one nuclear test compared with the United States' eight. Have you brought it up with Bush? asked U.S. Representative Tom Downey. "It was on the agenda," replied Gorbachev. "As you'll notice, it's still on the agenda."

It was still on the agenda when the delegation met with U.S. national security adviser Brent Scowcroft, two days after meeting Gorbachev. Scowcroft—co-author of a 1986 Council on Foreign Relations report that backed a CTB as a "significant contribution to containing proliferation"—did say the administration knew the world had changed and some new thinking might be necessary. "If you mentioned a Test Ban under Reagan, you'd be considered a lefty outsider," said Spector. "A few years ago it meant tying our hands. Now we can make the argument that it's a way to contain the programs while we're at the top of the hill."

Benefits of a Total Test Ban

The CTB would ensure that the NPT is renewed for a significant period of time. It would also slow regional arms races. The drama of a nuclear test tends to jolt rival countries into a response. India accelerated its program after China tested. Pakistan did so after India tested. Both nations, however, say they'd abide by a CTB. If both had known from the start that the other would never be able to test a bomb, they might not have even begun weapons research.

In addition, a CTB would limit proliferation to simple gun-style fission bombs, of the kind that wiped out Hiroshima. Although these can be built without testing, their unreliability means they could never be used with confidence or integrated fully into a country's strategic planning. Even crazed dictators care about getting their targets right. Testing is so crucial for everything else—Nagasaki-style implosion bombs, thermonuclear weapons, bombs on ballistic missiles—that building them under a CTB makes no sense.

Perhaps the best argument against the CTB is that it is naive to place our faith in treaties in this dangerous world. The answer is that the problem with the NPT is not that it's a treaty, but that it is a treaty resented by exactly the same countries it sought to contain, and one without enforcement provisions. A CTB would be different. The near universal enthusiasm for it makes it possible to do something that isn't possible with the NPT: set up real sanctions through the U.N. to enforce it. If a country tests—and we'll know because Iraq couldn't dig a test hole big enough to house the Statue of Liberty without getting caught—other nations could seize the proliferator's foreign assets, multilateral institutions could cut off loans, and U.N. forces could even bomb the violator's nuclear facility. "If the atomic club stops its testing, there might be the possibility for the world to accept that nuclear weapons are not the prerogative of any state," Kazakhstan deputy Olzhas Suliemenov told me in Moscow. "Take what's going on in Iraq. All humanity could look at this model of how to deal with one aggressor. In the future we could act together against regimes that find it necessary to possess nuclear bombs."

Other crucial measures could be added to a CTB. One is strengthening the NPT's safeguards. The IAEA is woefully understaffed, and its budget hasn't increased in six years. There should be more inspectors. The time between inspections should be less than the time it takes to make a bomb after diverting material. Inspectors should be able to drop in without warning and visit a greater range of facilities.

Sanctions should be imposed on arms sellers. Although the German government has been shamed into behaving better, nuclear trading continues. As late as 1990 U.S. companies were still selling U.S. government-approved technology to Iraq—$1.5 billion worth of which, according to the *Washington Post*, found a use in the Iraqi nuclear program. There's also a new class of Third World nuclear supplier. Brazil sold uranium and enrichment technology to Iraq. North Korea helped Iran's weapons program. Argentina helped Libya. Recent relaxations of controls on technology exports to the Soviet Union and Eastern Europe have opened new avenues for proliferators. In March 1990 a U.S. Customs sting operation caught Iraq trying to smuggle krytrons—nuclear switching devices. "As of July 1, Iraq can simply go to Romania and buy them over the counter like bags of onions," says Gary Milhollin, director of the Wisconsin Project on Nuclear Arms Control.

Ban Nuclear Weapons Fuel

While we're at it, why not also ban the production of the two materials used in weapons—plutonium and highly enriched uranium? Breeder reactors—the sole civilian use of plutonium— once touted as the path to cheap energy, have turned out to be electricity gluttons. . . .

Things are surely getting out of hand. The specter of the Iraqi bomb is now jolting us awake to the need for serious nonproliferation measures. The implosion of the Soviet Union now gives us the chance to take them without compromising U.S. security. The tougher and more credible U.N. offers the mechanism for a treaty that will work. It is now up to the Bush administration to abandon its cold war attitude to nonproliferation, thinking that has predictably and methodically made the world safe for nuclear terrorism.

203

*"Military action should be seriously considered
as a selective means to control nuclear
proliferation when other means [have] failed."*

Swift Military Action Can Prevent Proliferation

William R. Van Cleave

Unsuccessful efforts to dissuade or prevent an adversary from seeking nuclear weapons may prompt consideration of one last resort: military action, according to William R. Van Cleave. In the following viewpoint, Van Cleave argues that conventional military strikes against enemy nuclear weapons facilities can be highly effective in removing a nuclear threat and preventing proliferation. Van Cleave contends that not only will the targeted nation's weapons facilities be destroyed, but neighboring nations will feel less threatened and have less incentive to seek nuclear weapons as a defense. Van Cleave is director of the Center for Defense and Strategic Studies at Southwest Missouri State University in Springfield and a senior research fellow at the Hoover Institution at Stanford University in Palo Alto, California. He has served as chairman of the President's General Advisory Committee on Arms Control.

As you read, consider the following questions:

1. According to Van Cleave, why may it be difficult for a nation to gain international approval for military action?
2. In the author's opinion, how should the United States and other countries defend against potential nuclear missile attacks?
3. Why does Van Cleave believe it would be appropriate for the United States to undertake its own military action?

William R. Van Cleave, "Assertive Disarmament in the New World Order," position paper written expressly for inclusion in the present volume, June 1992.

On Sunday, June 7, 1981, Israel's air force, operating with surgical precision, destroyed Iraq's nuclear reactor complex, thus preventing Saddam Hussein from producing nuclear weapons. The Israeli government announced to the world that it had "decided to act without further delay, to ensure our people's existence," after all diplomatic efforts had failed.

This was the first exercise of "Assertive Disarmament," the use of military force specifically to stop a threatening nuclear weapons program.

A decade later, during Desert Storm, the United States also bombed Iraq's nuclear facilities, which were once again intended to produce nuclear weapons. Even though this occurred during a war in which the United States and its coalition partners destroyed many strategic targets in Iraq, the action could nonetheless be considered the second use of military force to halt the spread of nuclear weapons. This time, in contrast to 1981 when Israel was widely condemned for its unilateral action, the American action was sanctioned by the international community through the UN Security Council.

The Origin of Assertive Disarmament

The first discussion of "assertive disarmament" appeared in print in 1968 in the context of the nuclear weapons program of the People's Republic of China. The authors of the article explained: "By 'assertive disarmament' we do not mean the species of aggressive acts usually referred to as preventive war. . . . We mean solely a precise, surgical disruption of China's present capability to produce nuclear weapons."

The article argued that this option of military action should be seriously considered as a selective means to control nuclear proliferation when other means had failed. While directed at states whose acquisition of nuclear weapons could be particularly destabilizing, and not meant to be a general or indiscriminate policy, the authors believed that judicious application of assertive disarmament would have a potent anti-proliferation effect. First, it did not leave the control of proliferation entirely to diplomatic and voluntary means. Second, it would put dictators and predators on clear notice that their efforts to acquire nuclear weapons would be in vain and their labor and expenses lost. Third, it would free others, particularly neighboring states, from the need to acquire nuclear weapons of their own in defense.

The question with which we are dealing is simply how civilized nations, and a stable world order, can deal with the acquisition of nuclear weapons by dangerous or unstable regimes, and prevent their proliferation?

It is true that, to date, the "proliferation" of nuclear weapons states has been relatively modest—far more limited than many alarming predictions of thirty years ago when some (including John F. Kennedy) were projecting twenty or twenty-five possible nuclear weapons states by 1990. Nonetheless, as we move into the 1990s, more and more states are capable of acquiring not only "primitive" nuclear weapons, but a deliverable variety of such weapons, as well as missile delivery systems, which add a new and more threatening dimension to the proliferation problem. For the first time, we are facing the chillingly realistic prospect of nuclear-missile weapons in the hands of a number of regimes of questionable stability, responsibility, and intent.

No Alternative for Intervention

There is no alternative to confronting, deterring and, if necessary, disarming states that brandish and use weapons of mass destruction. And there is no one to do that but the United States, backed by as many allies as will join the endeavor.

Charles Krauthammer, *Foreign Affairs*, vol. 70, no. 1.

Secretary of Defense Richard Cheney has projected that twenty-four or more third world countries will have ballistic missiles by the year 2000. How many of these countries will also possess nuclear weapons cannot be reliably predicted. It could be several. Several currently non-nuclear weapons states have nuclear programs that could now secretly be weapons programs, or could rapidly be turned into such programs.

It is more than an assumption that among the states that could attempt to acquire nuclear weapons will be those quite capable of monstrous use of these weapons. In the hands of such regimes, even a very few nuclear weapons could present an intolerable threat to a stable "new world order." (One need only recall the "War of the Cities" in 1988 when Iraq and Iran hurled over 500 missiles at one another, mostly at cities, and then add nuclear weapons to such a scenario, in order to appreciate the potential magnitude of the problem.)

Traditional Nonproliferation Measures

In the face of an increasing threat, traditional means of dealing with proliferation, which are essentially based upon goodwill and cooperation, are not likely to be adequate. That is not to say that they should be abandoned; in combination, they are not unhelpful. But they cannot prevent determined troublemakers from acquiring nuclear weapons.

Some might argue that the Non-Proliferation Treaty has been

effective in curtailing nuclear proliferation, and that arms control remains a reliable way to deal with the problem. But such agreements are voluntary. They "work" when there is no real problem; when all relevant states share the goal to begin with, or are otherwise deterred from weapons programs. When there is a real problem—a determination to acquire weapons—they do not work. Consider, for example, Iraq's determined quest for nuclear weapons, even though, as a party to the NPT, it agreed to remain non-nuclear. Consider also Iraq's use of chemical weapons against Iran, even though it signed the Geneva convention that outlawed such use.

So, too, with technology transfer controls. Tighter control over the transfer to the likes of Saddam Hussein of the technology and components for the production of nuclear weapons and ballistic missiles, or the finished systems themselves, is much to be desired. The effort should be intensified. But at the same time the inadequacy of this civilized approach has to be recognized. Many countries, even U.S. allies, simply will not cooperate, or will be unable to do so effectively. Export controls can be evaded; if laws exist, they are frequently not tightly enforced. Some major supplier states—e.g., the People's Republic of China, Russia, North Korea—have refused to cooperate at all. In any case, this approach is too little, too late; many troublesome states already possess the necessary technology and equipment.

Security and Nuclear Umbrellas

More effective in limiting nuclear proliferation, perhaps, have been security alliances and guarantees, such as those constructed by the United States. These have satisfied the security needs of states that might otherwise have sought nuclear weapons. But these states have not been and are not now the problem. The United States, the United Kingdom, France, and Israel (presumably) are examples of stable, democratic, and responsible states that do not threaten peace by having nuclear weapons. In their hands, nuclear weapons are forces for peace and stability.

Although nuclear umbrellas or guarantees extended by the United States and its nuclear allies to non-nuclear states may have been relatively effective in the past, there is evidence that such extended nuclear deterrence is eroding. There are clearly threats for which U.S. nuclear guarantees are not an effective deterrent. In fact, the apparent erosion of traditional means of deterrence (through threats of retaliation) adds yet another new dimension to the problem of proliferation. The Persian Gulf war demonstrated, for example, that missile attacks cannot be reliably deterred even by target states possessing both superior military power and nuclear weapons (i.e., the U.S. and Israel). In fact, Saddam Hussein launched missiles against Israel precisely in an effort to provoke military retaliation by Israel; and had any of his missiles had a nuclear warhead, he would surely have succeeded.

The specter of the proliferation of ballistic missiles with nuclear warheads certainly underscores the urgent need for missile defenses, which provide one means for coping with the problem. In January 1991, the U.S. Government refocused the SDI program specifically toward providing protection against third world country or limited missile threats, and redesignated the program "GPALS," or Global Protection Against Limited Strikes. Other countries are considering similar programs. It is noteworthy that Russian President Boris Yeltsin even proposed a cooperative global system of defense against nuclear-missile proliferation in his January 1992 speech to the UN. He said, in essence, that deterrence must now be supplemented by the means to defend against attack.

The Use of Preventive Force

The war against Iraq was a preventive war in the minds of many Americans. A primary goal of the war was to destroy Iraq's potential to make and deliver nuclear, chemical, and biological weapons—to make war now, rather than later when Iraq might be armed with long-range weapons of mass destruction. The destruction of the Iraqi Osiraq reactor by Israel is another example of a preventive use of force. The use of force, especially on the scale of U.S. actions in Iraq, will generally be limited to the most exceptional circumstances and the most obviously aggressive and nefarious governments.

Steve Fetter, *International Security*, Summer 1991.

But missile defense, while essential, is only part of an effective strategy for dealing with the dangers of nuclear and missile proliferation. To be effective, such a strategy must include the option of using military force to prevent destabilizing proliferation. This idea will be distasteful to many: to some, it may even seem contradictory to American political and legal values. But it must be weighed against the likely costs of failure to act decisively. Would not a limited use of force be preferable to an increased risk of nuclear war? To a situation where aggressive and irresponsible regimes can credibly threaten their neighbors with nuclear terrorism? To retaliation only after the fact of a nuclear attack?

Let us briefly examine the use of assertive disarmament.

Assertive disarming attacks obviously may be conducted as

part of a broader military engagement. In such cases, the political costs could be negligible and there would be less concern about the means and destructiveness of the attacks. Or assertive disarmament may need to be carried out as a discrete act on its own merits. In that case, the type and scale of military action necessary must be carefully weighed in making the decision. Divorced from a military conflict, assertive disarmament should be a "surgical" operation, limiting damage as much as possible to the targeted facilities, which should be relatively few in number.

This suggests precise use of force; for example, with highly accurate non-nuclear guided missiles or stealthy air strikes, or with Special Operations Forces such as Delta or Seal teams. Use of these forces in Iraq demonstrated that they could be covertly inserted into a country and could operate effectively in small units largely on their own. It would almost certainly be possible for such units to destroy or critically damage key elements of the weapons production process by explosive, electronic, or manual means. Fake accidents or unidentifiable sabotage may also be possible in some cases.

If these restrictions on assertive disarmament are accepted, they underscore the importance of timely decision and action. Critical elements of the weapons program should be identifiable and vulnerable to an appropriately limited attack. The more developed the weapons program, the more diversified, dispersed, or concealed its facilities, the less appropriate this option becomes, as its difficulty and likely destructiveness increase.

The assured destruction option, then, is most appropriate against incipient weapons programs in lesser industrialized societies—and, again, only those with radical, unstable, and threatening regimes.

A Question of International Support

The destruction of Iraq's nuclear facilities during and after Desert Storm, authorized by the UN Security Council and conducted in the name of the international community, clearly demonstrated that assertive disarmament is not an uncivilized act, or in itself an aggressive one. This may have established a precedent for a more agreeable exercise of assertive disarmament than unilateral action, and it may turn out to have an anti-proliferation effect. But this may also be a unique case: Openly brutal aggression had taken place, the UN Security Council agreed to react to this aggression, a diverse coalition of responsive states was formed, and Iraq was soundly defeated militarily. It is rare for international bodies to act with such cohesion and resolution. It may not happen again. Had it not been for Iraq's invasion of Kuwait, it is difficult to imagine international action against its nuclear facilities. Perhaps the only lesson learned by third world regimes that would acquire nuclear weapons is not to aggress prematurely, to act more carefully until they possess the weapons.

Should the United States be prepared to act alone? It would obviously be preferable to have the open support of the UN Security Council, or of a broad and representative "concert" of powers, or at least of most of the states in the particular region involved. But the United States could legally and morally act alone, in self-defense, and as the most powerful state in the world with a unique responsibility for world order. As the world's leading nuclear power, it could be argued that the United States has a special obligation to act to help avert the dangers of nuclear proliferation.

Assertive Disarmament as Self-Defense

The UN Charter obviously permits and legalizes the collective assertive disarmament that took place against Iraq. But the principles of the Charter also recognize the right of individual national acts of self defense, including the right to act against threats before they become the overt use of violence. As the American statesman and international lawyer, Elihu Root, once pointed out, under international law every state has the right "to protect itself by preventing a condition of affairs in which it will be too late to protect itself."

Unable to rely entirely on cooperation in non-proliferation or on cohesive and timely action by the international community, it would be folly for the United States to exclude the assertive disarmament option and not make contingency plans for carrying it out. Proliferatory and aggressive regimes should understand clearly that the United States reserves for itself a preemptive defense against their weapons facilities or stockpiles. The alternative would be to leave the United States, other peaceful nations, and the new world order vulnerable to disasters simply waiting to happen.

Recognizing Statements
That Are Provable

We are constantly confronted with statements and generalizations about social and moral problems. In order to think clearly about these problems, it is useful if one can make a basic distinction between statements for which evidence can be found and other statements which cannot be verified or proved because evidence is not available, or the issue is so controversial that it cannot be definitely proved.

Readers should be aware that magazines, newspapers, and other sources often contain statements of a controversial nature. The following activity is designed to allow experimentation with statements that are provable and those that are not.

The following statements are taken from the viewpoints in this chapter. Consider each statement carefully. *Mark P for any statement you believe is provable. Mark U for any statement you feel is unprovable because of the lack of evidence. Mark C for any statement you think is too controversial to be proved to everyone's satisfaction.*

If you are doing this activity as a member of a class or group, compare your answers with those of other class or group members. Be able to defend your answers. You may discover that others will come to different conclusions than you do. Listening to the reasons others present for their answers may give you valuable insights into recognizing statements that are provable.

P = provable
U = unprovable
C = too controversial

1. The United States and Russia possess the largest nuclear arsenals in the world.

2. Only a few countries have ever conducted nuclear weapons tests.

3. Arms control agreements remove the threat of aggression by one nation against another.

4. Nuclear proliferation will inevitably lead to a nuclear war.

5. Iraq is the only nation that has had nuclear facilities destroyed by another country.

6. Nuclear weapons are the most effective type of weapons a nation can ever hope to possess.

7. Weak international laws governing nuclear-related exports are mainly responsible for nuclear proliferation.

8. The Partial Test Ban Treaty of 1963 prohibits nuclear weapons tests in the oceans and atmosphere.

9. American scientists were the first to develop an atomic bomb.

10. Nonproliferation efforts are futile since the materials and technology to build nuclear weapons will always exist.

11. Militaristic dictators cannot be trusted with nuclear weapons.

12. A country that has nuclear weapons garners much respect and can increase its influence over international affairs.

13. A worldwide ban on nuclear testing will encourage nations to reject nuclear weapons as worthless.

14. Almost all of the world's nations have agreed not to acquire or spread nuclear weapons.

15. Humankind's resolve to protect the welfare of the human species will ensure that a nuclear war will never occur.

16. The world would be safer without nuclear weapons.

17. The world's only nuclear attacks occurred when the United States dropped atomic bombs over the Japanese cities of Hiroshima and Nagasaki.

18. Mikhail Gorbachev's policies of openness and reform in the Soviet Union during the 1980s expedited U.S.-Soviet nuclear arms reductions.

19. The former Soviet Union is responsible for nuclear proliferation in Asia.

20. Nuclear weapons tests cost the United States millions of dollars annually.

21. In 1974 India became the first Third World nation to test a nuclear device.

22. The worldwide nuclear threat is decreasing.

23. Because of its policy of continued nuclear testing, the United States shows a reckless disregard for global nonproliferation efforts.

24. A 1992 agreement among more than twenty nations to tighten nuclear export controls will prevent future secret nuclear weapons programs.

25. The United States has not produced new supplies of plutonium for nuclear weapons since 1988.

26. A reduced nuclear arsenal still offers a nation the means to deter attack.

Periodical Bibliography

The following articles have been selected to supplement the diverse views presented in this chapter.

Bruce B. Auster and Tim Zimmermann	"America and Russia Set a Good Example," *U.S. News & World Report*, June 29, 1992.
James A. Baker III	"Supporting Scientists of the Former Soviet Union," *U.S. Department of State Dispatch*, February 24, 1992.
Brian Bremner	"The Techies vs. the Techno-Cops," *Business Week*, June 15, 1992.
William J. Broad	"Twenty-Seven Countries Sign New Atom Accord," *The New York Times*, May 3, 1992.
The Bulletin of the Atomic Scientists	Special issue on arms control, November 1991.
The Bulletin of the Atomic Scientists	Special issue on disarmament, May 1992.
George Bush	"Initiative on Nuclear Arms," *Vital Speeches of the Day*, November 1, 1991.
J. Bryan Hehir	"The Proliferation Problem," *Commonweal*, October 25, 1991.
Charles Krauthammer	"Why Arms Control Is Obsolete," *Time*, August 5, 1991.
Carl A. Posey	"Nuclear World Order," *Omni*, March 1992.
Eduard A. Shevardnadze	"Nuclear Disarmament," *PSR Quarterly*, vol. 1, no. 4, December 1991. Available from 428 E. Preston St., Baltimore, MD 21202-3993.
Aaron Tovish	"Ending Nuclear Weapons Production Worldwide," *Nuclear Times*, Spring 1992.
U.S. Department of State Dispatch	"U.S. Nuclear Testing Policy," August 19, 1991.
Lincoln Wolfenstein	"End Nuclear Addiction," *The Bulletin of the Atomic Scientists*, May 1991.
World Press Review	Special issue on nuclear proliferation, December 1991.

Glossary

arms control The process of negotiations between two or more nations to limit or reduce arms. Usually refers to efforts to control **weapons of mass destruction**.

atomic bomb A bomb whose energy comes from the **fission** of **uranium** or **plutonium** atoms.

ballistic missile A missile powered on takeoff by rocket engines, but which descends to its target in a free-fall after the engines burn out.

bilateral Action taken equally by two sides or nations.

calutron Acronym for the California University **cyclotron**. The calutron was an accelerator used to enrich **uranium** for the Hiroshima atomic bomb. This technology has now been abandoned by Western nations.

centrifuge A device used to spin low-grade **uranium** into **weapons-grade material**. The spinning action concentrates and enriches the **uranium**, making it powerful enough to be used for nuclear weapons.

cyclotron An accelerator in which charged particles are propelled by an alternating electric field in a constant magnetic field.

deterrence The threat of nuclear retaliation that keeps a nation from launching a **first strike**.

DOD Department of Defense.

DOE Department of Energy.

enrichment The process of increasing the concentration of one **isotope** of a given element, for example, **uranium**-235.

first strike An attempt to gain a military advantage by launching a nuclear attack against an opponent's nuclear arsenal before the opponent can launch its weapons.

fission The process by which a neutron strikes the nucleus of an atom and splits it into fragments, releasing heat and radiation.

fusion The formation of a heavier nucleus of an atom from two lighter nuclei, with an attendant release of energy.

IAEA International Atomic Energy Agency. An organization affiliated with the United Nations that oversees many nations' civilian nuclear programs and that monitors the **NPT**.

ICBM Intercontinental **ballistic missile**. A long-range **ballistic missile** capable of reaching targets on the other side of the globe.

INF Intermediate-range nuclear forces. **Tactical** nuclear missiles with a range between three hundred and thirty-four hundred miles.

INF Treaty A 1988 treaty between the United States and the Soviet Union eliminating all **INF** missiles.

isotope A form of an element that contains an unusual number of neutrons in the atomic nucleus.

kiloton The explosive power equivalent to one thousand tons of TNT.

megaton The explosive power equivalent to one million tons of TNT.

NATO North Atlantic Treaty Organization. A military alliance among the United States, Canada, and many European nations.

NPT   Nuclear Nonproliferation Treaty. A treaty first signed in 1968 by nations that promised not to spread or acquire nuclear arms.

plutonium   A highly toxic and radioactive element produced by nuclear reactors and usually used for the **weapons-grade material** of nuclear weapons.

preemptive   *See* **first strike.**

proliferation   The continued increase in the number of nuclear weapons. Horizontal proliferation refers to the spread of nuclear weapons to other nations while vertical proliferation refers to the upgrading of nuclear weapons technology within the arsenals of acknowledged nuclear weapons states.

R&D   Research and development.

START   Strategic Arms Reduction Treaty signed in 1991 by the United States and the Soviet Union that drastically reduced certain classes of **ballistic missiles.**

strategic nuclear weapons   Nuclear weapons with the range to reach deep inside the opponent's territory and destroy strategically important targets.

tactical nuclear weapons   Short-range nuclear weapons that can only be used in nearby battlefields.

Third World   Developing nations of Africa, Asia, and Latin America.

unilateral   Action taken by only one side or nation.

uranium   A radioactive element found in natural ores and used in the manufacturing of nuclear weapons.

verification   The process of confirming compliance with arms control treaties through satellite monitoring or on-site inspections.

warhead   The device in missiles containing the nuclear explosive. The term "bomb" is usually reserved for gravity bombs dropped from the air.

weapons-grade material   The type of **plutonium** or **uranium** most suitable for nuclear weapons.

weapons of mass destruction   Biological, chemical, and nuclear weapons capable of causing widespread damage.

yellowcake   A concentrate of approximately 80 percent **uranium** oxide used for uranium **enrichment.**

yield   The explosive power of nuclear weapons measured in the equivalent amount of TNT.

Chronology

1942

August 13   U.S. Army Corps of Engineers establishes the Manhattan Project to develop an atomic bomb.

1945

July 16   The United States tests the first atomic bomb at Alamogordo, New Mexico.

August 6   The United States drops the first uranium bomb on Hiroshima, Japan.

August 9   The United States drops the first plutonium bomb on Nagasaki, Japan.

1946   The United States proposes the Baruch Plan, which would prevent nuclear proliferation by placing all nuclear materials and technology under international control. The Soviet Union rejects the plan.

1949   The Soviet Union begins testing nuclear weapons.

1950

January 31   President Truman directs the Atomic Energy Commission to develop a hydrogen bomb and tactical nuclear weapons.

1952

October 3   Great Britain begins testing nuclear weapons.

1957   International Atomic Energy Agency (IAEA) is founded under the auspices of the United Nations to help nations develop peaceful nuclear programs. Careful monitoring ensures that materials are not diverted for nuclear weapons.

1958

October 31   Nuclear test ban negotiations among the United States, Great Britain, and Soviet Union start in Geneva, Switzerland, and officials from those countries announce a test moratorium.

1960

February 13   France tests a nuclear weapon in the Sahara Desert.

1961

September   The United States resumes limited underground nuclear testing.

1962

October 22-28   Cuban missile crisis. The United States imposes a naval blockade on Cuba because of the placement of Soviet nuclear missiles there. After a declaration to defend its rights, the Soviet Union finally relents and removes the missiles.

1963

October 10   Partial Test Ban Treaty is ratified by the United States, Great Britain, and the Soviet Union, prohibiting nuclear testing in the atmosphere, in space, or under water.

1964	China begins testing nuclear weapons.
1965	Multilateral negotiations begin on a formal treaty to prevent the spread of nuclear weapons.
1967-68	U.S. inventory of nuclear weapons reaches a peak of about thirty-two thousand weapons.
1968	
April 22	Treaty for the Prohibition of Nuclear Weapons in Latin America (also known as the Treaty of Tlatelolco) takes effect.
June	The United States, the Soviet Union, Great Britain, and fifty-nine other countries sign the Nuclear Nonproliferation Treaty (NPT).
1970	
March 5	Nuclear Nonproliferation Treaty is ratified.
1971	Anti-Ballistic Missile (ABM) Treaty limits the United States to two hundred nuclear interceptors.
1972	
May	Strategic Arms Limitations Talks (SALT I) agreements signed by the United States and the Soviet Union.
November	Negotiations begin on SALT II, a long-term treaty on strategic nuclear weapons.
1974	India tests a nuclear bomb but claims that the test is for peaceful purposes.
July 3	The United States and the Soviet Union sign the Threshold Test Ban Treaty, limiting nuclear tests to 150 kilotons.
1978	Congress passes the Nuclear Nonproliferation Act, requiring tighter restrictions on the sale and the use of plutonium.
1979	
June 18	President Carter and General Secretary Brezhnev sign the SALT II Treaty, limiting the number of nuclear weapons in the United States and the Soviet Union.
September 2	A U.S. satellite detects an apparent South African-Israeli nuclear test off the South African coast.
1981	
June 7	Israeli jets destroy Iraq's Osirak nuclear research reactor.
1982	U.S. nuclear weapons inventory reduced to about twenty-four thousand weapons, of which about half are strategic and half tactical.
June 29	Strategic Arms Reduction Talks (START) begin in Geneva, Switzerland.
1985	Australia, New Zealand, and nine other nations sign the South Pacific Nuclear-Free Zone Treaty (also known as the Treaty of Rarotonga).
1987	
December 8	President Reagan and Soviet general secretary Gorbachev sign the Intermediate-Range Nuclear Forces (INF) Treaty, eliminating short- and intermediate-range nuclear weapons.

1990

February 8   A Soviet KGB report concludes that North Korea "continues scientific and design-testing work leading toward making nuclear weapons."

March 20   British agents in London intercept a shipment of capacitors used to trigger atomic bombs. The devices were bound for Iraq.

July 15   Iraq's ambassador to the United States, Mohamed al-Mashat, says in a newspaper interview that "there is no plan to develop nuclear weapons in Iraq."

1991

April 3   U.N. Security Council passes Resolution 687, ending the Persian Gulf War, and orders the destruction or removal of all of Iraq's prohibited nuclear material and facilities.

May 6 and 12   The United States and the Soviet Union destroy their last remaining intermediate-range missiles in compliance with the INF Treaty.

May 14-22   The IAEA's initial inspection in Iraq following the Persian Gulf War discovers that Iraq has produced small quantities of plutonium.

July 9   South Africa signs the Nuclear Nonproliferation Treaty (NPT).

July 31   George Bush and Mikhail Gorbachev sign the START Treaty, the first accord requiring reductions in strategic warheads.

September   Pakistani prime minister Benazir Bhutto announces that her country has the capability to produce a nuclear weapon.

September 27   President Bush announces a major disarmament initiative: the removal of ground-launched nuclear weapons from Europe and of all nuclear weapons from South Korea, ending ground alert for nuclear-armed bombers, and accelerating the elimination of strategic nuclear weapons covered by START.

October 5   Soviets respond to the U.S. initiative with a similar initiative: the removal of all tactical nuclear weapons from ships and submarines; reductions to five thousand accountable warheads, one thousand less than agreed to under START; and the destruction of all nuclear artillery projectiles, nuclear land mines, and nuclear warheads for nonstrategic missiles.

October 11-21   IAEA inspectors find traces of weapons-grade uranium at Iraq's Tuwaitha nuclear research center.

October 17   NATO decides to eliminate 80 percent of its nuclear weapons—leaving only seven hundred air-delivered atomic bombs at European bases.

December 13   Argentina and Brazil agree to place all of their nuclear facilities and materials under IAEA safeguards.

1992

January 28   In his State of the Union Address, President Bush announces the cancellation of the Midgetman missile program and an end to advanced cruise missile and Trident II submarine missile warhead production.

January 29	Russian president Boris Yeltsin announces a halt in production of all long-range nuclear air- and sea-launched cruise missiles.
January 30	North Korea signs an agreement with the IAEA—six years after signing the NPT—allowing inspection and monitoring of all its nuclear facilities and activities.
March 9	China signs the Nuclear Nonproliferation Treaty.
April 3	Members of the twenty-seven-nation Nuclear Suppliers Group agree to voluntary international rules limiting the sale of machinery and materials that can be used to build a nuclear weapon.
May 11-16	IAEA director Hans Blix tours several of North Korea's nuclear facilities.
May 22	China sets off its largest ever underground nuclear test. The explosion is estimated to be in the one-megaton range.
May 23	Russia, the Ukraine, Belarus, and Kazakhstan agree to abide by the START Treaty signed by the now-defunct Soviet Union.
June 16	The United States and Russia sign an agreement reducing both of their nuclear arsenals to thirty-five hundred strategic weapons each.
June 19	France signs the Nuclear Nonproliferation Treaty.
July 2	President Bush announces that the United States has completed its withdrawal of all tactical land- and sea-based nuclear weapons outside the country.

Organizations to Contact

The editors have compiled the following list of organizations that are concerned with the issues debated in this book. All have publications or information available for interested readers. For best results, allow as much time as possible for the organizations to respond. The descriptions below are derived from materials provided by the organizations. This list was compiled upon the date of publication. Names, addresses, and phone numbers of organizations are subject to change.

The American Civil Defense Association (TACDA)
PO Box 910
Starke, FL 32091
(904) 964-5397

TACDA is an organization that advocates civil defense and preparedness to ensure the protection of the United States. The association believes that as long as other countries test nuclear weapons, the United States must continue to do so to maintain its security. It also supports keeping a nuclear arsenal equal to the largest of any other nation. Publications include the quarterly *Journal of Civil Defense* and the *TACDA Alert* newsletter.

American Defense Institute (ADI)
1055 N. Fairfax St., 2d Fl.
Alexandria, VA 22314
(703) 519-7000

ADI advocates a strong national defense. It supports continued nuclear weapons testing until the adoption of a comprehensive test ban, a reduced nuclear arsenal to act as a deterrent, and a stronger Nuclear Nonproliferation Treaty to reduce proliferation. The institute publishes the quarterly newsletter *American Defense Initiative* and the monthly *ADI Briefing*.

American Security Council
916 Pennsylvania Ave. SE
Washington, DC 20003
(202) 484-1676

The council is a research institute that studies national defense issues. It advocates a large arsenal of nuclear weapons and continued testing as part of a strong national defense. Publications include the bimonthly *National Security Report* newsletter and policy papers and briefings.

America's Future
PO Box 1625
Milford, PA 18337
(717) 296-2800

America's Future seeks to educate the public about the importance of the principles upon which the U.S. government is founded and of the value of the free enterprise system. It supports continued U.S. testing of nuclear weapons and their usefulness as a deterrent. The group publishes the monthly newsletter *America's Future*.

Arms Control Association (ACA)
11 Dupont Circle NW
Washington, DC 20036
(202) 797-4626

The association is dedicated to promoting public understanding of arms control and disarmament policies and programs. ACA seeks to increase public appreciation of the need to limit arms, reduce international tensions, and promote world peace. It publishes the monthly magazine *Arms Control Today*.

Campaign for Peace and Democracy (CPD)
PO Box 1640
New York, NY 10025
(212) 666-5924

CPD brings together members of the peace, feminist, and environmental movements, among others, to work to eliminate all nuclear weapons. It believes that the United States, IAEA, and NPT have failed to prevent nuclear proliferation. It also supports a comprehensive nuclear test ban to help end the development of new nuclear weapons. CPD publishes the biannual *Peace & Democracy News*.

Carnegie Endowment for International Peace
2400 N St. NW
Washington, DC 20037
(202) 862-7900

The Carnegie Endowment for International Peace conducts research on international affairs and U.S. foreign policy. Issues concerning nuclear weapons and proliferation are often discussed in articles published in its quarterly journal *Foreign Policy*.

Center for Defense Information (CDI)
1500 Massachusetts Ave. NW
Washington, DC 20005
(202) 862-0700

CDI comprises civilians and former military officers who oppose excessive expenditures for weapons and policies that increase the danger of war. It advocates a comprehensive nuclear weapons test ban and believes that the optimum means of preventing nuclear proliferation is to grant the United Nations Security Council broader powers and the IAEA additional authority, resources, and support to inspect and safeguard nuclear facilities and material. The center publishes the *Defense Monitor* ten times per year.

Center for Security Policy
1250 24th St. NW, Suite 600
Washington, DC 20037
(202) 466-0515

The center is concerned with issues of national defense and foreign policy and advocates continued U.S. testing of nuclear weapons to maintain national security. It publishes periodic *Decision Brief* reports on nuclear proliferation issues.

Center for War/Peace Studies
218 E. 18th St.
New York, NY 10003
(212) 475-1077

The center's purpose is to eliminate the institution of war. It seeks global disarmament to levels of peacekeeping forces and advocates a strong United Nations to verify arms control, disarmament, and on-site inspections of nuclear facilities. The center publishes the quarterly newsletter *Global Report* and occasional papers about nuclear weapons.

Foreign Policy Research Institute (FPRI)
3615 Chestnut St.
Philadelphia, PA 19104-9817
(215) 382-0685

FPRI studies international affairs and U.S. foreign policy. Nuclear proliferation issues are often discussed in the institute's quarterly journal *Orbis*.

The Heritage Foundation
214 Massachusetts Ave. NE
Washington, DC 20002
(202) 546-4400

The foundation is a conservative think tank that favors a strong national defense. Several of its publications have addressed START and regional arms control negotiations. Among its periodic publications are the *Heritage Lectures* and the Asian Studies Center *Backgrounder*.

Parliamentarians for Global Action
211 E. 43d St., Suite 1604
New York, NY 10017
(212) 687-7755

Parliamentarians for Global Action is a network of legislators from around the world concerned with the survival and well-being of humanity. It favors a complete ban on nuclear testing and supports nonproliferation actions such as arms control negotiations and an increased United Nations role in nuclear inspections. The group publishes the periodic *Parliamentarians for Global Action Update*.

Physicians for Social Responsibility (PSR)
1000 16th St. NW, Suite 810
Washington, DC 20036
(202) 785-3777

PSR is a group of medical professionals, students, and others concerned with the threat of nuclear war. It supports a comprehensive nuclear test ban and disarmament. Publications include the bimonthly newsletter *PSR Monitor*, which focuses on nuclear arms control legislation, and the quarterly newsletter *PSR Report*, which provides information on the medical consequences of nuclear weapons tests.

SANE/FREEZE: Campaign for Global Security
1819 H St. NW, Suite 1000
Washington, DC 20006
(202) 862-9740

SANE/FREEZE is committed to nuclear disarmament. It advocates a comprehensive nuclear weapons test ban treaty, arms control negotiations, and a stronger United Nations role in inspections of nuclear facilities. Publications include two newsletters, the bimonthly *Grassroots Organizer* and the quarterly *SANE/FREEZE News*.

Union of Concerned Scientists (UCS)
26 Church St.
Cambridge, MA 02238
(617) 547-5552

UCS is concerned about the impact of advanced technology on society. It supports nuclear arms control as a means to reduce nuclear weapons. Publications include the quarterly *Nucleus* newsletter and reports and briefs concerning nuclear proliferation.

United States Strategic Institute (USSI)
67 Bay State Rd.
Boston, MA 02215
(617) 353-8700

USSI is a conservative think tank that studies political and military topics and U.S. national security policy. The council publishes a variety of opinions on both sides of issues such as nuclear testing and deterrence in its quarterly journal *Strategic Review*.

The White House Office of the President of the United States
1600 Pennsylvania Ave. NW
Washington, DC 20500
(202) 456-1414

As commander-in-chief of the armed forces, the president formulates policies and strategies on arms control, nuclear testing, and nuclear proliferation. Contact the office for various reports and speeches.

Wisconsin Project on Nuclear Arms Control
1900 L St. NW, Suite 610
Washington, DC 20036
(202) 223-8299

The Wisconsin Project researches and publicizes several nations' suspected secret nuclear weapons programs and the illegal exports that aid them. It supports arms control measures and tough export laws that restrict transfers of nuclear material and technology. The project publishes articles and reports on the weapons programs of individual nations, including *Bombs from Beijing: A Report on China's Nuclear and Missile Exports*.

Bibliography of Books

Kenneth L. Adelman   *The Great Universal Embrace: Arms Control—A Skeptic's Account*. New York: Simon & Schuster, 1989.

Kathleen C. Bailey   *Doomsday Weapons in the Hands of Many*. Urbana: University of Illinois Press, 1991.

Frank Barnaby   *The Invisible Bomb: The Nuclear Arms Race in the Middle East*. London: I.B. Tauris, 1989.

Peter R. Beckman, ed.   *The Nuclear Predicament: Nuclear Weapons in the Cold War and Beyond*. 2d ed. Englewood Cliffs, NJ: Prentice Hall, 1992.

Bruce D. Berkowitz   *Calculated Risks: A Century of Arms Control, Why It Has Failed, and How It Can Be Made to Work*. New York: Simon & Schuster, 1987

Gary Bertsch, Richard Cupitt, and Steven Elliott-Gower   *International Cooperation on Nonproliferation Controls*. Ann Arbor: University of Michigan Press, 1992.

Bruce G. Blair   *The Logic of Accidental Nuclear War*. Washington, DC: Brookings Institution, 1992.

Philip Cohen, ed.   *Nuclear Proliferation in South Asia: The Prospects for Arms Control*. Boulder, CO: Westview Press, 1991.

Congressional Budget Office   *The START Treaty and Beyond*. Washington, DC: U.S. Government Printing Office, 1991.

Paul P. Craig and John A. Jungerman   *The Nuclear Arms Race: Technology and Society*. 2d ed. New York: McGraw-Hill, 1990.

Ivo H. Daalder   *The Nature and Practice of Flexible Response: NATO Strategy and Theater Nuclear Forces Since 1967*. New York: Columbia University Press, 1991.

Lewis A. Dunn   *Containing Nuclear Proliferation*. London: Brassey's for the International Institute for Strategic Studies, 1991.

Anoushiravan Ehteshami   *Nuclearisation of the Middle East*. McLean, VA: Brassey's, 1989.

David Fischer   *Stopping the Spread of Nuclear Weapons: The Past and the Prospects*. New York: Routledge, 1992.

David Fischer   *Toward 1995: The Prospects for Ending the Proliferation of Nuclear Weapons*. London: Dartmouth, 1992.

M.P. Fry, N.P. Keatinge, and J. Rotblat, eds.   *Nuclear Non-Proliferation and the Non-Proliferation Treaty*. New York: Springer-Verlag, 1990.

James L. George   *The New Nuclear Rules: Strategy and Arms Control After INF and START*. London: Pinter Publishers, 1990.

Kurt Gottfried and Jonathan Dean	*Nuclear Security in a Transformed World.* Cambridge, MA: Union of Concerned Scientists, 1991.
Tom Harkin with C.E. Thomas	*Five Minutes to Midnight: Why the Nuclear Threat Is Growing Faster than Ever.* New York: Carol Publishing, 1990.
Vilho Harle and Pekka Sivonen, eds.	*Nuclear Weapons in a Changing Europe.* New York: Pinter, 1991.
Selig S. Harrison and Leonard S. Spector	*Nuclear Weapons and the Security of Korea.* Washington, DC: Carnegie Endowment for International Peace, 1992.
Seymour M. Hersh	*The Samson Option: Israel's Nuclear Arsenal and American Foreign Policy.* New York: Random House, 1991.
Regina Cowen Karp, ed.	*Security with Nuclear Weapons?: Different Perspectives on National Security.* New York: Oxford University Press, 1991.
Charles W. Kegley Jr. and Kenneth L. Schwab, eds.	*After the Cold War: Questioning the Morality of Nuclear Deterrence.* Boulder, CO: Westview Press, 1991.
Paul L. Leventhal and Sharon Tanzer	*Averting a Latin American Nuclear Arms Race: New Prospects and Challenges for Argentine-Brazil Nuclear Co-operation.* New York: St. Martin's Press, 1992.
Chong-Pin Lin	*China's Nuclear Weapons Strategy: Tradition Within Evolution.* Lexington, MA: Lexington Books, 1988.
Jonathan Medalia, Paul Zinsmeister, and Robert Civiak, eds.	*Nuclear Weapons and Security: The Effects of Alternative Test Ban Treaties.* Boulder, CO: Westview Press, 1991.
Gary Milhollin and Gerard White	*Bombs from Beijing: A Report on China's Nuclear and Missile Exports.* Washington, DC: Wisconsin Project on Nuclear Arms Control, 1991.
Ziba Moshaver	*Nuclear Weapons Proliferation in the Indian Subcontinent.* New York: St. Martin's Press, 1991.
Joseph E. Nation, ed.	*The De-escalation of Nuclear Crises.* New York: St. Martin's Press, 1992.
Office of the President of the United States	*Activities to Prevent Nuclear Proliferation.* Washington, DC: U.S. Government Printing Office, 1991.
William C. Potter	*International Nuclear Trade and Nonproliferation: The Challenge of the Emerging Suppliers.* Lexington, MA: Lexington Books, 1990.
Thomas Schmalberger	*In Pursuit of a Nuclear Test Ban Treaty.* New York: United Nations Institute for Disarmament Research, 1991.

William A. Schwartz and Charles Derber

The Nuclear Seduction: Why the Arms Race Doesn't Matter—and What Does. Berkeley: University of California Press, 1990.

Jennifer E. Sims

Icarus Restrained: An Intellectual History of Nuclear Arms Control, 1945-1960. Boulder, CO: Westview Press, 1990.

Leonard S. Spector

Nuclear Ambitions: The Spread of Nuclear Weapons 1989-1990. Boulder, CO: Westview Press, 1990.

Shelley A. Stahl and Geoffrey Kemp, eds.

Arms Control and Weapons Proliferation in the Middle East and South Asia. New York: St. Martin's Press, 1992.

John G. Tower, James Brown, and William K. Cheek

Verification: The Key to Arms Control in the 1990s. McLean, VA: Brassey's, 1992.

U.S. Senate Committee on Foreign Relations

Nuclear Proliferation: Learning from the Iraq Experience. Washington, DC: U.S. Government Printing Office, 1992.

Frank von Hippel and Roald Z. Sagdeev

Reversing the Arms Race: How to Achieve and Verify Deep Reductions in the Nuclear Arsenals. New York: Gordon and Breach Science Publishers, 1990.

Index